ISBN: 978-1-7372123-0-0 (Ebook – EPUB)
ISBN: 978-1-7372123-2-4 (Paperback)

Library of Congress Control Number: Pending

Cover Design by Angelo DiLullo

Website

SimplyAlwaysAwake.com

Guided Meditation App

Simply Awake: Meditations for Awakening

Developer: Mark Lackey

Dedication

*This book is dedicated
to those who have come before us,
who were willing to forego comfort
and predictability to venture into the
unknown in the name of truth.*

*This book is dedicated
to anyone who, from this moment
forward, is willing to forego comfort
and predictability to venture into the
unknown in the name of truth.*

*This book is dedicated
to you.*

Table of Contents

Introduction 1

Chapter 1: A Word of Caution..17

Chapter 2: First Steps 24

Chapter 3: What Is Awakening?..46

Chapter 4: Paradox..73

Chapter 5: Attention 93

Chapter 6: Resources 106

Chapter 7: Teachers..110

Chapter 8: Practices and Techniques 130

Chapter 9: Traditions 165

Chapter 10: Stages of Awakening 171

Chapter 11: Mind-Identification...220

Chapter 12: Thoughts..257

Chapter 13: Beliefs 296

Chapter 14: Emotions 322

Chapter 15: Inquiry 378

Chapter 16: Awakening...403

Chapter 17: Post-Awakening Guidance 457

About the Author...466

AWAKE

It's Your Turn

Angelo DiLullo MD

Introduction

Y ou can wake up from the dream of separation. If you know what that means, then you're in luck, this entire book was written for you! If you're unsure but curious, let me assure you that no matter what your background, belief system, views, or religious orientation, this possibility is just as available to you as it is to anyone else. Simply stated, waking up from the dream of separation means living a life of spontaneity, wonder, freedom, and unbroken peace. It means realizing your true, undivided nature and living out of an instinctual interconnectedness that is undeniable and immediately available at all times. It means expressing yourself authentically and without hesitation and feeling comfortable in your own skin no matter the situation. Ultimately, it is about the end of suffering in this lifetime. I understand this is quite a promise. You might wonder how in the world a book can guide you to a life free of suffering. Well, I have a secret. What makes this possible is nothing special about this book or its author. What makes this possible is something about you. You carry a possibility with you at all times. It is encoded in the very fabric of your existence. In fact, you already have everything you need to make this journey-less journey into moment-to-moment freedom. It's simply a matter of access and realization. It's a matter of waking up to the living truth of what you already are. You've always known this was possible in some deep recess of your being, have you not?

"Still, there are moments when one feels free from one's own identification with human limitations and inadequacies. At such moments, one imagines that one stands on some spot of a small planet, gazing in amazement at the cold yet profoundly moving beauty of the eternal, the unfathomable: life and death flow into one, and there is neither evolution nor destiny; only being."

—*Albert Einstein*

Now if waking up from the dream of separation sounds like something you know little about, that doesn't mean this transformation isn't available to you. It absolutely is available to you. What we're talking about isn't about knowledge. In fact, what we're talking about may be revealing itself in your experience already. This may have been going on for some time in your life. It may be that you simply haven't noticed it. Most likely, you've noticed it but didn't know what to call it or what to do with it.

It is quite common for people to have experiences that are precursors to awakening, without recognizing them. Because we have no context for these experiences, we may not appreciate their value and so we don't consider investigating them more directly. Amazingly, these "clues" can go almost unnoticed for many years. If we do notice them, they often feel so odd or unexpected in comparison with our usual experiences that we just think we're different from others in some fundamental way. Indeed, many of the people I have worked with who have awoken to the most profound depths didn't initially know what was happening within themselves. So take heed, you may well be in the early stages of awakening already! You have simply had no context to understand what is going on or what to do about it. That is, until now. With this book you have a clear and actionable resource to help you access and actualize your deepest promptings—your true nature.

I understand if you are skeptical. I would have been had I not seen this transformation occur in myself and in others again and again. Perhaps you could take a few minutes to read to the end of this chapter. By that point, you will have enough of a sense of what the process of awakening is all about to properly decide whether this book is for you.

The Purpose of This Book

My intention in writing this book was to lay out a clear, potent, and comprehensive guide to help you navigate the endeavor of waking up to your unbound, undivided nature. Its purpose is to provide a practical and relatable means by which anyone who has the inclination to wake up can do so. It's a roadmap that shows you how to use the tools that you already possess to access that which is your birthright.

I'm not only interested in discussing initial awakenings, which are still uncommon yet indescribably transformative. I mean to show anyone interested in taking realization beyond the initial awakening, the depths of what is possible. I am talking about liberation, or what in spiritual circles might be called enlightenment. If you dislike the word enlightenment or spiritual terminology in general, then we are on the same page. There is an immense amount of unnecessary confusion in spiritual circles about the awakening process. I will address this throughout the book. One of the main things that drove me to write this book is that the awakening process is actually quite simple and accessible, yet often made to seem unattainable and complicated in contemporary spirituality. It often frustrated me that finding good pointers along the way was more challenging than seemed necessary.

It's a common belief that the path must be obscure, confusing, or nearly inaccessible to lead to authentic realization. This turns out to not be true at all. Isn't that great news?

This book is result of going through the awakening process myself and working with many others as they have gone through it. Throughout all of this, I have made a point to look as closely as I could at the nuances of what works and what doesn't work to facilitate this process. It has been an endeavor that has played out over more than twenty years. Don't worry, it needn't take you nearly that long if you apply yourself sincerely, consistently, and with an orientation to your own deepest truth. The contents of this book lay out a practical, accessible, and adaptable path to liberation. Just as important, they point out the many roadblocks that tend to occur along the way. Luckily, these obstacles are rather predictable. With some humility and willingness to learn from those who have walked this path ahead of you, they needn't derail you. However, knowing about them ahead of time and cultivating the wisdom to learn from others' mistakes will save you a lot of time and unnecessary confusion.

This Is Not a Philosophy, Paradigm, or Belief System

This is about your awakening, not mine. It is about your deepest truth, not mine or anyone else's. I make you this promise from the outset: I will not try to teach, convince, or encourage you to believe anything, period. Nothing I believe about reality or truth is helpful to you. Indeed, if I do convince you of some belief system, way of thinking, or specific view, then I have failed in the aim of this book. The whole point is for you to awaken to your own deepest truth should you choose to do so. Your deepest truth is a living truth that could never be contained by a set of beliefs or views. It is far too vast and free and, paradoxically, too intimate and self-obvious to be contained by a belief system or a paradigm.

Awakening is not about belief. This process is not conceptual in nature nor is it about rearranging concepts or beliefs in new ways to arrive at a more comfortable or peaceful way to view life. It is far more fundamental than that. As your awakened nature is realized and that realization is matured, you will have absolute freedom to utilize any belief system you choose. More important, you will be free from the need to take reference from any specific belief system to feel fulfilled or find purpose in life.

Is This About Spirituality?

If you are turned off by spirituality or religion, or have little interest in spiritual culture, belief systems, or practices, then you are in good company. A common reaction people have when an authentic awakening occurs is, "This does not feel spiritual. It feels natural, free, remarkably familiar. It is far more vast and intimate than the reality I thought I was living in, but it doesn't feel spiritual." I would like to add that the further a realization progresses beyond the initial awakening, the less spiritual it feels. One of the major aims of this book is to strip away as much spiritual terminology as possible and offer a practical means by which you can wake up to your true nature exactly how it manifests for you. At that point you can decide whether you want to call it spiritual or nonspiritual. I'll wager you won't want to call it anything because at that point you will experience so much freedom, wonder, and ease that you won't care to conceptualize. Moreover, it will be clear that to stuff that experience into a concept would be impossible. The awakened state is far too real, too close, too unbound to attempt to condense it into any description or label. You'll be too busy being absorbed into the flow of life and loving every minute of it to waste time with unnecessary conclusions, descriptions, and judgements.

If you do move in spiritual circles, resonate with spiritual culture, and/or are involved in spiritual practices, that is certainly no problem. You likely already have some context for what awakening is about. With that said, you may be even more surprised than someone who has no expectations when awakening does come about. I've had many people tell me, "Wow! This is not at all what I thought it would be, but it's more astounding than I ever imagined!" Indeed, people who have spent many years as spiritual seekers are completely dismayed when they realize that what they had been seeking all that time was a dream, an imaginary goal, and that it had nothing whatsoever to do with what is actually going on in natural (awakened) reality.

Is This Book for Me?

This book is designed to assist you at every level of the awakening process. If you relate to any of the following, you might benefit from its contents:

➤ You have felt that life up until this point has been unsatisfying in a way that is hard to pinpoint. This unsatisfactoriness seems to overshadow or "color" all your experiences. It is commonly described that one's life circumstances appear to be what most people would consider the makings of a good life, but none of it is truly fulfilling or satisfying. You feel like you are missing something big about the way life is supposed to feel.

➤ You feel like you live inside a prison of self-referential thoughts. The more you try to use thought to solve this problem, the tighter the cage gets. You want to find a way out of this pain but are unsure how to go about it, or whether it is even possible to do so.

➢ You don't know what awakening is but feel that a fundamental shift into a more intimate, authentic, and naturally free way of living sounds like a valuable undertaking.

➢ You have a sense of what awakening is and want to wake up, but you do not know how to proceed.

➢ You think you have had "tastes" of awakening but are unsure if they are authentic and do not know what to do next.

➢ You know a lot about spirituality, awakening, and/or enlightenment but have not had direct experience in a way that is nonconceptual and authentic beyond any doubt.

➢ You have had an awakening, and there has been some progress or clarification beyond it, but you still feel stuck. You have difficulty finding good advice about how to proceed. You aren't sure whether there is something more, or you believe that true liberation is out of your reach.

➢ You have experienced deeper stages of realization but seem to be endlessly "fluctuating" between awakeness and separation, between spontaneous presence and that heavy sense of isolation and contraction. You have integrated realization in various ways but still don't have the ongoing moment-to-moment realization as a living reality in your daily life.

➢ You believe you are awakened or enlightened, but external circumstances would suggest otherwise. For example, friends, family, or even your students tell you in one way or another that you have more work to do.

➤ You feel as if your realization has gone deep and has stabilized. Externally, life has become peaceful, and you find presence and flow nearly all the time. Yet there is still some doubt, even if it is subtle and fleeting. You recognize a profound responsibility to fully embody this realization and would like to investigate subtle dualistic tendencies that may still be a hindrance.

This Book Is a Catalyst

When we read a nonfiction book, we are usually expecting to learn something. We are hoping to gain a new perspective or see things in a fresh, new, or empowering way. This is not that type of book. This book is a living catalyst. It will help you to actualize thoroughgoing, authentic, and definitive transformation that is wholly outside any belief system or perspective. The function of this catalyst is to assist you on a journey directly into the deepest reaches of who and what you are. When you come through the other side, the living truth of what you are will be vibrant, immediate, and fundamental to all of your experience. You will no longer have doubts about who you are or what is real, nor will you care to live from belief systems. You will express realization in the exact way that only you can express it. What's more, you will do so with spontaneity, sincerity, and the joy of moving through life unencumbered.

*"All the darkness in the world cannot extinguish
the light of a single candle."*

—St. Francis of Assisi

Anyone Can Wake Up

Awakening is an equal opportunity employer. I have seen both spiritual and nonspiritual people wake up. I have seen logical, scientific, skeptical, intuitive, artistic, and emotional people wake up. I have seen people wake up who had a clear intention to do so and worked hard at it. I have seen people wake up who had no idea what was going on and for whom the process seemed to have begun spontaneously. What determines your qualification for awakening is nothing you believe, identify with, or do. What determines your qualification is one simple thing: you have a desire to open to the deepest truth of what you are. That's it, nothing more.

"I always thought this was something that only happened to other people—special people, lucky people. Now I realize this has always been here. I remember the wonder and ease of this from childhood, maybe before. There is absolutely nothing apart from anything else. True freedom is the nature of everything. Spontaneity and enjoyment aren't 'states' they are the immediate experience of natural reality. There is no problem to be solved, and there never was! There is just this timeless moment of total absorption. Even what I had perceived as difficult thoughts and emotional states are seen to simply be fluctuations in what I already Am: pure aliveness. This peace is profound, uncaused, and permeates all of experience. Even these words cannot touch the astonishment of this reality."

—Several people after awakening, who use surprisingly similar words

How This Book Came About

Many years ago, I had an awakening. Later in the book I will describe what led up to it, how it played out, and the aftereffects. For now, I will just say that it was radically transformative at the most fundamental level. It permanently changed how I experience everything. It was and continues to be a pervasive restructuring of my experience of life, myself, others, and the world. One of the interesting things that I recognized coming out the other side was that I had absolutely no capacity to explain what had happened to me. I certainly knew it wasn't something that could be explained in words or that I could teach. I will go into why this is later. For now, I just want to emphasize that there was no sense of being able to effectively communicate what had happened. Moreover, I didn't have the inclination to share the experience or even talk about it, really, although I did on rare occasion. When I would share about it, the responses I got from people suggested to me it was best to just continue to integrate and work with what had been directly realized, but not necessarily to try to communicate it. This was intuitively obvious and not something I had to think about. I certainly never aspired to become a teacher of awakening, spirituality, or anything of the sort. So, I just went on with my life.

Several years later I began to notice that, on occasion, while in the midst of a casual conversation, the person I was talking to would have a shift in experience. I didn't feel like I was talking about anything special; it actually felt mundane, like talking about the weather, or feelings, or life. It would only come up with certain people and in certain situations. With the majority of people I encountered, it didn't come up at all. It seemed to "know" when to come up. The strange part was that I had no investment in relaying any particular message. Yet the conversation would continue in an intuitive way and felt a bit like dancing. People would ask more and more directed questions relating to their own experience. I was genuinely surprised when I would seem to have the answer in the moment. Sometimes I would wonder, Where did that come from? even as it came out of my mouth. It is still like that, more so maybe.

Then people started having awakenings. I can't tell you what that is like, but I will say that the only thing better than waking up yourself is going through awakening all over again, alongside another person. Anyways, that's how this all progressed. At some point I was talking, messaging, and video conferencing with many different people in various stages of awakening. It still mystifies me, but somehow it works. Over time I started noticing distinct patterns in the ways the conversation would flow and commonalities in what was discussed and where people's sticking points were. One day I sat down and wrote the first chapter of this book. It came spontaneously and simply. It really is no big deal, but if it is helpful to anyone, how can I not write it?

Awakening Is a Real Thing

I clearly remember the exact moment it dawned on me that there was a certain possibility, a way of experiencing reality, that was altogether outside of the anxious and uncomfortable ways I had learned to view myself and my life up to that point. I was a first-year college student, and I was sitting in a course called Introduction to Eastern Religions. I genuinely enjoyed the class and thought Eastern religions were fascinating, although the fascination was limited to intellectual curiosity. One day the usual professor was out due to illness, so we had a substitute lecturer. He was an American who was a practicing Buddhist at a local temple. He began lecturing on Buddhism and was talking about suffering and enlightenment. I had read and heard about these topics before and found them interesting. What he was talking about seemed similar to what I had previously heard. Then something unexpected happened. It struck me in an instant that what he was talking about wasn't a topic, nor was it a subject or a set of beliefs. He was pointing to a way out! A way out of the usual way of living, thinking, and trying to survive as a person that had caused me so much pain. It was a way out of suffering—completely. I don't know how I knew this, but suddenly it was exquisitely obvious. Up until that moment, the whole endeavor of trying to be a human with all the accompanying expectations, trying to fit in, and trying to be happy when I really wasn't was all I had ever known. In an instant, it became obvious that I had been living in a sort of false reality. At that moment it clicked that I had been trying to live inside of a very small conceptual world, one which had been causing me tremendous pain.

I was listening to the lecture, "Buddhism . . . blah-blah . . . suffering, enlightenment . . . blah-blah," and suddenly the words he was saying faded into the background as if someone had turned down the volume. At the same time, the surroundings seemed to dim. It was almost as if color in the periphery had faded into black and white. There was something extraordinarily alive and deeply present that was palpable in the room. The aliveness wasn't otherworldly or anything magical. It was actually remarkably familiar, yet markedly potent. All my senses seemed to be acutely attuned to the experience. Time stopped (literally). As the substitute professor was talking, I realized he was conveying a message totally outside of the spiritual or religious material. It was as if he had walked right up to me, ignoring everyone else in the room, and said, "This has nothing to do with the subject matter I seem to be lecturing on. All this suffering, this mental prison and all of what you take yourself to be? Yeah, it's not like that at all. You can wake up out of that. This can happen at any time. It's not about religion or spirituality." Although he didn't say these exact words to me, I responded as if he had.

My hand shot up and I began rattling off questions before he nodded for me to speak. "This that you're talking about, is it real? I mean does that actually happen?" He locked eyes with me and his gaze told me he knew that I had gotten his subliminal communication. He paused before answering to make sure I understood the gravity of his answer. "There is no doubt."

13

He continued to look at me for a couple of seconds longer and then went on lecturing. I had no clue at that moment what would come of the seed that had just been planted, but I knew beyond doubt that this was real. I also knew intuitively that I would find a way to make it a reality in this lifetime. It has taken me many years to really grasp how profound that moment was. As I will describe later, this "little taste" was only a miniscule foreshadowing of what was to come, but I am grateful beyond words that it happened.

Although I didn't appreciate the full magnitude of what had been transmitted to me in that moment, a fire had been lit inside me. I didn't know what it was or how to attain it, but I somehow knew that there was something far more real than this story I had always believed about myself and my life. I also had the intuition that it wasn't somewhere else. I wouldn't have to join some special group to realize this possibility. I didn't know the path or what would be required of me to "attain" it, but it didn't matter. That one taste was enough. It was a confirmation of a living truth with a depth that I sensed was unfathomable.

A Way Out

Please understand that when I say, "a way out," I am not talking about escape from life or from our responsibilities as humans. I'm talking about a way out of a false reality and set of beliefs that had imprisoned me for years. I just knew somehow that there was an exit point being described that would lead to a life much freer and more real than anything I had heretofore experienced. I also knew that what this lecturer was pointing to, almost no one knew about. If they did, why hadn't I heard of it before? Why weren't people shouting it from the rooftops? If this possibility was common knowledge, why was this not being taught in schools? Why would physicians and therapists not recommend it for the endless numbers of people adrift in an ocean of angst and suffering? I sensed that the others in the room thought he was talking about the subject of enlightenment, just as I had always

14

assumed when listening to such lectures, instead of the living reality of it. I'm pointing this out not to make awakening seem unattainable, but to clarify why I had never heard of it in this way before. It was because most people simply don't know that this possibility exists.

I want to point out one other thing about this experience. Although this "transmission" occurred in the context of a lecture on Eastern religions, specifically Buddhism, I somehow knew even in that moment that it wasn't about religion. Although Buddhism may be a vehicle for some people, it is only a vehicle. The living truth itself, this vast reality that I sensed in that moment, has nothing to do with spirituality or religion. It was far more intimate and familiar than it was mystical. It had to do with me and the way I was suddenly relating to the rest of reality—a way that felt more real than I had remembered real feeling. It was as if the very core of what I was, which I had somehow learned to avoid looking directly into, was itself the portal to interconnectedness with everything. I couldn't have described it as such in that moment, but intuitively it was quite obvious. This was a potent "taste."

The first step in the awakening process is what I sometimes call recognition. It is the taste of something more real than real, something that lights a spark inside of you. It is my intention that reading this right now is that moment for you. I hope that by sharing this story with you, I have planted a seed in you just as that lecturer did in me so many years ago. Yes, awakening is a real thing, and it can happen to you . . . there is no doubt. If there is only one thing you take away from reading this entire book, hopefully it's that awakening is absolutely possible, and that it is possible for you in this lifetime. Even if you read no further than this sentence, yet you can simply glimpse the possibility of a living truth that is more vast, free, and real than the ways you typically experience life, then this endeavor was worth the effort.

I have seen people wake up many times. I have observed awakening and realization from many sides and perspectives and have made an exhaustive study of exactly how this process unfolds and what the obstructions are that can hinder it. I have done this for one reason: so I can impart it to you. It's your turn now.

Chapter 1:

A Word of Caution

The Ultimate Adventure

E very human on the face of the Earth has the capacity to live a life of spontaneity, peace, and wonder beyond what can be imagined. You have the potential to put an end to suffering in this lifetime. It is natural to have doubts when hearing statements like these. As a discerning reader you might be wondering, Is this an exaggeration, or is this some sort of positive thinking strategy? I assure you this is no exaggeration, and it has nothing to do with positive thinking. These are simple statements of truth that I've found to be accurate again and again in those who are willing to sincerely investigate their deepest nature.

By the way, your deepest nature happens to be synonymous with the deepest nature of the cosmos. Out of that parity arises the fundamental and unshakable realization of interconnectedness and synchronicity with all things, beings, and situations. Many people, myself included, have gone through this process and have been astounded again and again by the ever-deepening clarity and radical absorption into all of life. This truly is the ultimate adventure.

> **Luke Skywalker**: *"I won't fail you! I'm not afraid."*
>
> **Yoda**: *[grimly] "Oh! You will be, You will be . . ."*

With all of that said, I would be remiss in my duties if I didn't caution you on a few points. It goes without saying that no endeavor of this magnitude comes without discomfort, change, and sacrifice. While these elements will certainly come into play, it may not be in the ways you might think. This process isn't about dropping out of life to meditate in a cave for years on end. It isn't about giving up all your material possessions. It isn't about giving your will over to some religious figure or system. In a sense, it's more challenging than any of those scenarios. This is about waking up in your life exactly as it is. Stated this way, it may not sound like sacrifice, change, or discomfort will be necessary, but make no mistake about it, you will be challenged in ways that will surprise you and that you can't really prepare for. You will see things in yourself that you never knew were there. In fact, you will face every distorted belief and repressed emotion that is hidden inside you at one point or another. What's more, the old strategies of avoidance, distraction, and resistance will become less viable options as realization deepens. You will never be left empty-handed or completely out in the cold. You will be given many tools to navigate these sometimes unpredictable and challenging waters, but you will have to navigate them.

There will be shifts in the way you perceive reality. There will be moments when you will feel disoriented. Those moments will pass. There will also be times when you (or at least part of you) will wish you had never begun this journey. Those times will pass as well. You will never be given more than you can tolerate, but this will not always

18

be a walk in the park either. You won't always face this process courageously or even by choice. The investigations, contemplations, and practices described in this book are exceptionally potent. By following them you are initiating a process that will, in many ways, overtake you. That may sound scary, but the "you" that is overtaken is a limited version of what you truly are. This false identity must be seen through in order to wake up to the boundless and timeless reality that is your essential nature. We will be working at the level of your identity, which is the most foundational sense of who and what you take yourself to be. This is the most radical transformation that is available to you in this lifetime, bar none.

I'm neither saying these things to scare nor impress you. I'm saying them simply because they are true. Anyone I've ever worked with who has genuinely taken up this investigation will tell you that this is no exaggeration. It leads to processes that cannot be undone once started. Please keep in mind:

➤ First and foremost, the techniques, contemplations, and inquiries described in this book are extremely potent. These transformations occur at the identity level. Alterations and disentanglements will occur in the fabric of what makes you you! Unconscious places will become fully conscious. You will see things you don't always want to see in yourself. You are voluntarily coming into contact with forces that are vastly more powerful than you (or anyone) can begin to imagine.

➤ Awakening plays out on its own schedule, not yours. There will be aspects of this process that seem to be taking way too long. There will also be aspects of this process that come way too fast for your comfort.

➤ There will be experiences and events along this path that will surprise you. In many ways, this is a mysterious process, and things will arise at times and in ways that you cannot prepare for. Ultimately, this turns out to be okay because you have the innate capacity to integrate these eventualities. You do have the capacity for this, just know it is largely dormant; therefore some internal shifts will have to occur to allow you to tap into it.

If this all sounds like what you are interested in, then great. You will find this to be the adventure of all adventures. If it's not your priority at this time in life, then by all means, put it aside and pursue what most authentically moves you. This book will always be available if you choose to return and readdress this matter. There is no judgement from me or the Universe. If you genuinely feel that it is your path to be an exceptional parent and raise a family, then that is exactly what you should be doing. If you want to throw yourself fully into art or music, then that is exactly what you should do. If you feel genuinely moved to pursue a life of scientific investigation, then by all means go do that. This is your life, so doing what feels most authentic and relevant to you regardless of social expectation is what will be most fulfilling.

Liberation or Bust

If you decide to begin this undertaking or feel that the awakening process is already unfolding for you, then I strongly urge you to take it to completion. In actuality, there is no absolute completion. However, in this context I mean until the progression of awakening becomes spontaneous and individual suffering ends for you in this life. The word I will use for that stage is liberation. Liberation will be explained in detail later in the book.

It can be a painful and confusing place to find yourself when the awakening process has begun and then is abandoned after some initial insight. Most of the time this occurs, it is because there is confusing, contradictory, and/or uninformed guidance out there. This is especially true with the later stages of realization. The ubiquity of confusing and contradictory guidance is one of the major reasons this book was written. You will be given the tools needed to take this process to liberation. As well, you will be versed in the many potential pitfalls along the way and how to avoid them. It is on me to make sure you have a clear, adaptable, and effective means by which to navigate each stage of the process. It is on you to do the work.

"Nothing is so fatiguing as the eternal hanging on of an uncompleted task."

—William James

The Barrier of Belief

In coming chapters, we will investigate the nature of beliefs and how they affect our experience of reality. Interestingly, it doesn't matter what set of beliefs you have when you begin this journey. The nature of your beliefs ultimately has little to do with your ability to wake up. Whether you are liberal or conservative, religious or secular, Buddhist, Christian, or atheist makes little difference. What makes a considerable difference in how smoothly this process will go is not what you believe but rather your relationship to beliefs themselves. To put it simply, if you are willing to question or at least examine your beliefs and let go of the ones that are found to be inaccurate or that cause you suffering, then you are in a good place as far as awakening is concerned. On the other hand, if you pride yourself on having strong and rigid beliefs and have no willingness to examine them at all, this will be an extremely difficult path for you. I didn't say impossible, because it is still possible, but you will be fighting yourself at every turn.

Psychological Considerations

I had severe anxiety in my younger life. After my first awakening at age twenty-four, it improved tremendously, and for that I am forever grateful. Intermittently during the post-awakening phase there were some recurrences. They were milder versions and were experienced quite differently than before awakening. They were seen as guides to help facilitate a deeper investigation—an investigation that ultimately illuminated the roots of the anxiety. Over time, the anxiety completely subsided. This was my experience, and I know many others who had similar experiences with both anxiety and depression. With that said, I am not prescribing this process as a cure for any psychiatric disorder, nor is treating such ailments the point of the book. I am simply illustrating by example that it is okay to proceed on this path having these diagnoses with a few caveats.

If you have a history of attempting suicide or feel that you are suicidal or at risk of harming yourself or others, I cannot recommend this book as a sole resource. That doesn't mean that awakening isn't possible for you, but this can be a steep path, and trying to go it alone may not be safe for you. Working closely with someone who has walked this path ahead of you is advisable. Navigating this territory with someone who can effectively guide you and be available to you on a personal basis is the safest, most prudent way to go. Additionally, if you are having or have had psychosis, it is best to consult with someone who can help you decide when and how to approach awakening. The last word of caution is that this type of endeavor should never be expected to replace treatment by a medical or mental health professional. Please continue treatment plans and medication regimens as prescribed. Always work closely with a health care professional to make any changes or discontinuations.

If you feel there is any sort of instability in your life related to medical or psychiatric disorders that I have not mentioned, please consult a professional before attempting a process like the one I will be mapping out.

Chapter 2:

First Steps

Introduction

If you've read this far, I want to congratulate you. The mere acknowledgement that an investigation into your deepest truth is of value to you is incredibly powerful. You might not see the effect of this acknowledgment immediately, but it is like a message sent from your conscious self into the deeper recesses of your being. A communication has been dispatched to the fundamental forces that govern who you are and how you relate to yourself and to all of life. Transformation is already underway.

This chapter sets forth a set of simple suggestions that can be useful as orienting principles to get you started on the right foot. Keeping them in sight can make things much smoother for you. They can help to avoid a lot of confusion, frustration, and unnecessary detours. Do keep in mind these are only suggestions. While I wouldn't recommend ignoring them outright, they aren't meant to be rigidly applied.

Some of these suggestions are general frames of reference that help to cultivate a fertile soil for awakening. Others are strategies to read and incorporate the material in this book more effectively and efficiently. Still others are pointers to help dispel certain beliefs about awakening that can be a hindrance if not examined.

Scope

My original intent was for this book to cover the entirety of the awakening and realization process from the beginning, through awakening and the various insights and challenges that follow awakening, all the way to liberation. It became clear about halfway through the writing of the book that to do this would result in a book far too long to be practical. I decided to cover the territory up to and including awakening, leaving discussions specific to later stages largely for the next book.

With that said, the vast majority of the inquiries and practices laid out in these chapters are just as applicable after awakening as they are before—perhaps more so. Much of what I've included in this book comes from working with people who have gone through awakening but haven't yet realized liberation. Ninety percent of what I discuss with people who are in that in between phase you can find in these chapters. Much of the work after awakening is reminding oneself again and again of the nuances of what was realized during that initial awakening. With each round of inquiry, refinement, release, and integration, another level of clarity is realized that is irreversible.

The majority of the subsequent book will be descriptions of the specific shifts that occur after awakening and how to avoid the pitfalls that prevent them. There will be discussions of how and when to apply certain inquiries specific to those shifts in insight and understanding. As I mentioned, most of these techniques and inquiry points are included in this book, I just don't always go into great detail about how and when to apply them at later stages. There is a chapter included in this book called Stages of Awakening that also references these later transformations. In addition, there will be a brief chapter covering post-awakening guidance, describing basic practice approaches to those later stages of realization.

Participation

If you take the time to apply the various techniques, inquiries, and investigations in this book as you read through it, you will undergo a radical transformation. If you read it from cover to cover and don't take the time to apply anything you read, you will get far less out of it. I would suggest reading a little at a time and applying what you've read. If I were to prescribe a ratio, I'd suggest 5 percent reading and 95 percent putting what you've read into practice. As an example, you could read one section per week and then sit with, contemplate, and/ or apply what you've read before moving on.

I also want to say a word about repetition. You will undoubtedly notice certain themes and motifs being repeated at various times and in different contexts as you move through this book. This is purposeful. There are certain distortions in the way we process our experience that are rather insidious. I know from experience that we will have to readdress them multiple times and from different angles to really get under them, as they tend to reassert themselves in our perception. If you recognize this repetition, then you have the opportunity to address these distortions at a deeper level each time they are pointed out.

Foundations Are Foundational

As you begin to navigate this process, it can be tempting to get overly excited about learning everything about what comes later, such as the more advanced aspects of awakening. This enthusiasm is natural and simply a part of the process. However, I want to caution you that a

healthy appreciation for the fundamentals remains important throughout. Even at later stages of realization, much of what I discuss with people and the ways I guide them are similar to what I discuss with beginners. Moreover, the most confusing and tricky places I've seen people get themselves stuck have to do with overlooking something foundational. Losing sight of the basics can become quite a hindrance if not addressed. I'll use the analogy of building a house. If the foundation is complete and structurally sound, it will be a sturdy, functional, long-lasting house. As other aspects of the construction
are addressed, it is always a good idea to return to and inspect the foundation on occasion. This is especially true if you are having some trouble in later stages of the construction process. It's always possible that some part of the foundation has been damaged or was overlooked initially, and addressing that will make further construction go much smoother.

In this spirit, I suggest returning to this and the other foundational chapters on occasion. The purpose of doing this is twofold. First, you can be sure the foundation of your understanding and practice is intact and that nothing big has been overlooked. Second, by returning to the basics at various times throughout the realization process, you will gain a deeper understanding than you gleaned on the previous reading. This will cultivate a refinement in experiential insight. You will incorporate things at a more subtle level each time you return and remind yourself of the basic orientations. You might be surprised when, having read something five times, it suddenly stands off the page and hits you at a very deep level. What was previously an intellectual understanding suddenly becomes a profound living insight. This has happened to me more times than I can count. If I had a nickel for every time someone said to me, "I've heard you say that so many times. But for whatever reason, this time it hit me differently and everything changed."

A One-on-One Conversation

As you have probably gathered, the writing style of this book will be in the form of a one-on-one conversation. I am speaking directly to you, and solely for your benefit. I have no interest in philosophical discussions, especially about spirituality or enlightenment. I am only interested in what works. As I mentioned in the first chapter, this book grew out of one-on-one conversations with various people in the process of awakening. Now you are in on the conversation. As I write, this feels exactly how it does when I am working closely with an individual who is going through this process. This is not meant to be topical, textbookish, or even instructional. It is a catalytic transmission. I'm giving you everything I've got.

For the Moment Only

I always teach in the immediate. When I am working with someone, I don't concern myself with where they are in the realization process or a specific trajectory. In this way, the teaching can be immediate and not "loaded" with preconceived ideas of where someone is coming from or where they are headed. Hence the exchange is intuitive, instant, and fully in the present. It is a dynamic process and tends to change quickly and often. I will commonly say, "Don't worry about anything I've said before. It has no value here. I'm only concerned with what is immediately available and in direct experience for you right now." I urge you to treat everything you read in this book in the same way. If you are reading something, then give it your full attention. Don't worry about trying to fit it in to a paradigm with some other portion of the teaching. Instead, let it permeate you. Let it sink into your depths. Let it germinate inside you and find its own fruition. Let every suggestion, inquiry, and investigation stand on its own and reveal its own intelligence as a living experience in that moment. Even if you've read something before and are tempted to gloss over it, thinking, Oh, I know this, try to remind yourself to read it with fresh eyes. Let it be the first time you have read it, once more. Let it be the only thing you are concerned with in that moment. Let it fill up the moment. Let that moment fill up all your senses. Then, let it go . . . completely. Don't hold on. Don't collect information or strategies. Just allow and embrace whatever comes next.

Direct Experience Trumps Information

If at any point you are reading along and find yourself overtaken by an experience of expansiveness, interconnectedness, or deep stillness, then just stop reading and turn your attention directly to that experience. Relax into that experience. Give the experience permission to be the only thing there is. The words on the page aren't going anywhere. They will be here when you return. It is always best to honor your immediate experience. So if something peaceful, wordless, or "exceptionally real" comes over you, just sit with it. Don't try to make it stay or go, just let it merge with you. Let it show you its splendor. Let it reveal its nature to you directly, outside of words or concepts. You can even close your eyes and meditate for a few minutes, or longer if it feels relevant and spontaneous. Better yet, be meditated! This is what you're here for, after all.

The Need to Understand

We are fully immersed in the Information Age. We have ready and efficient access to vast amounts of data on any subject almost anywhere we go. This has a tremendous practical benefit to us. There is a side effect of this, however; we are inundated throughout the day with massive amounts of information through various electronic conduits. It really can have an overloading effect on our psyche. It can also be addictive. Our brains are wired so that the more times we use specific neural pathways, the stronger they get. In this way, we have wired ourselves as voracious information collectors and comparers.

When we are deciding where to go on vacation or comparing new cars to purchase, this faculty serves us well. When we are investigating our deepest nature, it can be detrimental. No set of descriptions, data, or information could possibly define the complexity and vastness of what you are, could they?

As you read through these chapters and apply the material, please keep in mind that intellectually grasping this material is not your primary goal. If you perceive that conceptual understanding is the point of this endeavor, then you will read in a way that is somewhat like data collection. On the other hand, if you read with the intent to experientially incorporate what is pointed to, you will be oriented in a different sort of way. So, I might suggest that while you read and incorporate this information, always give more weight to the sense of what is behind the words. Be more interested in what the words reflect inside of you in an intuitive and physical way than the words themselves.

Give Yourself Permission

When I was younger, I had a lot of difficulty in certain social situations. Celebratory environments such as parties often caused me anxiety and frustration. They had exactly the opposite effect on me of what I'd hoped for. I remember looking at people and feeling jealous because they looked so carefree and could enjoy themselves totally. They naturally had fun and moved so spontaneously. No one at these events had to work at being carefree; it was natural for them. It truly dumbfounded me because I was a smart person and good at problem solving. I thought it should be easy to kick off my shoes and relax in a social setting. But I never could. It took me a long time to realize that at those times in my life my heart wasn't into celebrating, escaping, and distracting myself endlessly. Now if you had asked me then, I would have told you that that is exactly what I wanted. It seemed like the thing to do. I thought I wanted to work and take care of my responsibilities so that when the opportunity arose, I could just let go, have fun, be silly and free. In retrospect, that was the fallacy of false alternatives in operation. I had an unexamined belief that the selection of activities that were available to me was limited to what I had seen others engage in. It seemed that outside of work, school, and family responsibilities, the choice of pastimes was limited to athletics, reading, partying, more work, or various hobbies. Of course, all of these are perfectly acceptable ways to spend free time. The problem for me was that I had believed that these were the only possibilities. They were not, but I had never come across a resource or met anyone who presented me with the possibility that I was genuinely interested in. I had to figure it out on my own, and it took me quite some time. Ultimately, I had to give myself permission to acknowledge a possibility I hadn't seen or heard anyone describe, then pursue it. So, what was this possibility? I wanted to investigate and ultimately live the deepest truth of what I was. I wanted to live out of an intuitive understanding of the fundamental nature of reality. I also wanted to end my own suffering.

"The truth is so lovable that it has only to be known to be embraced."

—Plutarch

It is simply not common to find a context for these interests in the usual social situations that we humans encounter on a day-to-day basis. If you want to see what I mean firsthand, you could try the following experiment. The next time you are having a casual conversation with someone, whether it be a friend, family member, or partner, address this directly. Say something like, "You know I do have some interest in what we usually talk about, such as our goals, our families, work related matters, etc. However, what I'm really interested in right now is the absolute truth. What is true for you right now? What is the most fundamental sense of reality as you are experiencing it at this moment?" The look on their face will say it all. Certainly, there are individuals and groups of people who are interested in these types of conversations, but they are usually found by intentionally seeking them out. It is taboo to talk about a radical and uncompromising pursuit of inner truth. I hope that changes, but until it does, we have to give ourselves permission.

I don't mean to criticize the practical ways we communicate or suggest that having an interest in waking up to our true nature is better than other pursuits. I don't think it is. However, if a yearning to embody your deepest truth is what is really stirring inside you, then there is no substitute. You have every right to address it. You have every right to answer its call. It is possible that no one you know right now would understand this intention, but that doesn't matter. You don't need an external context to validate this natural curiosity and inclination toward truth. You have the right and the power to give your yearning for truth the top priority in your life. This is primarily a heart-level commitment, so you don't need to figure out all of what that means in your life right now. It is simply a matter of acknowledging and giving yourself permission to orient toward the most fundamental and important yearnings in your life.

"I have lived on the lip of insanity, wanting to know reasons, knocking on a door. It opens. I've been knocking from the inside!"

—Rumi

What You Want Is Already Here

You carry the innate potential to end your suffering in this lifetime. Even that statement doesn't quite hit the nail on the head. I'll do you one better. Would you believe that the state of nonsuffering, the actuality of nondivision is here already? It's not "out there" somewhere. It's not something you will go out and find. It's not something that will occur in the future, even though our thoughts will make it appear to be that way. I know this doesn't make sense intellectually. That's perfectly okay. It doesn't have to make sense for it to become a living reality. There's no need to think about or contemplate this truth. At some point it will hit you over the head. It usually comes in an aha moment.

You might wonder what value there is in something that cannot be grasped intellectually. Well, it can be helpful to remind yourself of this principle when you start to see the machinery of seeking ramp up in your mind. When you start to notice thoughts or daydreams surface, such as, When I'm finally enlightened, it will be like this and that, you can remind yourself of this simple truth: "It's already here. Even if it isn't a moment-to-moment reality for me right now, I trust that it is here, not there, or something that will come later in my life." This affirmation has a way of bringing our attention back into the immediate. We can relax a bit and return our attention to the thoughts, feelings, and sensations of the moment instead of making ourselves endless false promises about the future.

"What we are looking for is what is looking."

—*St Francis of Assisi*

We will investigate the nature of thought and seeking in later chapters. It will become much clearer how something that is exactly here at all times could become so obscured and projected into an imaginary future. For now, you might take this as a suggestion to cultivate a measure of faith in your innate freedom and peace.

The Busy Life

Life keeps us busy, doesn't it? We have children to raise, relationships to nurture, grades to earn, and jobs to do. For some of us the demands are even more daunting. We might be taking care of a sick loved one. We might be a single parent with a just-barely-getting-by income, holding two jobs to make ends meet. We might be struggling with serious health issues ourselves, and at the same time trying to balance all our responsibilities. Regardless of the circumstances, life moves on and the demands can seem overwhelming at times. So where is there room for the work of investigating our deepest nature?

It is a common perception that to wake up we would have to abandon life as usual and dedicate ourselves to decades of contemplation or meditation in a secluded environment such as a monastery or temple. This turns out not to be true at all. That kind of seclusion can even be counterproductive in the deeper stages of awakening. The most deeply realized people I know are not monastics, priests, monks, or nuns. They are living among us with outwardly ordinary lives. They work full-time jobs and maintain relationships. This can be counterintuitive, but the texture of the busy life is the perfect environment for awakening to occur. One reason for this is that "life as usual" presents us with situations that can reveal to us the subtlest and most insidious ego structures (tendencies to contract into a sense of separation). Stressful environments and challenging interpersonal situations add the necessary texture to bring out deeply buried resistance patterns that can be quite hard to see in a life dedicated solely to quiet contemplation.

So how does one approach this awakening endeavor in the context of the busy life? First and foremost, it is important to understand that awakening doesn't just happen during meditation, on retreat, or when you are in the presence of someone who is awakened. In fact, it often comes out of the blue or in moments when we are not thinking about it or practicing in any specific way. It might seem as if awakening is something that you go out and find, like a buried treasure. It is not so much like that. It comes to you. It germinates and flowers in its own time. Your job is to cultivate the soil in preparation. When the soil is properly prepared, awakening comes as naturally as the day follows the night. It can and does come in all different life situations. It can come during a stressful time or even when life is in crisis. It can come when things are peaceful. It follows no rules.

It's also helpful to recognize that uninteresting, mundane, or seemingly boring moments in life are some of the best opportunities. Those times in our day for which we usually perceive no redeeming quality are ripe for investigation. Standing in line at the grocery store is a perfect opportunity to practice. Being stuck in traffic equally so. Even experiences of restlessness and confusion can be goldmines for inquiry and practicing mindfulness. Encountering people who trigger various emotional responses in you is valuable beyond measure when approached with openness and a willingness to let the situation reveal what it has to offer. Uncomfortable experiences are just as valuable as having peaceful or mystical experiences during meditation. Later we will cover how to apply practices or inquiries in these moments. For now, here is one of my favorite Zen quotes of all time:

"If you consider quietude right and activity wrong, then this is seeking the real aspect by destroying the worldly aspect, seeking nirvana, the peace of extinction, apart from birth and death. When you like quiet and hate activity, this is the time to apply effort. Suddenly when in the midst of activity, you topple the sense of quietude—that power surpasses quietistic meditation . . . by a million billion times."

—Dahui Zonggao

A million billion times! That is where you are headed. This is an expression of the natural state of reality and seamless immersion into it. If that is the natural state, you might wonder what is getting in the way of living it at this very moment. Well, it turns out very little actually. What this really comes down to is recognizing and reversing the ways in which we habitually reject life at various levels through perceptual distortion. By experiencing reality through layers of perceptual filters, we subtly, and at times not so subtly, reject our momentary experience. We do this through habituation, and we don't realize the cost. This rejection is human nature, or at least it is from the collective human delusion of separation.

When all is said and done, what liberation truly means is that we are so completely absorbed in the momentary flow of life that there is not the slightest rejection of the moment or situation. Only then is true freedom and radical intimacy seen to be the simple and obvious nature of things, rather than some goal to be achieved. So even though we often feel out of contact with the moment, we needn't become discouraged because life is so busy. The busy life continually exposes us to situations and textures necessary to realize and embody our innately free nature. For now, you needn't worry about knowing what to do in moments where you feel out of contact. It is enough to simply recognize and trust that your life, exactly as it is right now, is the perfect environment for awakening. Inquiries and practices will come later. For now, just make some room for the possibility that your day is full of endless opportunities to come in contact with your undivided nature. At deeper stages of realization, it becomes clear that every moment is perfectly choreographed for further deepening of insight and liberation. The Universe is on your side—fully on your side.

No Escape

Please never use the excuse of investigating your true nature or being on a spiritual path to justify irresponsible behavior. This process is not meant to be an easy way out, a way of escaping from the hardships of life, or a way to avoid responsibilities. In general, I recommend continuing to do what you've been doing and take your life responsibilities seriously. Go to work. Go to school. Treat your relationships respectfully, and give them the attention they deserve. If you are running from your responsibilities and telling yourself it is because of "spirituality," you might want to take a closer look at your motivations. Of course, we sometimes need to make changes in our lives. Sometimes we need to make changes in our relationships or vocations. Decisions such as these should be given the heartfelt consideration they deserve. What I'm suggesting is that if the reason you are giving yourself for making those changes has to do with the awakening process, you might be selling yourself a bill of goods.

Is it possible to build an ego around career, position, and accomplishment that can make awakening more challenging? Sure. It is possible to fixate anywhere, and some of this will happen no matter what we do. It is the way humans are wired. However, in my experience it is more common to fixate in the opposite direction. It is more common to use spirituality as an excuse to run away from our responsibilities or to avoid acknowledging truths that we find to be inconvenient or uncomfortable. Everyone has this tendency to some degree, but for some people this is a prominent distortion in their life. Without recognizing this misunderstanding, we can be derailed for many years without realizing it.

Micromanaging Life

We live in a society of myriad and easily available distractions. Consider the recently acquired appendage that has suddenly appeared on human bodies worldwide, mystifying scientists. Almost overnight, this abrupt evolutionary development we call the "smartphone" has dramatically transformed how we communicate and how we spend our time. Those little gadgets have the power to captivate our attention in innumerable ways. I have nothing against smartphones per se. They are practical and useful devices. But compare a room full of people today to a similar group before smart phones were invented, and you'll see what I'm getting at. Add to that all the other screen devices (television, laptops, tablets, video games, PCs) and we've got a veritable cacophony of distractions that can easily dominate our lives. On top of all the electronic distractions, we inundate ourselves with hobbies, pastimes, activities, social obligations, and on and on. Just as there are personality traits that tend toward escapism and avoiding responsibility, there are others that cause us to "overmanage" life. These tendencies can lead to ongoing distraction with activities, management, and details, resulting in wasted energy and even exhaustion. It is not uncommon for some people to fill every moment of their day with activities and tasks to actually avoid waking up. I have met people who have serious aspirations of realizing their deepest truth, but they continually overfill and overmanage their lives to the point where they undermine their own drive for realization.

What is often underlying this is a discord between thoughts and emotions. We can use the excuse of being overcommitted or generally busy to avoid feeling emotions in a natural and spontaneous way. I've had people tell me, "I get so exhausted with all of my commitments that I'll make time for myself to relax with no obligations. I think of how nice it will be to just sit and meditate. Yet when I try to relax, I feel restless and uncomfortable, like I need to go do something." At this point in the conversation, I'm usually thinking, Great! You've finally slowed down enough to start feeling what is underneath all of that frantic activity. Unfortunately, the next thing they often say is, "And since I couldn't relax, I went and did xyz." We can all relate to this at some level. However, if this pattern defines your life, day in and day out, then be wary of this overmanaging tendency. The adjustment here is the exploration of emotion and acceptance of what is happening, rather than always trying to "make" something happen.

We will discuss specific strategies to navigate these waters in later chapters. For now, I'd suggest beginning to open to the possibility of making space for "doing nothing" in your life. It is important to start with baby steps. At first, just begin to recognize when a moment presents itself to sit and relax and let attention come into the direct experience of what is happening. Give yourself a moment to let attention naturally move to the body sensations or to the sounds and colors in the environment. Don't hold yourself to some rigid standard (more management). Start where you can. Start with what feels natural and comfortable. If it's thirty seconds of silence and disengagement, then so be it. Let life come to you and show you how to attune to presence. Let natural peace and equanimity begin to reveal itself to you. These opportunities can come at any time throughout the day, so be open to the possibility. Cultivating a little receptivity in this way is helpful. The trick is to not try to manage or manufacture unmanaged space.

Also, don't hold yourself to unreasonable or rigid expectations because you feel exhausted. To tell yourself, "I'm just going to take an entire day off and meditate" when you have difficulty relaxing for thirty minutes at a time is probably an unreasonable demand to place on yourself. It will just lead to frustration and disappointment.

Remember... baby steps.

Effort

It goes without saying that investigating our deepest truths will require some effort on our part. We will have to be willing to be open to change. We will have to investigate or inquire in certain ways to cultivate the soil for awakening. Sometimes the work will be challenging, which often means facing difficult experiences, both internally and externally. However, we don't have to have the ability to work without reprieve or in some super-human way. Our body-minds do not naturally function in that way. If you just watch the body-mind, there will be times of intense activity and times of profound relaxation. There will be times of goal directed behaviors and there will be times of relaxed enjoyment of the surroundings. Observing these variations, you learn that letting the natural cycles governing your body (and all of nature) teach and inform you, can be balanced with developing a structured framework for practice. Over time what typically happens is that we learn to harmonize our practices, inquiries, and meditations with the natural movements and inclinations of the body-mind and the environment around us.

A common belief that often goes unexamined is the belief that we must work insanely hard and/or with machine-like consistency to wake up. This is simply not true, and believing it can lead to a lot of unnecessary discouragement. Please be kind to yourself and avoid holding yourself to unnecessarily rigorous standards. Don't judge yourself too harshly when things aren't going how you'd expected or planned for them to. There will be times when you had planned to meditate or practice, and then it doesn't happen for one reason or another. There will be times when you feel disciplined and practice seems to just flow along blissfully. There will be times when you feel hopelessly unfocused and distracted. There is no need to make a judgement about yourself due to any of these conditions. Just recognize that everything in nature is in flux and that this is all quite natural. These fluctuations happen to all of us. You will go through these cycles many times, so it is best to just accept that we are human, and humans aren't always consistent. In these instances, you might also notice a tendency to judge yourself: "I'm never going to wake up! I can't even keep to a simple schedule." Everyone has these thoughts; they are perfectly normal. I've had those thoughts more times than I can count. The important thing is to recognize that these are just thoughts. If we don't give them too much attention, they will come and go just like any other thought.

A little effort on a reasonably consistent basis is plenty. If you happen to go for some time without any sort of practice or attention to your path, it's okay. When practice or curiosity returns naturally, there's no need to look back and make a big deal about missed opportunities. By the time you've noticed it, the moment has already passed, so don't beat yourself up. Let the past rest.

Be Prepared to Be Uncomfortable

There will be some discomfort that goes along with this undertaking. There is no getting around this. It will never be unbearable, but at times your thoughts might tell you it is. We as humans can and do go to amazing lengths to avoid discomfort. As we discussed, we live in a society of endless distractions and any of these can be used to avoid discomfort. Well, when we take up an investigation of our deepest truths, we are voluntarily putting ourselves in situations that, by nature, make it hard to distract ourselves. As we do this, we will often notice some discomfort. Sometimes it is a mild uneasiness. Other times it might feel more intense. Either way it can be tremendously helpful to simply acknowledge the discomfort.

41

"Okay, I am feeling uncomfortable. What is it like? What does it feel like in my body at this moment? Do I have to do something to immediately distract myself like my thoughts or habits suggest, or can I just be with it?" You might be surprised. What you've been running from for years might turn out to be tolerable, even enjoyable after a time.

"The ultimate measure of a man is not where he stands in moments of comfort and convenience, but where he stands at times of challenge and controversy."

—Martin Luther King Jr.

Perhaps you can only sit with the discomfort for a few minutes at first, and that's perfectly acceptable. Over time you will start to recognize that you have an innate capacity to relax into whatever the body is feeling in the moment. With this relaxation, you may notice an alchemical process. The restlessness and discomfort will begin to transform into an experience of presence and wholeness. An intuitive realization might dawn—the discomfort itself was not what was making us distractible, restless, and irritable. These were only side effects of the habitual activity of running from our emotions. With this realization, we start to recognize that there is intelligence in discomfort. It is like a messenger telling you, "Look here." This will begin to replace the old habit pattern that seems to say, "Run away." As we experientially recognize our capacity to sit with these processes, a certain spontaneous willingness begins to emerge. We see that by voluntarily opening to the intelligence of these uncomfortable moments, we are simply acknowledging what is already within us. We recognize that to run from these experiences is to run from ourselves. We've done that for too long, haven't we? All that running is what is causing our suffering. This separation from ourselves is what perpetuates that sense of separation from others, and from life itself.

Don't Be a Jerk

I have committed to generally avoiding spiritual terminology in this writing. However, some terms are just too good to resist. The phrase "Zen stink" is one such example. This odd phrase refers to a very real phenomenon that occurs in practitioners at various stages along the path to realization. Zen stink is the belief that you are somehow superior to those "unenlightened people" who have not experienced, glimpsed, or realized what you have. This can occur at the conscious and/or the unconscious level. None of us wants to see ourselves as egocentric or having delusions of grandiosity, so this can be hard to detect in ourselves. It requires a measure of humility and self-reflection to recognize. To avoid unnecessary grief and confusion in the process of awakening, it is important to be aware of this tendency and be able to recognize its symptoms.

Without exception, we will all build a sort of "spiritual ego" as a byproduct of being engaged in the process of awakening. Depending on our personality, conditioning, and experiences, it might present itself in subtle ways or it might present itself in overt and overarching ways. On the extreme end of that spectrum are those that get a "taste" of realization and go on about the business of "saving the world" with a sort of messiah complex. I don't recommend this for obvious reasons. One of the major thrusts of writing this book was to help put an end to the potential for cult mentality or "spiritual teacher worship" by making it clear that thoroughgoing realization is available to everyone. If you stay on track, there is no reason your realization cannot be driven to depths well beyond those of well-known spiritual teachers, some having surprisingly large followings.

Zen stink can manifest in later stages of realization in subtle forms, but in early stages it is often overt and is usually a self-limiting phenomenon. It is associated with what I would call "foretastes" of awakening. When you start to open yourself to deeper truths, you will inevitably touch into experiences of interconnectedness or expansive mystical states. This is not yet awakening; however, you will instinctually know that you have come upon something more foundational and real than anything you had previously encountered in your life. As social creatures, it is natural for us to want to share something of this importance with people we are close to. We might not be able to contain ourselves, and out of sheer enthusiasm go on to describe our brush with mystical union with friends and loved ones in great detail. Their reaction is usually some combination of curiosity, interest, and bewilderment. Of course, sometimes a person truly picks up on the authenticity of our experience and can really resonate with what we're relating. It's nice to share in this way.

Unfortunately, our enthusiasm can take on a certain naive arrogance. We might graciously appoint ourselves the "local guru" and go about teaching people about "spiritual enlightenment," assuring them that we have the answers to help them awaken from their ignorant slumber. Aren't we surprised when the spiritually inept around us don't recognize our exalted status? They may even go so far as to laugh in our face or tell us that we're still the same schmuck we've always been, we've just become one degree more annoying. Can you imagine?

As I mentioned, this is usually self-limiting. We have our friends and family who love to keep us humble to thank for that. Don't be too disappointed if you are given some feedback that is a bit hard to hear after you get overly excited describing your newfound enlightenment to others. This goes with the territory. In fact, it is a lovely reminder that everything along the path to realization is here to show you the truth if you're willing to see it. I overdramatized this scenario, but it's often not too far off base. I recommend avoiding this type of thing to the degree you can. Remain humble and things will go much more smoothly for you. As things progress, you will have more and more opportunity to practice humility. Sometimes that practice of humility will be voluntary and enjoyable. Other times it will be less than comfortable and quite to your dismay.

Becoming a Spiritual Teacher, Counselor, or Guide

I think it's wonderful that meditation, mindfulness practices, and energetic practices such as yoga have become mainstream. This is a clear indication that humanity is in the midst of taking an evolutionary step forward in consciousness. I don't think there is anything wrong with teaching various spiritual practices if done with sincerity and good intention. However, if you really want to take this to liberation, I will generally caution against trying to teach people about or facilitate awakening until that occurs. A first awakening (what is covered in this book) is just the beginning. Deciding to teach or facilitate too early has much more potential to cause you distraction than it does to support your progress. Many people who have authentic awakenings decide to teach way too early and get themselves into situations where it is challenging to see that they are using the identity of the "enlightened one" to prevent the process from coming to fruition.

"Enlightenment is man's emergence from his self-incurred immaturity."

—Immanuel Kant

Chapter 3:

What Is Awakening?

We've finally arrived at the chapter where we get to discuss exactly what awakening is. There's only one problem though. I can't actually tell you what it is. In fact, no one can. I know that might sound disappointing, but once you understand why it is, you will realize it's a blessing in disguise. Awakening could never be explained or described accurately, and that is particularly good news.

To clarify this, it is important that we make a clear distinction between understanding and experience. Let's do a thought experiment. Suppose you had never tasted chocolate. Now imagine I had tasted chocolate and wanted to convey to you what it's like to taste chocolate. I could spend a lot of time describing the taste to you in great detail. I might use comparative descriptions referencing other flavor notes that you are familiar with. I could describe the texture, aroma, and color to you. I might even use poetic phrases to describe how it makes you feel to savor chocolate's complex flavor and aroma, and to feel it melting over your tongue. If I were a true wordsmith, perhaps I could come as close to describing the experience as words would allow. If you had listened intently, you could have assimilated all of the descriptions I'd used. Your imagination might be drawing on experiences you've had that pertain to those descriptions. You might even believe that you truly know what chocolate tastes like. In a certain sense, you do know. For instance, you could use descriptions you'd heard from me and go about the business of teaching others who had never tasted chocolate what it tastes like. You could say that a certain knowledge had been acquired in listening to and assimilating my descriptions. Your understanding of chocolate may be quite good at this point. You might even be able to quote technical or scientific references about the subtleties and varieties of its flavors.

Even so, if you'd still never tasted chocolate or anything containing chocolate, that knowledge, those elegant descriptions, even the ability to translate them to others, simply wouldn't give you the experiential insight gained by putting that chocolate in your mouth for the first time. The best descriptions would be a far cry from the direct experience, wouldn't they? To really drive this home, you can apply this thought experiment to other senses. For instance, if you had been deaf since birth, how could I convey to you the actual experience of the sound of a flute? If you had been blind since birth or for some other reason had never had the visual experience of the color red, there is no way I could describe that into direct experience for you, is there?

Awakening is exactly this way. It is by nature purely experiential. It has nothing to do with description or understanding. An awakening doesn't suddenly occur the moment you've collected enough information and descriptions to finally understand what it is. It simply doesn't work this way. This can be frustrating at times because we want to understand things, but it is important to convey this truth. You see, once we've accepted that trying to understand the awakening process won't make it happen, we begin to open to other possibilities. What are these possibilities? Here's where the good news starts. Setting aside the need for explanations or understanding as the primary mode of communicating the reality of awakening, we can explore what can be done to transmit the reality of it in a more direct and intuitive way.

There are many ways to plant seeds, in the form of these nonconceptual communications, that can ultimately germinate into awakening. I call this "transmission." Transmission is a term for inducing a direct insight into something that could never be conveyed through information. This can happen in a few different ways. One is that it can take place relationally. This means that hearing and vibing with someone's description of going through this process can induce and encourage similar processes in you. Listening to someone else's descriptions might sound like information exchange, but if done right, something can be related through a back channel. This is facilitated by our innate ability to empathize. Through empathy we communicate at a much more fundamental level than through the exchange of information. Empathy is our innate ability to synchronize our emotional states and our physiology with others we relate to.

A second way this transmission can occur is through direct pointing. This is a way of using language very purposefully to induce experiential insight in you. I have been doing this since the beginning of the book and will continue to do it throughout. The interesting thing about this method is it can happen right alongside the conveying of practical information. Sometimes it is not directly noticed in the immediate; other times it will be obvious that something is being communicated through the back channels.

The third method of transmission is the most important. That is, you can learn various strategies and inquiries to investigate directly for yourself. Further, I can teach you how to intuit and develop your own natural inquiries and investigations. Ultimately, you are self-transmitting. This is the most important method for obvious reasons. I can't wake you up; only you can wake you up. All I can do is show you how to gain access to parts of your experience that may be overlooked, forgotten, or ignored. Toward the beginning of the awakening process, this may not be very obvious. Yet it's already starting to happen. The intuitive part of you is starting to awaken and attune itself to its inherent awake nature. As realization unfolds, this type of transmission comes more into play. You will start to become more conscious of it functioning in an intuitive and intimate way. You will learn to trust your instincts as they come into alignment with your deepest truths, and your deepest truths will synchronize with the natural flow of life.

Each of these methods of transmission (relationally, direct pointing, and self-transmitting) is a means by which you can directly investigate your true nature. This investigation will begin to give you "tastes" of awakening, if that hasn't already begun to happen. At some point a sort of "event horizon" is crossed, and then—boom! At that moment you'll feel exactly what awakening is in every part of your being. You will not suddenly understand awakening; you will be the awakening! Everything will be seen to be awakeness. There will be not a hair's breadth of separation anywhere. You will move as your innate awakened nature, and all of life will move seamlessly with you. Even the word "awakening" and related concepts will seem silly to you. They will disappear like ice thrown into a roaring fire.

The following sections approach the question, "What is awakening?" from various angles, all of which are variations of the three methods of transmission described above. As you read on, please keep in mind that I am not trying to teach you something so much as dial you in experientially to your naturally awake frequency. Since the sections come from different angles, you may have a hard time logically putting them together in a structured mental framework. If you experience a bit of cognitive dissonance around that, it is okay. That is a sign affirming the transmission is having an effect.

A Shift in Identity

A practical way to describe what occurs during an awakening is to say that it's a shift in identity. It is a shift in what you take yourself to be. Specifically, it is a shift from continuously referencing concepts and beliefs about who you are for a sense of identity, consistency, meaning, and fulfillment to resting in and as consciousness. Until awakening occurs, we continuously and without noticing it, take ourselves and our experience to be defined by thoughts and concepts. This means that our identity is intimately tied into thoughts and beliefs whether we know it or not. We usually don't know it. Upon hearing that, it is common for someone to say, "I don't take myself to be thoughts and beliefs." To which I might respond, "Oh great, then what are you?" If they are sincere and curious, they will consider their direct momentary experience and say, "Hmm . . . honestly, I don't know." More likely the answer will be a list of statements, such as, "I am John. I am male and thirty-five years old. I am a human being made out of cells and tissue. I was born in Rochester." Hopefully, you picked up what I was pointing to here. That is that any and every description we use to describe who and what we are is a thought! Even clearly understood scientific principles about neurophysiology and psychological mechanisms are simply thoughts that you have accumulated in the past, aren't they?

If someone had some spiritual background, they might say, "Well, I'm formless consciousness." Of course, what they are saying is partially true. Identity rests not in concepts or beliefs but in consciousness itself. However, to probe deeper I might ask, "Okay, so how do you know that is not just another belief?" I'm not picking on them, by the way. I am pointing out something important and fundamental to what we are discussing. That is that as long as we have our identity tied into beliefs, thoughts, and concepts (even spiritual ones), it is exceedingly easy to reidentify with any concept and not recognize that it (reidentification) has happened. You could say that self-referential thoughts and concepts are "sticky" in this way. We're sort of addicted to thinking about ourselves, aren't we?

Since I introduced the term "consciousness," I should tell you what I mean by it. Consciousness can be defined in many ways. I use the term differently at different times, depending on what I am pointing to. In this instance I'm using the term to describe that space that feels like "you" right now. It feels sort of like that aware region inside you. Take a moment to consider that and see if you can find it in your experience. It's not something you reach out to find. It's more like something you settle back into. Another way of approaching consciousness is to rest in that place where your thinking seems to be happening. You can relax attention there whether or not there is thinking going on. This is what I mean by consciousness. Also note that you don't have to think about consciousness, because consciousness is more fundamental than, or primary to, any thought. It is that spaciousness that is the center or core inside you that is reading and evaluating these sentences at this very moment. For example, if you suddenly think, I don't understand this, or Wow! This makes so much sense, consciousness is that space in which you became aware of those thoughts. Importantly, it is also the "stuff" that the thoughts are made out of.

So, consciousness is that mutable, flowing space that is always there when you are awake, that feels like you. It is also the space in which all concepts, thoughts, and beliefs form and subsequently dissolve back into. It can be said that it is the source of thought. At times, consciousness will feel quite calm, especially once you learn to purposely rest your attention back into it. Other times it can feel rather tumultuous, like choppy water. Once identity shifts from thoughts to the source of thoughts, a dramatic transformation in the way you relate to reality has taken place. This doesn't mean there will be no thoughts. What it means is that your identity isn't threatened and fractured by fluctuating and inconsistent beliefs about yourself and the world on an ongoing basis. We will go into the relationship between thoughts, identity, and consciousness in detail in later chapters. For now, I will use an analogy to clarify this fundamental shift in identity.

Imagine you are standing in a meadow at night. You're looking out onto a clearing. In that clearing is a large pond. The sky is cloudless and there is a full moon shining brightly on the pond from directly overhead. There is a brisk breeze sweeping across the meadow. Because of the wind, the surface of the pond is turbulent. Due to this turbulence, there is no complete reflection of the moon appearing on the surface. There are only tiny dancing shards of light shimmering here and there. You could say the moon appears "fractured" into many pieces on the surface of the water. As you stare at the surface of the pond, you are mesmerized by the dazzling display. Let's further assume that since you've been standing in the meadow, you haven't averted your gaze away from the surface. You have no knowledge of anything but the surface of the pond. For all you know, there is no meadow, no wind, no sky, and no moon. Furthermore, the water hasn't calmed enough to see the full lunar reflection as a single whole. Since you haven't looked away from the surface of the pond, you fail to recognize the moon in the sky as the source of the reflection on the pond surface. Indeed, you have no memory or experience of the moon at all, either as a reflection or as the source of reflection. You are completely unaware that all those dancing shards of lights are fractured pieces of one coherent image. You could say that your entire paradigm for reality, your world map (as concerns the moon and reflection) is the surface of this pond as it is in its current turbulent condition, with dancing shards of light reflecting in a seemingly chaotic pattern.

In this analogy, thoughts and beliefs are represented by the dancing shards of light, which are, in essence, fractured pieces of the moon. Consciousness (the capacity for thought) is represented by the reflective surface of the pond. Whether they know it or not, everyone derives their identity from thoughts and beliefs until an awakening occurs. This may be obvious to some individuals and may completely escape the notice of others.

What then are the ramifications of deriving identity from thoughts and beliefs? Well, returning to the analogy can help to answer this question. What if the only source from which we recall deriving our identity, our sense of self, is that unpredictable, fractured display of short-lived shards of light? Take a moment to consider that question. If you truly identify as a shard of light, you will have an immediate sense of being one fleeting entity apart from, and often opposed to, many others. Remember, you have no memory or context that these light shards are pieces of a whole. You will feel small and isolated. Worse than that, you will perceive that your nature is easily threatened and at the mercy of local conditions such as small waves and the various interactions with other light shards. In fact, its integrity is not dependable, as it can easily be fractured into other various pieces and scattered across the surface in seemingly chaotic patterns. It is just a matter of time before that shard wholly disappears and is replaced by something else. When we recognize that clinging to and deriving our identity from one light shard is a source of pain, uncertainty, and instability, what do we do? We begin to develop coping mechanisms, don't we? One way or another we cope by beginning to identify with other light shards (beliefs). Perhaps we choose one that is close by. Or maybe we look for one that is similar in shape to what we've been clinging to. Either way, we are trying to maintain a sense of continuity, of predictability. Yet all of these efforts just require more and more energy and ultimately suffer the same fate.

This paints a picture of a pretty miserable existence, doesn't it? Well, this is exactly what we do with thoughts and beliefs. As in the analogy, once we recognize that beliefs about ourselves (and the world as it relates to us) lack consistency and integrity, we begin to purposely align ourselves with other beliefs and principles. We generally choose those that somewhat align with previous beliefs about ourselves. Sometimes if the previous set of beliefs were particularly uncomfortable, we take a more radical strategy. We decide to abandon one set of beliefs and adopt a set of beliefs that are opposed to the first set. This is the movement of rebellion. It is designed to release us from suffering, but it simply causes us to bind ourselves in a different way.

Regardless of our strategy for choosing and aligning with beliefs, we never seem to question the fundamental paradigm of clinging to beliefs and expecting them to preserve our sense of identity. At some point we might start to suspect that continually trying to derive our sense of self from thoughts or beliefs is uncomfortable, requires a lot of energy, and is ultimately fruitless. This recognition is the raw material that brings about the conditions for awakening. This recognition is something of a paradox. In one sense it motivates us to find a way to "break through." At the same time, it's quite uncomfortable because we sense that we have been living in a sort of false reality. For some, living in this false reality is unsatisfying, like a pebble in your shoe. For others, it is downright excruciating. By trying to force our identity into such a small container, we created a positive feedback loop of exhausting ourselves, trying to fix an imaginary problem using the exact mechanism that "caused" the problem in the first place.

This can begin to sound discouraging. However, it's only discouraging from the point of view of the strategy that wasn't working in the first place. What if we adopt an entirely new approach? What if instead of clinging to various thoughts and concepts, struggling to maintain a network of beliefs about ourselves, we step back and radically readdress our approach? What if we find an entirely different way to go about solving this problem? What if we suddenly saw this whole thing from a vastly different perspective? What if we found a way to experientially realize that we were never contained in any one of those shards of light? Instead, what if we "woke up" from the dream that we are one tiny, isolated shard of light, to the living truth that we are the entirety of the radiant moon?

When identity shifts out of concept and belief and into consciousness itself, you realize in a deeply instinctual way that you are and have always been the magnificent wholeness of the lunar reflection. You are also every single shard of light dancing on the surface. Just as no single shard of light could ever be other than their natural identity as the lunar reflection, you will know beyond doubt that no thought or belief could ever move you one inch away from your ever-present, oceanic nature. You are the movement, and you are the stillness. You are the particular, and you are the wholeness.

You are the light and the darkness. You are the reflective surface, and you are the unfathomable depths.

Self-Validating

The most salient feature of awakening is that it is self-validating. This self-validating nature is somewhat paradoxical. Before awakening, it is exceedingly hard to describe what I mean by self-validating, yet afterwards it becomes exquisitely clear. The awake nature itself is the most real thing there is. By the mere experience of it, one knows instinctually that it is far more real than the illusory world they had been living in before awakening. Its very nature fully supports and validates its own presence. When I talk to someone who has gone through an awakening, this is the thing that is most obvious to me. It's nothing specific they say, but how they say it that is so striking. Instead of communicating from beliefs and concepts, they are communicating, even transmitting, from the very substance of unbound identity.

Let's look at this through the lens of the pond analogy. The moment you suddenly realize you have always been that entire reflective surface, including the reflection of the moon and each and every shard of light, an undeniable wholeness and integrity emerges. Similarly, once you see clearly and definitively that you are the reflective nature of consciousness, and that that consciousness is the source of all possible thoughts and beliefs about you, you experience yourself and all of life in a clear and integrated way. This experience is not conceptual; it is instinctual and utterly real. It's as if a huge weight you'd been carrying around for as long as you remember is suddenly lifted. It's the kind of thing where you can't appreciate the magnitude of what you'd been struggling to carry until the shift occurs and the struggle ceases.

If you had been living in an exceedingly small room all of your life, how could you know that small room was actually nested inside a much larger space? Well, you couldn't until you opened the door and walked out of that tiny room. Awakening is like walking out of that small room into a vast and mysterious reality that is far more natural. A big part of the relief is that once we walk out of the small room, it is clear that the exhaustion was caused by expending our energy struggling to stay inside that little room. What a welcome relief it is to let go of all that struggle.

A natural and relaxed confidence emerges. It is a pervasive feeling of "alrightness" that you had totally forgotten was possible in life. Some people remember it as a distant experience from early childhood or even before. There is wonder, mystery, and awe in moment-to-moment living. Most important of all, there is a knowing that there is nothing in your true identity that could be threatened, there is nothing to defend, and everything is okay and could never be otherwise. This isn't a thought or belief; you feel it in your marrow. The most enlightened person in the world could tell you that you are mistaken, and you'd laugh in their face. It wouldn't shake your confidence in the realness of this natural awakened state one iota. It is more obvious than the sun when you look directly at it.

Not only is this unshakable knowing the hallmark of awakening, I would say that it is the most enjoyable aspect. It doesn't carry a big emotional charge (after the initial surprise wears off). It is quite neutral, actually. Yet to know with every ounce of your being that no matter what happens, everything is deeply alright, that there's nothing you have to do to make it alright, is the blessing of all blessings.

It's Always Been Like This

Perhaps one of the most bizarre and unexpected features of awakening is that once it occurs, you know beyond a shadow of a doubt that it had always been like this. I remember this clearly after my initial awakening. It felt like the biggest relief in the world that I was finally back to this natural state. It's not a memory exactly. Memories can fade and become altered with time. No, this is a gut-level instinct that tells you it simply couldn't be other than this. You look back at the way you were perceiving yourself up until awakening and it's clear that that was what was unreal and contrived. This is without limits, natural, and not apart from anything or anyone.

I remember being dismayed, thinking, How did I ever forget this? It was like that moment you wake up from a bad dream and realize everything is completely fine. It's a huge release and a wonderful relief. This is true relief as it isn't tied to a single event, but is ongoing, moment by moment.

The Timeline of You

This section will be a little different. It will be an experiential journey designed to induce some sense of your natural awakeness. If you take a few moments to engage the questions and earnestly look where they point, you will get a lot more out of this.

Take a moment to consider your life. What can you say that's true about your life? What is true about you? I'm sure you can provide many facts about who you are, where you came from, and where you're going. You may be a mother, a father, a sister, or brother. You might be athletic or artistic. You might be in school or you might have a full-time job. You might be religious or spiritual. You might be skeptical or scientific. Do you consider yourself to be generally happy or generally melancholy? Or something in between? Do you have a clear idea of how your future will go? Maybe you don't plan anything and haven't the first clue what will happen next week. Have you had health challenges or a lifelong disability? Are you relatively young, or more advanced in years?

There are so many facts about our lives that we can refer to that seemingly define who we are. We frequently communicate these facts to ourselves (thought) and to others. We do this all day long, don't we? When we refer to any specific fact or defining experience to describe ourselves, one thing is consistent. That is that we will refer to something on the timeline of our life. If you considered any of the descriptions or questions above, you had to refer to the timeline of your life, didn't you? Specifically, you would have had to refer to either the past or the future. If you take a moment to really consider this, you might notice something quite interesting. In the way that we recall facts about ourselves from our internal timelines, we never actually refer to this moment; we refer to a thought. So, these facts that define our life are never derived from this exact present experience. Isn't that sort of bizarre?

Now, someone hearing this might respond, "Well, I know I'm a husband in this moment." I would simply ask, "Okay, so how do you actually know that? Where, specifically, is the evidence you are referring to?" If they were honest, and looking where I'm pointing, they'd have to say that all of the evidence to support such a statement is via a collection of memories, which are made out of thought. Then they might say, "Well, I could go dig up my marriage certificate to prove it!" If I were feeling particularly feisty, I'd point out that they are now referring to a thought about the future. In this very moment there is actually no evidence to support the belief that they are a husband, aside from a thought. Without going into a lot of examples or making this into a philosophical argument, you can probably get the gist of what I'm pointing to: in truth, all of what we know about ourselves is fact-based, and those facts can only be supported by referring to the past and the future in thought. To drive the point home, imagine you had no ability to recall the past or future in this moment, yet you were awake and alert and able to communicate normally. Just because you couldn't answer a question about yourself based on past facts or future plans, does that mean that you don't exist? Of course not.

So, considering that, here you are right in the present moment, neither in the past nor the future. Even though you think and talk about thought-based facts about yourself all day, that doesn't detract from the very obvious reality that here is where you exist, which has nothing to do with thoughts, memories, past, or future. If you get a sense of that mysterious recognition, then this analogy might shed some light on the nature of awakening for you.

Let's liken your life to a corridor that represents a timeline. In one direction it leads off into your distant past. You can see several years back, but the farther that portion of the corridor goes off into your past, the less clear it gets. In front of you the corridor stretches off into your future. You have a general idea of the nature of that corridor and facts about it, but it isn't as clearly seen as the past. For instance, it seems more difficult to pull facts out of the future corridor. However, if you are particularly goal-oriented, you may have some definite ideas about what lies in that corridor ahead. One thing is certain, however, and that is that past events are "back there," and all possible future events are "up ahead." Neither the past nor the future portions of your life are right in the portion of the timeline in which you are currently standing. Even something that happened just yesterday can only be found in the corridor behind you (memory). Similarly, something that you expect to happen, even in a short time from now, such as an upcoming meal, can only be found in the corridor in front of you. When you really consider the significance of this you, might start to wonder, "If every single defining fact and event about who I am can only be found in the past (memory corridor), or in the future (imagination corridor), what am I right now? What am I without all those facts and experiences that always seemed to define me? What can I find right here that is somehow provable to be 'me' without looking into those corridors of past and future?"

What are you when you don't think about yourself, or your past, or your future? This is quite mysterious indeed. It may seem eerie, confounding, or just plain bizarre. However, if you persist in inquiring in this way, "Who am I?" not settling for any memory (past) or referring to your imagination (future), you might find that you actually have no idea who or what you are. Even stranger, regardless of what was just recognized, your sense of "I" or "me" is quite strong and obvious with no facts, thoughts, or references attached to it. You find yourself in a space with no past and no future. This space does not rely on any concepts to define who you are, and yet here you remain. Undeniably here, awake, alert, and aware of the senses. The sounds haven't gone anywhere, have they? The colors and shapes in front of you are still there. In fact, they are a bit more vivid, aren't they? The sensations in the body are right here. Yet there is no story, no past, no future, no "substance" of what you always thought of as you. At this point you have a choice. You can start thinking again and just forget this little exercise, or you can decide you really want to find the answer and so you keep asking and keep investigating directly in this moment, "What am I without referencing the past and future?" If you do proceed in this way and find yourself in a thoughtless space, it's okay to just remain there. You don't need to continue to ask the question unless you get lost in thought.

If you do this in the right way and with some persistence, something might happen—something surprising, something life-altering, something radical. What can happen is that all of a sudden that corridor, with all of its facts and experiences, can suddenly be seen to be what it is: merely a collection of thoughts. When this happens, there is far less interest in these thoughts. When that occurs, the entire timeline and identity tied into it is suddenly seen to be quite illusory. It's as if a hole has been blown in the side of that timeline, and you are able to stick your head out the side and see what's really going on. What's "out there" is wholly indescribable, but let me just say that it's unimaginably vast and radically intimate.

Although the timeline has stopped operating, what is left feels far more like you than anything you've ever experienced. It feels like an intuitively obvious, pure "I" that is undeniable and free from subjugation to thought. It has the feel of "everything is already I," so there is nothing to threaten your existence anymore. This often comes with a massive release of tension and doubt. It usually brings with it an unshakable sense of peace and freedom. You feel lighter than you've ever felt. There is a pervasive feeling of simplicity and okayness. You instinctually know what you are but cannot define it. It

60

is a pure sense of oceanic Being. There may be thoughts, but they are of no concern. They are mere waves on the infinite ocean of your cosmic Self. Struggle is nowhere to be found. Effortless flow is seen to simply be the nature of what you always were.

This timeline analogy is just that, an analogy. Even if you had an experiential sense of how extraordinary awakening is by reading it, I assure you the actual (non)event is far beyond that.

The Value of Curiosity

As you start diving into an investigation of your true nature, it's natural to have a lot of curiosity. Curiosity is a wonderful attribute, and it will serve you well. Initially that curiosity will, at least in part, take an intellectual form. You might find your thoughts repeatedly asking, "Yes, but what is awakening?" Innocent curiosity is natural and harmless. It can even be enjoyable. When we add urgency with thoughts such as "But I just have to know!" it can become uncomfortable. So, when curiosity comes, just feel into it. Trust it. Let it be there. Don't try to "cure" curiosity with information. It doesn't need a cure. If impatience comes, that's okay too. It can feel like a yearning to be in on the "big secret." Well, the funny thing is that you are already in on the secret. The curiosity itself is an opening. The frustration is also an opening. It's an opening to the mystery. That mystery is right here and is unfolding at this very moment. My suggestion is to enjoy it. Embrace it. Plunge right into it. Trust the curiosity and trust the mystery. Innocent curiosity won't take you somewhere else; it will bring you right back here, again and again and again. As this inward unfolding occurs, you will become more receptive, more open, and more curious.

Patience

If you are prone to impatience and find yourself saying, "Okay, okay, but when do we get to the good stuff?" I understand. The excitement is natural and well placed. Just know that all of the foundational chapters are important. Without them, the techniques and inquiries would not be nearly as effective. Also, you can remind yourself that the transmission is already going on and that transformation is already at hand, whether you are aware of it or not.

That Moment

I always love that moment. The moment I'm talking to someone and I see the sudden recognition. It's the recognition that what I'm pointing to is altogether outside the contexts of what they typically consider to be their "life" and how they think about it. It's striking because it's a taste of a far bigger reality, and yet it's familiar and intimate in a way that no thought or idea could be. It's an experiential sharing between the two of us in that moment. It's as if we both just got into a rocket ship and launched off the surface of planet "Boring Old Reality" together. In this wondrous sharing, we are not two. I always feel a little giggle percolating up from the fabric of the Universe in these moments.

I remember talking with a friend over dinner a couple of years ago. Even though I had casually mentioned the possibility of awakening to her several times before, for whatever reason this time the mention of it stopped her in her tracks. She had been talking about some situation in her life, then suddenly dropped what she was saying like she was discarding a gum wrapper. The conviction with which she had been relating a recent event in her life just vaporized. Her demeanor immediately shifted, and she became quite present. You could feel it in the environment, not just in her. She looked me right in the eye and said, "Wait back up, what do you mean by 'waking up'?" I felt a big energetic smile inside expanding out into boundlessness. I don't remember exactly what I said in response, but at that moment it was clear to me that the awakening had already begun. This is the living truth, the deepest nature inside all of us, suddenly recognizing itself as it moves through the human body-mind. This moment of recognition is not yet awakening, but it is an important milestone. It is when something vast and eternal steps forward into your conscious experience and recognizes itself in a very direct way.

You may have already touched into a similar recognition some time in your past. Maybe it struck you while reading the previous chapters. Perhaps not. It doesn't matter either way, because as you read on, the opportunities for this recognition to occur will come more frequently. This chapter marks a transition point. From this moment on, a lot of what you will be reading will be directly transmitting. The purpose is to have an immediate and direct effect on you. We will discuss practical guidance, but it will be intermixed with "catalyst" material whose purpose is to trigger experiential, nonconceptual insight.

Foretastes

It's quite common to experience glimpses of awakening before it occurs. It's not exactly accurate to call them mini-awakenings, because they are limited to the realm of experience, whereas awakening goes beyond the confines of experience. However, experientially speaking, they are short glimpses or tastes of what is to come. These can occur at any time. For many people, they happen intermittently for years before awakening, even before the person is familiar with the subject of awakening. I'll call these experiences "foretastes." In the previous section I talked about "recognition" as that initial glimpse of something altogether beyond the ways you usually experience
yourself and your life. A foretaste is like that initial glimpse
on steroids. These occurrences can be so remarkable and all-

encompassing experientially, that you think you're enlightened for a few hours. You could say that they are as close as you can get to awakening without any transformation of identity. You may or may not have had them in the past. As we approach awakening, they are more likely to occur, and/or be more pronounced. However, there's no need to be concerned if you don't have these types of experiences or don't recognize them. They are not necessary for awakening to occur. This section merely addresses how to regard foretastes should they occur.

Foretastes vary considerably in their quality and duration. There is also a wide variation in how people interpret them. Many people consider them sacred or mystical experiences. Others consider them odd or unexplainable happenings. Sometimes they are overlooked entirely. There have been many times I have been discussing this topic with someone and their memory is suddenly jarred. They will say something to the effect of, "Oh! I've had something like that happen. I just didn't know what it was. I had forgotten all about it until just now." When they relate the story to me, it becomes clear to both of us that something had happened to them, causing a significant perceptual shift. They had forgotten about it because it didn't fit into the ways they would usually think about themselves and their life. It's one of those things that, because it's never talked about, we don't file it away as "important" in the way that we typically would with other life experiences. Has this ever happened to you? Take a moment to feel into what you've just read, and you might be surprised what comes.

Foretastes are generally short-lived. They may last a few moments, a few hours, or on occasion, a few days. There might be deep peace, a flow, or a connectedness that is unusual in your life. Sometimes it feels as if time has stopped for a few moments. A friend described her foretaste experiences this way:

"I would be going on with life as usual, and all of a sudden time would stop; like everything in the room, people and such, would be moving in slow motion. It was like there was something else holding all of this visual experience. I would stand still in a room full of people, and it was clear that no one would even notice the whole room had started moving in slow motion. It was like 'Ahh . . .' and I would become really curious about it, then everything would return to normal speed again."

Here is another example of a foretaste in a story someone related to me. I will paraphrase with her permission. It came to her in an aha moment when I was talking to her about awakening. She recalled a mysterious event that had happened to her years before. She felt it had changed her in some fundamental way. She described a particularly stressful time in her life when she had recently had her first baby. The child was still an infant and was having health problems. She and her husband were understandably anxious about the health issues. The stress of learning to be new parents while dealing with their child's health challenges was overwhelming. At one particular moment, she and her husband were extremely frustrated because her daughter wouldn't stop crying. They both felt helpless and overwhelmed. She said something just took over her. She had never felt anything like it before. She turned and walked right out the door without thinking about it, leaving her husband behind with the baby. She told me, "I guess I went for a walk, but I don't remember it because the best way I could describe it was I went to 'nowhere' for a while." She didn't remember how long she was gone but said when she returned, her husband looked concerned, so it might have been an hour or two. Remarkably, when she returned, she had a feeling of deep peace. What's more, all of her previous concerns about the baby and the stress of worrying about its health issues were completely gone. She said she hadn't even wondered why it had happened because the experience felt so natural and seemed to have no content. Her husband was bewildered by her sudden equanimity and relaxed confidence. He asked about what had happened and she couldn't recall. She said from that moment on she never worried about her child in that way again. Parenting had become more peaceful and enjoyable, and that never changed, even up to this day.

Can you relate to these descriptions? Maybe you've never had an experience similar to these, at least in the narrative sense. Even so, if you take a moment to feel into them, a glimmer of something from your past might come to the surface. Some memory of an unexplainable but very real event might come back to you that had been overlooked or forgotten. It might have had a sense of intense presence or even felt like you went away for a moment. The circumstances or descriptions you use might be different, but the feel of something extraordinary, unexplainable, or outside the contexts of what you would typically consider "normal" experience might be there. This is what I mean when I say awakening is about you. It is a very intimate process; it comes from the inside not from the outside. It's more about letting something come to you from your own depths than it is about going about finding something "out there." It's far less about a script or a path and far more about being receptive to the possibility that you've been trying to wake yourself up all along. Cultivating receptivity to these experiences, these foretastes, can be quite potent.

So, what should we do about foretastes if and when they occur? First of all, remind yourself that they are a good sign that transformation is at hand. Even if they seem confusing or out of place, nothing has gone wrong. Also remember you don't need them for awakening to happen, nor should you go looking for them as a sign of progress. For some they are obvious, for others they aren't.

Second, a foretaste should never be interpreted as awakening itself. I have met many people who refer to an event they call their "awakening," and after talking with them for a few moments, it's pretty clear they are referring to a foretaste or another type of experience.

Some foretastes can be quite extraordinary, including visions, states of ecstasy, and mystical union experiences. They are all valid in their own right. However, interpreting them as awakenings can lead to a lot of misunderstanding and even become a roadblock if one gives these events too much attention.

> Mistaking a spiritual or mystical experience for
> awakening can be used to reinforce a false identity,
> rather than allowing a shift to occur, which breaks us
> free of our false identities.

I'm not saying this to be critical or elitist, I'm saying it because it's quite easy and common to underestimate the true magnitude of the shift that is authentic awakening. I come from the point of view that anyone can awaken, so I'm not pulling any punches. I want to give you the best possible chance, which includes pointing out the common roadblocks. If you get what I'm saying here and have had foretastes or other experiences that you are really invested in, then this is good news. Can you imagine that something even beyond what you had previously thought of as awakening is available to you? In this case, there is something quite extraordinary ahead for you. The magnitude and thoroughness of the transformation I am talking about is not comparable to any individual experience or life event—not even close. The shift is not subtle, fleeting, or unclear.

Beyond Experience

Awakening is beyond experience. For one thing, experiences come and go. When an awakening occurs, it's quite clear that there's been a fundamental shift into a way of being that is not subject to time in the way we think about and experience it. That being the case, coming and going doesn't even apply. It is a shift into pure, unbound being that is clearly seen and felt to be more real than what you had experienced before the shift occurred.

So then, how should you think about or view these pre-awakening experiences? Well, the simplest and most practical advice is this: If they do occur, don't make a big deal about them. They are a good sign that things are happening. But once the moment has passed, they really have no value. Let them go. Be alert for the tendency to daydream about them or recreate them. We all tend to do this to some degree, so don't be surprised if you see thoughts along these lines. Just don't actively encourage them. Recognize that these experiences had their time and place, and now something else has its time and place. Honor what is happening, which is far more valuable than using memory to try to resurrect something that has already passed and can never come back.

Also, if you move in spiritual circles, watch that you don't subtly or not so subtly use these experiences as spiritual currency with others. It is tempting and common to wear experiences as badges of honor, subtly competing with others or trying to impress others with our spiritual adeptness or accomplishment. This will not help you awaken. It is actually counter to the movement of awakening because it is really just reinforcing the false identity by spiritualizing it. It is far better to be humble and not settle for experiences. Don't settle for anything short of realization!

Uninterrupted Peace

Awakening and realization is ultimately about living your life in uninterrupted peace. I'm not talking about the idea of peace. I'm not talking about walking around in life believing that you are a peaceful person or that you are creating peace in the world. These are merely conceptual or practical views. In fact, some people who have built identities around being peaceful are actually deeply divided on the inside and energetically attract and cause unpeaceful life situations. What I'm talking about is uninterrupted peace as primary to all your other experiences. I'm talking about living life with peace being interwoven into the fabric of all experience. This isn't something you

68

do, by the way; it is a realization of the nature of what is. You see, life doesn't push against itself in any way. Life has no way of pushing against anything because there is no other to push against. Life knows no separation. There is no strain. It flows effortlessly into existence, and dissolves without a trace just as effortlessly.

So, what is this peace that I'm talking about? What is its nature? How do you know when it's being embodied in your life? I'll answer the last question first: You will know. Trust me on this. It's almost like you're getting away with something. It's like, "You mean I don't have to suffer at all, and I can just enjoy all of this effortlessly and without strain of any kind?" It's like winning the lottery in every moment. The rub is that I'm making it sound like something you have to acquire . . . it's not. It is the natural state before the unsettled, endlessly seeking thought process starts to move. It's already here. We've just sort of forgotten it. We've learned to habitually overlook it. It's not easy to overlook, actually. It takes tremendous energy to do so on an ongoing basis. This expenditure of energy is why we feel exhausted and why we suffer. It's why life often doesn't feel quite right. Sure, we have our stories about that. We blame people and situations for our suffering, but ultimately it comes down to an ongoing expenditure of energy trying to hold distance between ourselves and life. In doing so, we perpetuate the forgetting of our own true nature. Crazy, isn't it?

I want to say something about what peace is not. Peace is not the absence of anger, sadness, or discord. It is full acceptance of these and all other experiences with no resistance whatsoever. You might ask, "How can I fully accept anger? I've learned to avoid it in my life so that it doesn't cause destruction." This is one of those things you really have to feel deeply into. The answer is that because of learned resistance to certain feelings, we suppress and distort their natural expression. This ultimately leads to destructive behaviors. Once anger is fully accepted, it is no longer a problem. It has an important role to play in life. It is a guardian of personal boundaries. Sadness has its place as well. It is a normal and healthy response to grief or to letting go. When anger gets suppressed, it eventually surfaces as violence (emotional or otherwise). When sadness becomes suppressed it surfaces as depression and/or anxiety. So the emotions that we've judged as negative or unwelcome in our lives are not the problem, nor have they ever been. The problem, if there can be said to be one, is the resistance to these emotions and experiences. Resistance, then, becomes a way of describing the ongoing rejection of the uninterrupted peace that is our deepest nature. Through acceptance we hold all the keys to the freedom to know uninterrupted peace as the canvas on which our lives are painted.

How do we reclaim this uninterrupted peace that is our birthright? First, it's not something you do or acquire; it is already here. This takes a measure of faith at the outset, but if you've read this far it probably makes sense to you. Second, the only way in is to be fully authentic. Don't hide from yourself. If you're feeling fear, then own it. If you're feeling anger, then own it. If you're feeling sadness, then own it. If you're feeling shame, guilt, or resentment, then own those. Most importantly, if you're feeling angst, trepidation, or fear about feeling these emotions, then own or admit that. Authenticity is the starting place. The starting place is always where you are when you are being fully honest with yourself. Why? Because life is authentic. Life is simply what it is, and it makes no excuses for that. It is not embarrassed about any part of itself. Life never holds back. Life doesn't second-guess itself or think that part of itself should not be there. Only the divided human mind can do that.

Third, be patient. Simply wanting to feel peace won't get you there. That's just more thought-stuff. Wanting is about not allowing. I want because I'm not okay with what I'm feeling right now. I don't like this restlessness, boredom, dis-ease, so I'm going to imagine an alternative reality. Imagination is fine. However, when we imagine because we have a deep sense of dissatisfaction, then our imagination becomes the machinery of division. Worse, this imagining ourselves out of the truth of the moment becomes habitual, involuntary, and at least partially unconscious. This is why we find ourselves on the wheel of suffering and end up asking questions like, "How did I get here again?" Just start with authenticity to the degree you can right now, and then be patient. Understand that to come into the deepest authenticity, and as a result begin to reclaim the deepest peace that is what we all really want, can take some time. Your job isn't to decide how long it will take for unbroken peace to return. Your job is to be authentically here, to honor each moment. That's it. What I've seen is that the more authentic, present, and willing to feel uncomfortable emotions someone is, the faster they wake up and open to the underlying peace. I've seen some extraordinary transformations in just a couple of years in people who are fully willing to face life in a raw and vulnerable way. Try it.

What Awakening Is Not

❖ Awakening is not a new way of looking at life.

❖ Awakening is not adopting any belief system.

❖ Awakening is not a spiritual or religious practice.

❖ Awakening is not about someone else.

❖ Awakening is not a form of positive thinking.

❖ Awakening is not about getting everything you want.

❖ Awakening is not about changing your lifestyle.

❖ Awakening is not a way to get "one up" on anyone else.

❖ Awakening is not a way of avoiding emotions or escaping life.

❖ Awakening is not a way to get magical powers.

❖ Awakening is not the end of the realization process; it is only the beginning!

Chapter 4:

Paradox

Introduction

T aking up an investigation into your true nature will lead you directly into a world of paradox. If you haven't noticed this yet, you will soon enough. Here are the definitions of paradox, according to Merriam-Webster:

❖ "a statement that is seemingly contradictory or opposed to common sense and yet is true;" and

❖ "a situation, person, or thing that combines contradictory features or qualities."

In time you will become quite familiar with paradoxical emotions, perceptions, and experiences. Indeed, you will become familiar with the unfamiliar. In fact, the more you wake up, the more this will be the case. The more you wake up, the less "you" you will be able to find apart from the flow of phenomena. Moreover, paradox isn't a side effect of awakening—the truth of the matter is that the natural state of things, let's call it "reality," is by its very nature entirely paradoxical.

"How wonderful that we have met with a paradox.
Now we have some hope of making progress."

—Niels Bohr

In this chapter we will explore various paradoxical elements you will encounter as this process unfolds. My aim is that by discussing them ahead of time, you will be better equipped to recognize and thus cultivate some understanding and acceptance of these elements as they arise. With acceptance, there can be a sublime and wondrous enjoyment, even as we find ourselves more and more intertwined with a mysterious and paradoxical reality. On the other hand, the inability or refusal to accept the paradoxical aspects of unfiltered reality can cause a lot of frustration and confusion.

When the Other Shoe Drops

There's a biphasic phenomenon that often occurs when we get a "taste" of unfiltered reality. When we touch into something vast, eternal, and beyond the usual human dimension, the experience will often be followed by a period of dysphoria, with or without intense emotion. If we are not particularly in touch with our emotions, it may be experienced as disorientation or a certain kind of mental upheaval. When we have little to no experience in this arena, these intense experiences will often be judged as "not good." They can range in intensity anywhere from uncomfortable to terrifying. This biphasic aspect appears to be universal in early stages of awakening, meaning you don't often get the first phase without the second phase following close behind. This phenomenon is commonly encountered in spiritual practice, such as during sustained meditation (retreat) or with intense inquiry. However, it also occurs in unexpected situations and nonspiritual settings. I've met many people who have experienced this phenomenon in various contexts, often unexpectedly and with little knowledge of what was happening. It's even more distressing if you don't have a practice context or a mentor to explain that this is a totally natural process. If you think back, you may be able to identify one or more similar experiences in your own life—times you had an intense or even terrifying emotional experience that seemed to come out of the blue. Yet if you look more closely, it may have followed some period of clarity, or an opening to your unbounded nature. We often fail to associate the two experiences because they seem so divergent (paradoxical). Here are some examples:

- ➢ We listen to a talk or read something written by a person who has some degree of realization and we experience a shift in consciousness. A few days later we find ourselves in the midst of difficult or confusing emotions.

- ➢ While having a deeply moving experience, such as falling in love, observing powerful art, having sex, experiencing the sublimity of nature, or even taking a hallucinogenic drug, there is an experience of expansion or unity. After "coming down" from that experience, not only is that indescribably pleasant experience gone, it has been replaced by a sense of isolation, grief, or anxiety.

> After some practice or inquiry, we have a "pre-taste" of awakening and for a time feel unusually free, relaxed, and intimate with life like we never have before. This lasts for a few hours or perhaps a couple of days. Then it's suddenly nowhere to be found, and we find ourselves feeling more awful than we had before.

Regardless of the circumstances, the key is to recognize that this is exactly how the process is supposed to go. Having an uncomfortable or distressing experience after having a direct taste of reality doesn't mean you aren't cut out for awakening or that you've made a mistake. It means that the process is working. Moreover, it's irrelevant whether this experience was a result of some intentional practice, or whether it seemed to just come upon you out of nowhere. In the latter case, this is life waking you up, giving you a "nudge."

Let's look at the mechanism behind this phenomenon. When we come into contact with living truth, there is often an expansion of consciousness and a momentary dissolving of the sense of being a discrete, separate, isolated being. I'll call this the "expansion" phase. This gives us a glimpse of the natural truth that there are no actual boundaries anywhere. There are only apparent boundaries. These glimpses are precursors to awakening. They remind us experientially that this natural state of fluidity, unbound intimacy, and freedom is our birthright. The next thing that usually happens (but doesn't have to) is that consciousness contracts back down and we are suddenly faced with resistance patterns and challenging emotions. This movement has equal value to the expansion movement. In actuality, these two movements are different aspects of the same phenomena, both being necessary for awakening. They just appear to be separated in time due to the way our minds process these experiences. If I were to give the expansion movement a voice, it would say something like, "This is how unfiltered reality actually is." Then the contraction movement would say "And this is what's preventing you from experiencing unfiltered reality on an ongoing basis." By this I mean that we are shown not only the unbound possibility, but also the resistance patterns that cause us to distract ourselves by binding our attention into an internal hiding place (thought). Isn't that ingenious? When seen in this light, we start to recognize that this biphasic phenomenon is grace giving us exactly what we're looking for—and it's doing it in a powerful and efficient way. Here are a few key points that will help keep things in perspective when you experience this expansion/contraction phenomena:

> It's helpful to recognize that these contracted experiences, consisting of repressed emotions (doubt, fear, confusion), as well as resistance patterns, are temporary just like every other experience. They don't last forever (even if fearful thoughts sometimes say they will).

> The emergence of these painful emotion states doesn't mean that the awakening process caused those emotions to be there. In actuality, you've been carrying them around with you; they've just been locked away inside you in a way that prevents you from experiencing natural intimacy, flow, and equanimity. This is not the fault of the emotions. Rather, it is caused by our resistance to them.

> These repressed emotion states and associated resistance patterns coming to the surface are truly a gift. They have the potential to cause us to act in unconscious ways if they remain repressed.

➤ When resistance patterns and repressed emotion states inevitably come to the surface, you have many resources—first and foremost, acceptance and the recognition that this is unconditional love moving in your life. The chapter on emotion will offer many helpful approaches for these situations.

➤ It's helpful to remind yourself that emotions, in and of themselves, are never a problem. This is true regardless of their quality. We don't need to eradicate, solve, heal, intellectualize, justify, or explain any emotion we encounter. The emotion's very existence is its own justification for being.

➤ The first few times this happens, we may be faced with resistance patterns and emotions that we really aren't used to experiencing. This can be quite unsettling, even overwhelming if we don't recognize that this is just part of the process that everyone goes through. It can be helpful in these moments to remind yourself that the mental chatter, stating, I can't handle this or This is overwhelming me is simply thought. These thoughts, or conclusions, aren't necessarily true, and they will pass just like the emotions will. Oftentimes just sitting with whatever is happening internally is proof that you can indeed handle it. It may not be your choice of experiences in the moment. It may be quite uncomfortable, but the mere act of sitting with it, even for a few minutes, proves that you have the capacity for it. I've seen many people get exactly this far with the awakening process and then abandon the whole undertaking because they wrongly conclude they can't handle these experiences. Sometimes believing a single thought can be the difference between salvation and a lifetime of distraction and avoidance.

➤ Sometimes we instinctually know we can handle the emergence of this second-phase discomfort, but we'd rather not. We consider whether it would be easier to just go on avoiding looking at the repressed emotions and internal resistance-mass. Well, I can't make that decision for you, but I will say this: You can't actually avoid them. They are there, have life energy, and will express themselves one way or another. If we choose to actively repress and avoid acknowledging their existence, they will find expression by causing us to act in unconscious ways. We will continue to perpetuate divisive energy at some level, which will cause ongoing suffering in ourselves and others. In the end, you will be forced to face these unconscious mechanisms one way or another, so why not now? Life is giving you the most wonderful opportunity. Why not show up and be willing to see what's here?

Paradox and Language

Whether we realize it or not, before awakening our identity is tightly intertwined with our inner world of thought. Since thoughts are largely made out of self-talk (inner dialogue), we can say that our identity is bound up in language and concepts. This inner world of language and concepts is experienced quite differently than natural reality (how reality is experienced after liberation). Language is by nature divisive, so to live in a world of thought-bound identity feels limited, isolated, and fractured. Your true nature (natural reality) is indivisible, so when identity is disentangled from thought, we experience the natural world of unbound clarity, peace, interconnectedness, and freedom. The experiential difference between these two modes of experiencing is night and day.

A simple way of investigating this entanglement is to look at the practical function of language. Language is primarily a tool for communication. When we use language to communicate with another person, there is an assumption being made by the very fact that we are using language at all, and that is that we are separate from the person we are communicating with. It's inferred that there is a "me" over here that is exchanging some information with a "you" over there. Now I'm not suggesting that one instant of information exchange is enough to cause us to believe and feel that we are separate from everything "out there." However, when this event is repeated again and again, and more importantly, reflected inside our mind endlessly (how often do we reflect internally on conversations we've had or are about to have with others?), it starts to really feel as if we are separate.

Another way of looking at this is to consider the structure of language itself. One of the simplest aspects of language is the act of labeling. To even begin to use language we must learn names and labels for things, people, concepts, and events. Furthermore, we must agree on which labels match which objects for language to work. If I'm talking to you about a "chair," there is an assumption on my part that you and I share a belief about what that label is referring to. First and foremost, we assume that the label refers to the same object for both of us. If we used the same label for different objects in some arbitrary way, then we would get nowhere in communication. If I was talking about a "chair," but to you that label referred to a goat, then we aren't going to have a meaningful conversation. This is so obvious that it might sound silly to point out, but when we really investigate the power labeling has on our perceptions, we begin to see how intertwining our identity with language causes a pervasive sense of isolation.

The thing is that when we label something, we are asserting that the object is not everything else. For instance, when I speak about a chair, I may relate an image to you that looks in your mind like what I call a chair. But I have actually communicated much more than the shape and use of that object. Subtextually, I have communicated to you a million things that the object I'm talking about is not. In practical usage this is perfectly okay and is the function of language. However, when we internalize language (thousands of times per day), we label ourselves in various ways. While this might seem like a harmless or even valuable endeavor, we often don't notice the painful side effects. Every definition we apply to ourselves is a trap. Everything I believe I am comes with a subtext of a whole lot of things I'm not. When we label, evaluate, and critique ourselves internally many times per day, day in and day out, we start to feel isolated, discreet, and small. Also, because our identity has been so seemingly divided up by definitions and labels, we often feel like we always need to defend ourselves. At the same time, we live with an underlying fear that we actually don't know who we really are.

The insight of awakening turns this on its head. After awakening, we have little ability or desire to define ourselves. This is because we feel the natural fluidity and interconnection of all of life. At the same time, the sense of isolation and feeling of needing to defend ourselves is considerably diminished. These thoughts and labels that used to imprison us are now seen to be but harmless clouds floating across an endless sky. Paradoxically, although we find no need or use for internally self-labeling, there is finally a very settled sense of identity. This sense of identity is completely nonconceptual, and yet is satisfying and "true" regardless of the circumstances. We come to this strange and marvelous place where we are finally truly settled about the problem of who we are and how we fit into life, and yet we can't say a darn thing about it.

The Paradox of Teaching

This book is made out of language, and thus seems to be using language to convey concepts to you, the reader. Yet by its very nature, awakening is nonconceptual. I'm sure you see the disconnect here. I am aware that because I'm using language, the mind of the reader will automatically package this material into concepts and store it safely within its extensive conceptual framework. The sense of conceptual identity that is "receiving" this information will try to reconcile it with other information and conceptual frameworks that are already in place. This is the normal functioning of the mind, of course. The funny thing is that those conceptual frameworks aren't the intended target of this writing. Not at all. The intellect is simply the interface. My intention is not for anyone to develop a conceptual framework of what is written here, but I know it will occur to some degree. This is a side effect that is unavoidable.

In truth, the target of the message is far deeper than the conceptual mind. As identity disentangles itself from the conceptual, it will become more and more obvious that you are hearing this message from a totally different place. So, the paradox here is that when we set out on this journey, the part of us that feels the most like us (the intellect) will feel like it is learning or receiving something from this communication. It will interpret this communication to be for its own benefit. In reality, I'm doing my best to bypass that part of the receiver, and at the same time giving that conceptual apparatus just enough candy so that it thinks it is the one benefiting from this message. What I'm really doing is sending wake-up calls straight past that conceptual identity structure so that a more fundamental and vaster identity begins to "remember" itself.

*"Do I contradict myself? Very well, then I
contradict myself. I am large, I contain
multitudes."*

—Walt Whitman

When we listen to a talk given by someone who can effectively
point to realization, it may suggest that that person has something we
don't. Reading a book about awakening may seem to suggest that its
writer has realized something we haven't. In either of these situations,
it's natural to conclude that we need to figure out how they did what
they did so that we can replicate their methods or path to achieve the
same realization. None of these conclusions are accurate.

In truth:

➢ There are no teachers of realization. You can never have my
realization, and I can never have yours. Realization is the
most personal-impersonal thing possible.

➢ You won't get anything from that person giving the talk or the
author of the book.

➢ This book can't give you anything you don't already have.

➢ No matter how enlightened anyone seems, they don't have
anything you don't have.

➢ That person cannot wake you up.

➢ The best "teacher" is like a polished mirror. They simply reflect your innate awakened nature and demonstrate to you that you have the ability to access it at all times.

The Paradox of Knowledge

I remember having dinner with a good friend, and she said, "You know, I've realized I really don't know anything at all." She said this from a place of authenticity and peace. While I completely understood and related to what she meant by that, I found myself responding, "You know, it's funny. There's one thing I know with absolute certainty, but there's no way I could ever say anything about it."

There is something quite paradoxical about knowledge when it comes to realization. I'm using the term "knowledge" here in a far broader sense than the word usually implies. Once we begin to recognize and trust nonconceptual knowing, the whole game is changed. There is a profound knowing here that could never be put into words. It's too close, too simple, and too obvious to be conveyed with concepts or descriptions. What's even more bizarre is that I know with absolute certainty that this paradoxical knowing is also the case for you. If that is not immediately apparent, it doesn't mean you're flawed, it's just because the mind is creating certain types of perceptual filters that are getting your attention.

This knowing, which is not apart from the knower or the known, excludes nothing and has no boundaries. Thus, it's not possible for "part" of it to stand apart from the rest of it and say anything about itself. Also, it is not static or fixed, so it evades description. The moment you make a conclusion about it, it has morphed, disappeared. This knowledge is not limited in any way or subject to any definition. It can never be threatened because it can accommodate anything. This the paradoxical world where you know that you know absolutely nothing when it comes to conventional understanding, simply because conventional understanding can't accommodate living truth. Yet there is a profound certainty in your trust of life and moment-to-moment reality that goes beyond even life and death.

The Paradox of Letting Go

Much of the awakening process is about letting go. Of course, stated in the usual way it sounds like letting go is an entirely voluntary process. It isn't. Sometimes we welcome this letting go, other times not. When it comes to letting go of doubt, hesitation, and resistance, it feels pretty darn good to let go. When it comes to letting go of some of the ideas we have about ourselves, it can feel more sticky, more uncomfortable. This is especially the case when we have solidified those ideas into beliefs and identities and learned to use them as coping mechanisms or as a means to avoid the uncertainty and pain inherent in being human. Regardless of how we respond to it in a specific set of circumstances, the process of letting go is a natural one.

Here comes the paradox. The more we let go of what we think we want, the more we have access to what we really want. The more we let go of empty promises of imagined futures, the more we enjoy the radiant intimacy of this exact moment. The more we let go of seemingly "positive" beliefs about ourselves, the more we find that we don't suffer cognitive dissonance when we find that we don't always live up to our own ideals. We can then give ourselves permission to be naturally human. We see that this immediate immersion into all of life is what we were chasing with all of that endless mental seeking. When we finally stop expending so much energy looking for the missing piece somewhere outside of our immediate experience, the natural, undivided reality seeps up through the cracks in our perception. The more that is let go of, the more abundance, depth, and richness is revealed exactly where we are.

The Paradox of Spirituality

An important part of maturing as a human involves realizing that scattering our energies in multiple directions can be unproductive and exhausting. Living this way often feels like we are struggling against ourselves or driving with the brakes on. If we see this clearly, we will realize that sustained effort and attention in one area of life usually yields better results, more satisfaction, and so on. Once we discover this, we tend to apply this kind of effort in areas of our lives that we are passionate about. Realization is no exception. When we get a taste of undivided reality, it is often so striking and so "right" that this focus on our spiritual life intensifies greatly. For many of us, it takes priority over most or all other areas of our lives. What we hadn't heard of a few years before becomes the most important thing to us. I think this is great. I believe it's the most valuable thing you can do with your life, as long as you genuinely feel it is something you're willing to engage with an open mind and heart.

And yet . . . there really is no such "subject" as awakening, realization, or enlightenment. There is a great saying in Zen: "Zen is life." This simple statement points to what I'm getting at here. I'm not interested in you developing a new hobby called "awakening." I'm not saying that this is one of many paths you can choose. This is no path at all. What I'm pointing to throughout this book has nothing to do with paths, or processes, or parts of your life. What I'm pointing to is your life exactly as it is, unfolding in this very moment. What I'm pointing to is not special, because you have never been apart from it. What I'm pointing to is feeling every sensation you feel right now. It also is every one of those sensations. It sees everything you see, and it is the seeing itself. It is those colors and forms and shapes dancing before your eyes. It is the movement of thought right now, evaluating what you're reading. This that I'm pointing to isn't spiritual because then what is there that isn't spiritual? When awakeness wakes up to itself, it immediately recognizes itself as every part of life. Seamless and complete. If it had a voice, it would say,

"Here . . . Here . . . Here,"

and

"Now . . . Now . . . Now."

"Paradoxes explain everything. Since they do, they cannot be explained."

—Gene Wolfe

So, although we have the tendency to compartmentalize our lives, the truth of awake nature simply doesn't recognize compartments. It's there when you doubt; it's there when you are lost in thought; it's there when you work; it's there when you stand in line impatiently; and it's there when you argue with your partner. You've never been separate from your true nature, not in the slightest.

The Paradox of Effort

We can learn so much from nature. If you observe nature, you will see a perfect balance between effort and effortlessness. There is equanimity and synchronicity in the way that natural processes unfold. This is true from the quantum level all the way to the astronomical level. It's just as true for the laws that govern the interactions of gluons and quarks as it is for the laws that govern the birth of a star or the collision of two galaxies. If we recognize that our own practice and investigation of living truth is itself a natural process, we begin to intuit when we might be resisting this natural balance. There will be times when it feels like you have to exert quite a bit of effort. This is okay. There will be times when you feel like relinquishment is the only thing that feels natural for you to do. In these moments, it will feel as if all practice, effort, and desire has become fruitless and exhausting. This is also okay. These fluctuations are all part of the natural process.

"The best paradoxes raise questions about what kinds of contradictions can occur—what species of impossibilities are possible."

—William Poundstone

At some point you will start to recognize there is a magical place where effort and effortlessness meet. In this place it will be clear that in certain moments, applying effort is where true effortlessness can be found. At these times, relinquishment and willingness to be still means not trying to hold back the natural flow of energy and activity. Other times you will be physically still and yet know
the spontaneous activity of the cosmos as intimate display. This
is a wonderful place. A place of stillness in motion. A place of surrendered fascination. You won't be able to makes sense of this logically, but in your gut, in your bones and marrow, it will resonate Yes.

The Paradox of Awakening

The awakening "event" itself is paradoxical in many ways. I had my initial awakening in 1997 and immediately found myself in a world of paradox. Here are some of the observations I made.

Awakening seems like an event. It isn't.

The sense of being on a timeline, traveling through life, endlessly trying to put out fires, solve problems, and get things done suddenly subsided. The relief afforded by the freedom from always being "on the clock" was quite surprising. I had no idea just how confining that sense of time had been until it stopped. The experience itself is timeless, so it can't be described as an event in time. If you find this hard to imagine, I totally understand. Our minds need to subsume the paradigm of time to imagine anything, so it's just not imaginable. However, it is experienceable. Moreover, this timelessness was clearly natural, and more real than when I had perceived myself confined by time. You could say that the true "event" wasn't the awakening; it was the previous experience of being in an enclosed identity somewhere on a timeline. The event that I didn't remember the beginning of because it occurred at a young age was intrinsically uncomfortable. Yet until that event ended, I had no idea exactly how uncomfortable it truly was. The moment that event subsided is what I call awakening. So, you could say awakening is actually the cessation of an event, even if it is initially a temporary cessation.

Nothing changed and yet everything changed.

I could look around and see that life looked the same way as it always had. The objects were the same, the people were the same, the body was the same. Yet everything was radically different. Although outward appearances were unchanged, everything was infused with a certain depth and rightness. Things felt actually real for the first time in my life. The magic of early childhood had returned, and every moment was enjoyable, even the painful ones. I wanted to relate this to people I loved, but I knew I had no words for it because I couldn't put my finger on what specifically had changed.

It felt really good to feel bad.

It's really easy to hear a message about awakening and interpret it as a promise that you will live life feeling good all the time and will never feel pain or discomfort. This is a total misunderstanding of what awakening is about. In fact, awakening means waking up from the imprisoning paradigm that some things are good, and some things are bad. That paradigm is rooted in the delusion of separation and causes a near-constant seeking of some experiences and a simultaneous rejection of other experiences. In short, that paradigm is what causes us to struggle and to feel isolated. All of my life I had unknowingly avoided emotions and thoughts that I had somehow concluded were not okay or were dangerous. I really didn't recognize the degree to which I was doing this. With awakening, that avoidance stopped. Strangely, when there was no longer avoidance of internal experiences, every experience felt fine. Even those experiences I had run from in my mind for years were found to be enjoyable. What a blessing to be able to enjoy sadness, grief, confusion, even shame! I hadn't realized the resistance-fear was the problem and not the seeming object of the fear.

The simplest and most insignificant events were the most enjoyable.

In truth, there weren't things that were more or less enjoyable anymore, because that judgment system had dropped away. Yet in contrast to how things seemed before awakening, it was quite striking how much satisfaction and natural enjoyment there was in standing in line, scratching an itch, and looking at the sky.

My heart opened, and I stopped caring.

With the immediate and causeless intimacy I experienced with every moment, I suddenly found myself unconcerned with most of the things I used to think I cared about. It became clear that I had been fooling myself. All that overthinking, justifying itself as "caring," was just a way of distancing myself from the momentary flow of life. I took care of responsibilities naturally in the moment without having to think or worry about what did or didn't get done. What remained was a joy in everything, no matter how small or seemingly insignificant.

"None are born or die,
Nor are they stained or pure,
Nor do they wax or wane.

So, in emptiness no form no feeling thought or choice,
Nor is there consciousness.

No eye, ear, nose, tongue, body, mind,
No color, sound, smell, taste, touch, or what the mind takes hold of,
Nor even act of sensing.

No ignorance or end of it,
Or all that comes of ignorance.

No withering no death
No end of them.

Nor is there pain,
Or cause of pain,
Or cease in pain,
Or noble path to lead from pain,
Not even wisdom to attain."

—*Heart Sutra*

The Biggest Paradox of All

There is absolutely nothing wrong with you. There is nothing wrong with life. There is no you apart from everything. There is no separation anywhere. Nothing needs correction. Yet as we work at investigating our true nature, it can feel as if we are trying to overcome some flaw or correct some error. This is not the case. The work we do is seamlessly part of the whole and not a means to an end. It is simply an expression of natural and spontaneous perfection. Ultimately, we realize that suffering ends when we stop trying to end suffering.

Chapter 5:

Attention

Introduction

I was quite excited to write this chapter because I get to show you, in a direct way, that you carry a get-out-of-suffering-free card with you at all times. After reading this chapter, you will never have to be confused again about how to immediately access your primary faculty to awaken. You will know, without ambiguity, how to activate your innate capacity to investigate the deepest truths of yourself and of reality. Moreover, you will be able to recognize that this faculty is available at every moment, regardless of the conditions. At the outset, I'd like to point out a few things about this innate capacity:

❖ It isn't a teacher.

❖ It isn't a specific technique.

❖ It isn't anything outside of yourself.

❖ It is always available if you're conscious.

- ❖ It is immediately accessible and unambiguous.

- ❖ It doesn't have to be cultivated.

- ❖ It's not complicated, technical, or conceptual.

- ❖ Anyone can learn to utilize it in a short time regardless of intelligence, beliefs, or background.

What I'm referring to, of course, is your attention. The ability to modulate our attention is something we overlook almost constantly. Yet it is the fundamental capacity we have that allows us to focus, meditate, inquire, and investigate the nature of presence. Anytime you meditate, whether it is guided or technique based, what you are actually doing is modulating your attention (or allowing something else to help you modulate it).

*"One day a man of the people said to Zen Master
Ikkyu: 'Master, will you please write for me some
maxims of the highest wisdom?' Ikkyu immediately
took his brush and wrote the word 'Attention.' 'Is
that all?' asked the man. 'Will you not add
something more?' Ikkyu then wrote twice running:
'Attention. Attention.' 'Well,' remarked the man
rather irritably, 'I really don't see much depth or
subtlety in what you have just written.' Then Ikkyu
wrote the same word three times running:
'Attention. Attention. Attention.' Half angered, the
man demanded: 'What does that word 'Attention'
mean anyway?' And Ikkyu answered gently:
'Attention means attention.'"*

—*Roshi P. Kapleau*

In this chapter we will discuss the nature of attention, its qualities, and the benefits of utilizing attention in skillful ways. We will approach this by:

➢ Learning to recognize and remind ourselves that we have the choice to modulate our attention at any given time.

➢ Learning how to modulate our attention in specific ways.

➢ Learning the value of developing a habit of noticing and/or modulating our attention on a consistent basis.

There are a lot of hands-on exercises in this chapter. If you want to really grasp this subject with clarity and confidence, I highly recommend you make it a point to take some time to perform the exercises as we discuss them. If you just think about or evaluate what you think the exercises are referring to, this subject can easily remain conceptual for you. On the contrary, learning these simple and always available practices and then applying them can become an exceedingly transformative endeavor over time. Do not overlook the value of attention merely because it seems too simple. Its power lies in its simplicity. Suffering and mind-identification are complicated; reality is quite simple.

Let's Go!

The great thing about attention is that you learn its nature and its nuances by using it. In truth, you're always using your attention when you are conscious, but you are not always using your attention knowingly. To clarify this point, how many times today have you thought about where your attention was? Is this something you consider often? Can you remain aware of exactly where your attention is on an ongoing basis?

Let's start with a simple exercise:

1. Look at the palm of your hand.

2. Keep your gaze there for about five seconds.

Not too difficult, eh? Now let's modify the exercise slightly:

1. Look at the palm of your hand.

2. Keep your gaze there for about thirty seconds.

Did you find that more challenging than the first exercise? Did you notice distracting thoughts? Did your mind wander? Did you notice any sensations or feelings during that time? Now let's modify the exercise further:

1. Look at the palm of your hand.

2. Keep your attention there for five seconds.

3. Then shift your gaze to an object behind your hand, perhaps the wall.

4. Keep your attention there for five seconds.

Congratulations! You just modulated your attention and did so in a precise and clear way. It wasn't hard, was it? So, we've learned a few things with this exercise. First, we've learned through experience that we can easily put our attention on a visual object. Second, we learned we can modulate or modify our attention by moving it from one visual object to another. We also learned that it takes little to no effort to move our attention. A fourth thing we might have gleaned from this exercise is that attention sort of "becomes" its own object. For instance, when we put attention on the palm of our hand, we weren't aware of something separate from the visual object (palm) that we could call attention. You could say that during the moment of viewing, attention was the visual image, and that visual image was the attention.

Objects of Attention

In the preceding section, we practiced placing our attention on a visual object (the palm of the hand). There are, of course, other types of objects on which we can place our attention. Try this:

1. Move your attention to any sound in your vicinity.

2. Gently rest your attention on that sound for a few seconds.

You just focused your attention on a sound object. Did you notice that it was just as simple and effortless to move attention to a sound object as it was to move it to a visual object? Also, did you notice that although the sound and visual objects have different qualities of experience, the attention you placed on them was the same in both cases? You could say that attention is somewhat like a beam of light, similar to a spotlight. It can easily and readily be directed to any object in your environment.

So far, the two objects we've placed attention on were external to our body. Is it possible to direct this beam of attention inward? Let's check it out:

1. Move your attention to the sensations inside one of your feet. Just the sensations. They might be tingly, dull, cool, warm, or any combination of sensations. There might be sensations in only one part of the foot, or there might be sensations throughout the foot.

2. Gently hold your attention there for ten seconds.

Was it easy? Did the sensations shift or change? Did they come and go? Do you find it interesting that attention can just as easily be moved to an object (sensation) inside the body as it can be moved to an object outside the body?

We've covered three of the five senses so far: sight, sound, and sensation. What about smell and taste? Well, I'll leave you to try this simple practice on those senses when you get the chance. Next time you're eating, close your eyes and direct all of your attention to the taste of the food just like you did with visual and sound objects. You might be pleasantly surprised how saturated your attention can become with taste. Similarly with smell, if you close your eyes and focus some attention into a fragrance, you might be surprised how vivid that experience becomes.

We've discussed all five senses, but there is one more object of attention we haven't addressed. That object is thought. To be precise, what I'm referring to is thought-consciousness, but for simplicity, I will just refer to it as thought for now. Let's practice:

1. Imagine a plump, red strawberry.

2. Hold your attention on that strawberry for a few seconds.

Congratulations! You just directly experienced what it is to place attention on a thought object. Let's do it again:

1. Say to yourself (in your mind): "I am a good person."

2. Repeat that statement internally a few times and notice what it feels like to rest attention in that thought.

This is a second type of thought object. This is an auditory or conceptual thought, as opposed to a thought image (strawberry).

That's it, five senses and thought. Those are the only objects of attention. Does it surprise you that there are only six types of objects we can pay attention to? I challenge anyone to demonstrate that they can put attention anywhere else. For instance, anything you can put your attention on that is in the past, meaning even one second ago, is always a thought. Similarly, anything you can think about happening in the future is always a thought. So, you're left with your immediate environment, aren't you? What is the immediate environment made of? The five senses and thought-stuff. Nothing more.

Qualities of Attention

Functionally speaking, attention is rather simple as we deduced in the previous section. While it is easily directed and can refer to only six possible object types, it does have various qualities that can be examined. These qualities of attention exist on various axes. To understand what I mean by axes, consider that most human qualities can be described as existing on various axes. A given person at a given time will be somewhere on the axis of underweight to overweight, short to tall, introverted to extroverted, and so on. Here are the axes of attention:

Dilated vs. Narrow

If we use the spotlight analogy mentioned earlier, we can demonstrate that attention can be confined to a narrow beam, or dilated to something more like an area light. Let's check it out:

1. Pick one sound in your immediate vicinity.

2. Let your attention rest on just that one sound for ten seconds (narrow attention state).

3. Now "relax" your attention to open to all of the sounds in your environment at once.

4. Remain in that dilated attention state for ten seconds.

Were you able to do it? Was it challenging? Try moving your attention back and forth between narrow and dilated. You might find that by doing this for a few seconds, the whole experience starts coming alive with sound. In fact, this is an excellent practice in and of itself. Many hundreds of years ago there was said to be a person who achieved enlightenment by focusing intently on sound. Her name,

Guanyin, can be loosely translated as "perceiver of sounds," or "the one who hears the cries of the world."

This spectrum of dilated versus narrow attention also applies to the visual field. Notice how most of your attention is usually on the center of the visual field (what you're looking at). Now try to relax your vision such that you are just as aware of your periphery as you are your central vision. How does that feel? This alone can be a valuable practice. It can transform the usual focused and probing activity of looking into a diffuse, immersive experience of seeing.

Directed vs. Receptive

So far we have explored the faculty of attention largely based on active direction. We've directed attention to this object, then to that object. On the other end of this axis is the possibility to utilize attention in a receptive manner. Let's practice:

1. Rest your attention on the sensations in your lips.

2. Keep attention there (just on the way it feels) for ten seconds.

That is an example of directed attention. Now:

1. Dilate your attention to feeling roughly the space of your entire body.

2. Remain open and relaxed. Just notice which sensation in the body calls your attention first. Which area seems to be most prominent in feeling, or the most noticeable?

3. When you notice that area, allow your attention to naturally flow there.

This is an example of using attention in a receptive way. Can you feel the difference in quality? It might feel a bit more like you are opening to something rather than controlling or directing something. This distinction may seem a bit unclear at first, but if you practice in this simple way, it will clarify over time. Letting attention naturally flow to whatever sense calls it moment to moment can be a deeply meditative practice.

Experience-Close vs. Experience-Distant

This particular axis is harder to demonstrate directly because it is something you will get better at detecting as you become more aware of qualities of attention. At first when we practice these exercises, sense objects might feel somewhat distant in our experience. We may not even recognize this, as that experiential distance feels quite normal to us. One way to investigate this is to put our attention on any object as we have been practicing, and hold it there for about thirty seconds. Anytime during that thirty seconds you can ask yourself, "How close does this sound/image/sensation/thought feel in this moment?" Does it feel like it's "out there" somewhere? Does it feel closer—a little louder, brighter, and sharper than it did previously? Or does it feel like you are in contact with it? It might even feel like you are totally intertwined with that sensory object, and it with you. Keep working with this exploration and you will likely find that with sustained attention, experiences become closer and more intimate.

Singular vs. Split

It is also possible for attention to be split among more than one object or type of object. Let's try:

1. Rest your attention on something in your visual field that is brown.

2. Pick one brown object and let it absorb your attention for about ten seconds.

3. While your attention remains on that visual object, see if you can bring in some of the body sense. It can be any sensation in the body, whether it's in the belly, chest, head, arms, or legs.

Did you find that challenging? Did you find it enjoyable? You can practice this with any combination of senses. This can be an incredibly valuable practice if you feel inclined to incorporate it into your routines.

Subjective vs. Intrinsic

This is a more subtle axis of attention qualities, but as your insight into the nature of attention clarifies, it begins to mark a profound transformation experientially. When we described attention as a beam similar to a spotlight, that was a convenient way of describing attention. On this axis, that description is on the "subjective" end experientially. That is to say that it appears as if attention is a quality that moves outward from the sense of a "me" or a center of experience toward an object. As you clarify attention and are able to experience sense objects more fully, more experience-close, and more immersively, it will begin to appear as if attention is not so much a beam shining on an object; but more like a radiance emanating from that object. Here is a way to explore that:

1. Move your attention to any sound in the room.

2. Let attention rest there for about ten seconds. Just that one sound.

3. Does it seem more like that sound is coming to you as a receiver, or does it seem more like that sound is simply

here-there, arising from itself, and not specifically locatable?

4. Now ask yourself, "Can I detect the interest and attention attributed to that object from within that object to any degree?"

This distinction can be pretty subtle or even undetectable at first. If you keep inquiring in this way, you will begin to notice that the attention and the essence of that sense object seem to be originating simultaneously from within the object. With practice, you might notice that objects of attention such as colors, forms, sounds, and sensations begin to take on a sort of glow as a natural enjoyment of pure sensation begins to materialize. This can evolve to the point where there is no longer an object as such; instead, there is simply a glow of enjoyment and immersion. Along with this, a certain gratitude begins to arise.

"Be present in all things and thankful for all things."

—Maya Angelou

Benefit

Learning to direct our attention and investigate its qualities can pay huge dividends. Moreover, if we don't mindfully utilize this power we have to modulate our attention, our attention will, by default, remain in thought throughout most of our waking hours. There is a lot of momentum behind this tendency to keep attention bound into thought, so don't underestimate the force of habit. There is a wonderland of presence available to us at every moment. We can reclaim it through skillful practice with attention.

Chapter 6:

Resources

Humans are, by nature, doers. It is quite natural that we put effort into things we are interested in and passionate about. When we take on a new project, hobby, or venture, we have a natural instinct to draw upon various resources to gain knowledge and learn new skills to help us accomplish what we've set out to do. The types of resources we generally draw upon fall into three basic categories.

The first resource we often look for is a teacher of one sort or another. We seek out someone who has already accomplished what we are taking on so that we can learn from their experience. This is sometimes a formal arrangement, such as taking a course, hiring a tutor, or utilizing a mentor. Other times it is informal, such as reading a book or watching an instructional video.

The second set of resources we usually draw upon are tools, techniques, and strategies to help us leverage our efforts to accomplish our goals. One thing that sets humans apart from many other species is the ability to use tools in complex and flexible ways so we can adapt to our circumstances and environments.

The third resource we tend to draw upon is group support in one form or another. Group support can be as informal as discussing your plans with trusted friends or loved ones, or it might involve joining clubs, groups, or online communities. When we seek more formal arrangements, we might consider institutional support, such as a religious organization, an athletic team, or enrolling in a trade school or university.

These three categories of resources (teachers, techniques, and groups) are just as relevant when it comes to awakening and realization as they are with any other endeavor. Each has both benefits and pitfalls specific to this process. We will discuss these benefits and potential pitfalls in detail in the next three chapters. Each category has both obvious (conscious) benefits and drawbacks, as well as hidden (unconscious) benefits and drawbacks. It is important to be aware of our own motivations and our influences, both conscious and unconscious as regards each of these three areas. This is so we can utilize resources intelligently, rather than in unhelpful or detrimental ways that can slow or undermine the awakening process. Having this knowledge ahead of time can save you from a lot of unnecessary confusion and frustration.

Before we explore each of these resource types in detail, I want to delineate what I'm including in these categories as regards the awakening process. I am using the category terms, "teachers, techniques, and traditions," because the terms are useful and convenient, but I mean them in a broad sense. When I say teachers, I mean self-described spiritual teachers as well as those who specifically point out that they are not spiritual teachers, yet they seem to be teaching something about awakening. I also mean anyone who facilitates awakening through writing, individual or group interactions, or retreats. They may or may not use the term awakening, and some might even say they do not believe in awakening, but they still seem to be teaching something like it. Also in this category are guides, channelers, coaches, etc.

When I talk about techniques, I am referring to various types of meditation, mindfulness practices, energy practices, inquiry methods, and any other tools you may find and utilize along the path. These may be something you learn by reading a book or through some form of e-learning. They may be something someone teaches you personally, or that you learn in a group setting. They also include anything you have developed on your own, or a version of something you have learned elsewhere but have customized through your own experience and intuition. When I refer to traditions here, I mean spiritual groups and communities, religions (such as Buddhism), sects (such as Zen), and other systems (such as meditation systems that are secular in nature).

Lastly, before we jump into detailed discussions of these resources, I would like to lay out a few guiding principles. As always, these are mere suggestions, but they come from years of observation and experience, and their only purpose is to make things go more smoothly for you:

➢ The best teacher is your own intuition, when you are oriented to your deepest living (unlearned) truth.

➢ The most powerful technique is always a willingness to see/hear/feel as clearly as possible exactly what is happening in your immediate experience, whether it be a thought, emotion, or sensory phenomenon—also to allow this ability to evolve in subtlety and clarity.

➢ The best group, system, or tradition can do no more than show you practical ways to facilitate and hone the two above truths.

➢ You already have everything you need to wake up to the living truth of what you are. Resources can be helpful, but watch for the hidden belief that the reason you are not experiencing realization ongoing is because you have not found the right teacher, technique, or system. The responsibility ultimately falls on you to awaken to your own undivided nature.

Chapter 7:

Teachers

W hen we take up the matter of investigating our deeper truths, we will naturally find ourselves interacting with teachers in one form or another. How that interaction plays out can look quite different depending on the person, the situation, and the stage of realization. In some instances, this will be a long-term formal interaction with a teacher. In other instances, it might mean various informal interactions with different teachers. In contrast to these direct types of interactions, there are many good ways to utilize teachers indirectly, mainly through media, such as books and videos.

Direct Interaction

There are several direct methods of interacting with a teacher. You could meet and work with a teacher in person on a one-on-one basis. There are many good teachers out there available for these types of arrangements. Your interactions might be sporadic and informal or longitudinal, intensive, and formal in nature. If it is not possible or convenient to work with a teacher you resonate with in person, it may be possible to work with one over a video conferencing platform. There are some teachers who don't work one-on-one with people, only teaching in group settings. These group events may take the form of talks, guided meditations, workshops, or question-and-answer sessions. The duration of these types of gatherings can range anywhere from a few hours to several days. Longer group events of this sort are usually called retreats.

Another great way to interact with a teacher is through asymmetric communication. Email exchanges, direct messaging, and/or voice messaging may be available, depending on the teacher and situation. This is less direct, but the interaction can be powerful and valuable to you. One person I worked with comes to mind. She lived in a different state, so our main form of interaction was through text messaging. We video chatted a few times as well. Through this method of interaction, and a heck of a lot of inquiry on her part, she had an awakening in five months from the time we met and was liberated in eighteen months after our first video chat. This means the end of suffering for her in this lifetime. I tell this story so that you don't discount any form of interaction. When you decide to investigate your true nature, all sorts of forces come to your aid, and things are possible that we might not typically imagine or consider. Technology has given us amazing opportunities that weren't available throughout most of human history. If your intention is strong and you are willing to work at it and investigate earnestly, any form of interaction can facilitate great transformation, even text messaging.

I would encourage you to investigate the various modes of interaction with teachers. Read some books and watch some videos. Let the teachings sink in. Then, if you resonate with one particular teacher, see if you can set up a meeting or video chat session. Or you can attend one of their talks or retreats. See which styles of teaching/interaction work best for you. If at any point a relationship with a realized teacher develops organically, then great. Just keep in mind that it isn't necessary to have a formal relationship with one teacher to awaken and mature that awakening.

Timing

It might seem that taking on an endeavor of this magnitude requires you to immediately find a liberated teacher and develop a one-on-one relationship with him or her. While that arrangement might be helpful, it is definitely not necessary nor is it the most common path. This wasn't my path, and it may or may not be yours. I didn't develop a formal relationship with a teacher until after awakening. That relationship lasted for a few years, then dropped away naturally. Beyond that there were various teachers who I can say had profound effects, but my interactions with them were intermittent and informal. These interactions were often asymmetric or one-way interactions, such as reading their books or watching videos. The point is that everyone's path will be different, and the "right" path for you is the one you're on right at this exact moment. Don't make the mistake of trying to make your path, as it relates to teachers, "look" like anyone else's. Let the process surprise you and reveal itself little by little.

Guiding Principles

Keeping these pointers in mind can save you a lot of time and confusion when it comes to teachers:

> ➤ The most a teacher can do is point the way; you will always have to walk the path. Don't expect the teacher to do the work for you, because they couldn't even if they wanted to.

> ➤ The best teacher will always reflect back to you your innate awake nature and reinforce that only you can wake yourself up. They will show you that you are your own best teacher.

In practical terms, teachers (in various forms) will be part of this process at some point along the way. With that said, it's important to be open to the possibility that:

> The teachers you encounter might be in forms you don't expect. That situation at work that makes you want to quit, escape, or use an unhealthy coping mechanism to avoid? That is your teacher.

At some point, everyone and everything becomes your teacher. Every sound, every movement, every breath, every belief observed is offering you the most profound teaching if you are open to receive it. In that sense, life—exactly as it is—is the best teacher of all!

Advantages of Teachers

➢ Interaction with liberated teachers will dramatically accelerate the process of awakening. This includes direct interaction in person, through messaging or voice, or through video chat. It also includes passive interaction through reading their writing or watching their videos. I'll use the term "transmission" to describe this effect. This is a transmission outside of concepts, theories, and practices, and it is very real and very potent.

➢ Good teachers are like a mirror. They can help you see things that might be hindering or obstructing your natural movement toward realization. Some of the obstructions can be quite hard to see if working on your own.

> Their experience can help you to avoid some pitfalls and provide you with good advice on strategies and techniques, as well as advice about how to apply them effectively.

> They demonstrate by example that realization is possible and available to you.

Potential Pitfalls

The pitfalls of utilizing a teacher in the setting of awakening and realization fall into two general categories. The first category involves attributes and limitations of the teacher. The second category involves challenges regarding the student's knowledge of how to select a good teacher, their understanding of the role and the limits of the teacher, and unconscious obstructions that can come into play due to the nature of human interaction. Concisely, the potential pitfalls can be categorized as those that fall on the responsibility of the teacher and those that fall on the responsibility of the student.

Pitfalls Involving the Teacher

> There is tremendous variation in knowledge, teaching ability, and experiential insight among available teachers. Do not be discouraged if it takes some time and effort to sort through teachers with whom you don't resonate, to find the one(s) who really move you and stir your deepest yearning for truth. We will go into detail about characteristics of a good teacher as well as what to avoid, but ultimately it is up to you and your intuition. Never sell yourself short with a teacher who cannot address your most sincere questions and drive to awaken. If you're willing to look and have a measure of patience, the right teacher(s) will appear.

➤ There are teachers of spirituality and/or awakening that have a lot of conceptual knowledge but have little to no experiential insight (realization). Some may admit this openly, some may hide or avoid discussing this fact, and others might actively mislead students about this, describing themselves as enlightened. Practical and scholarly knowledge can be helpful, but experiential insight (realization) is essential to transmit living truth.

➤ Some people who present themselves as spiritual teachers are fraudulent. This means they profess to wanting to help you wake up but in actuality they have their own interests, not yours, in mind.

➤ There is considerable variation in teaching styles, and some of those styles even seem to contradict one another at times. This can be confusing for a sincere student, especially early on. The way to avoid this becoming a problem for you is to trust your instincts about which teaching style(s) you resonate with. Also recognize that your instincts about this matter will shift and evolve over time.

Pitfalls Involving the Student

Stereotypes

We all have preconceived, stereotyped ideas about how spiritual teachers look and act. Take a moment to consider this question: What does an "enlightened person" look like? What image is conjured in your mind when you consider that question? Do they wear long, flowing white robes and hang beads and/or flowers around their necks? Do they have long hair and a beard? Do they have that unmistakable look of "enlightenment" in their eyes? Do they speak slowly and mysteriously? Do they not have a job because they have renounced worldly interests such as vocation, money, and sex? How close was I?

I've met many liberated people, and none of them looked or acted like the picture that was painted above. Here are a few examples:

- ❖ A thirtysomething something female writer from the UK

- ❖ A twenty-year-old Latina college student and competitive athlete living in the United States

- ❖ A businessman in Southeast Asia

- ❖ An IT specialist living in the southern United States who is active in the recovery community

- ❖ A young, Jewish female artist with a particularly good sense of humor

- ❖ A sixtysomething male surfer who lives in California

- ❖ An electrician and father of two from the Midwest

None of these people wears a white robe or has taken vows of celibacy. None of them live in monasteries, having renounced the material world. You could easily walk right past any one of them on the street and not notice anything special about them. However, if you interacted with them, you would likely start to notice something different—a presence and authenticity that is uncommon in people you meet day to day. If you were to get to know them and interact with them over a longer period, they would have a profound effect on your life.

So why did I take so much time to point out this set of stereotypes and give counter examples? Simply because unexamined, these unrealistic and distorted views can cause a tremendous amount of confusion. Being aware of our stereotypes can help us to avoid making irrational decisions or assumptions. Broadly speaking, there are two ways that these stereotypes can hinder our ability to identify an authentic teacher.

The first is that we tend to assume a teacher is authentic solely because they look and act like the stereotypical "enlightened person." Unfortunately, a person's style of dress and manner of speaking is not a good indicator of their degree of realization or their ability to help others through the awakening process. In fact, there are unscrupulous people out there who know that most of us have these preconceived notions and therefore use that knowledge to manipulate people into believing they are an authentic teacher. They intentionally don a spiritual or "enlightened teacher" style and persona to dupe others for their own gain. What are they trying to gain? Usually validation, money, or sex. If you haven't seen the movie Kumare, I highly recommend watching it. It drives this point home in a clever way.

Please don't take this to mean that just because someone dresses or acts in a manner that our stereotypes would endorse as an authentic spiritual teacher, they are automatically a fraud. There are also liberated, effective, and well-intentioned teachers who do indeed wear white robes and have long hair and beards. The point is that the persona, manner of dress, and style of speaking is not, in and of itself, a good indicator of someone's teaching ability.

The second way these stereotypes can be a hindrance is the opposite of the first. That is that when we don't see "evidence" through dress, manner, livelihood, or speaking style of an enlightened person (based on our stereotypes), we might assume that the teacher is not authentic. This is a mistake and can lead you to totally overlook someone who can be of tremendous benefit to you. A friend of mine who is a very sincere, effective, and deeply realized non-duality teacher told me something that illustrates this point well. She happens to be a young, blonde, Caucasian, and attractive European woman. None of these qualities fall under the stereotypical list of attributes of the spiritual teacher or guru, and yet she transmits very powerfully and has helped many people to wake up. She told me one of the things that she gets the most criticism for is that she wears makeup. This demonstrates the exact evaluative mistake I'm pointing to. We might have an assumption that an "enlightened person" should have no need to beautify herself or that she should be completely "natural" in some way that we idealize. So, if we see someone who seems to be teaching about realization, but they display some characteristic that might not fit into our unexamined list of "enlightened qualities," we might dismiss that person outright. In the case of this teacher, the concern about wearing makeup is simply a preconceived notion that is being projected onto her. If we aren't aware that that is what is going on, we might entirely discount her ability to teach/transmit, which would be unfortunate as she is a particularly potent and adept teacher.

Another example of this phenomenon is a cautionary tale from my own past. When I tell this story, it tends to make people laugh, and looking back it is sort of funny. However, it wasn't funny to me at that time. It actually discouraged me from looking deeper into the possibility of realization for a time. It was shortly after that initial glimpse that I described in the first chapter. I was in a bookstore in the "spirituality" section, looking for a book that might help me investigate further. I came across a book about Indian "Sadhus." It mostly contained photos of these individuals in their natural environment. If you don't know anything about Sadhus (I didn't at the time), they are men in India who have renounced the world and all material possessions. Many of them were hanging around on heaps of trash and had ashes rubbed all over their faces and bodies. What's more, they were naked, and some had their penises wrapped around sticks to prove they had no need for them because they had renounced sexual desire. Well, I was a nineteen-year-old American male, and to me this was shocking and disturbing. I actually thought, Wow, I don't want to be that enlightened! It honestly scared me to think that if I take this too far, I might end up hanging out with those dudes. In retrospect, it was a pretty silly conclusion. Yet in that moment, making assumptions that weren't true based on limited experience, it seemed reasonable to me that at some stage of realization, you have to renounce all desires and material possessions. Turns out that's not actually true—which reminds me of a joke:

A new monk arrives at the monastery. He is assigned the task of helping the senior monks transcribe the old texts by hand. He notices that they are making copies of copies and not of the original texts.

So, the monk decides to inquire about this practice with the head monk. He points out that if there was an error in the first copy, that error would be duplicated in every subsequent copy. The head monk says, "I hadn't thought of that. We have been copying from the copies for centuries. I'll take this up with the abbot."

The head monk goes to the abbot of the monastery and repeats the concern of the new monk. "Master, if we have been making copies of copies for centuries, then how do we know that we have it right? Shouldn't someone at least confirm that we are being true to the original text?"

The abbot sits for a moment in silent contemplation, then his eyes meet those of the head monk. "This is our way and we have not deviated from it for hundreds of years. And yet what harm could be done in confirming that we are following the precepts as they were originally written?"

The Abbot descends to the basement of the monastery and is not seen for two days. The monks are becoming concerned about his absence, so the head monk descends the stairs to the basement. Walking to the very back of the archives where the original texts are kept, he finds his master leaning over an ancient tome, weeping. "Master! What is the matter? Have we made a mistake in transcribing these copies over the years?" Through red, teary eyes the abbot answers, "Only one . . . the word was 'Celebrate' not celibate!"

Takeaway points:

➤ Do not judge the value of a teacher based on their appearance, nationality, gender, style of dress, location, or speaking style.

➤ Be aware of the tendency to overlook a teacher that may be valuable to you simply because they don't come across as "spiritual" in dress or manner. Furthermore, waking up does not mean you will have to alter your style, vocation, or community to accommodate realization. Realization is infinitely adaptable. You wake up in your life just as it is.

Under and Overemphasis

Both underemphasizing and overemphasizing the role of teachers can be detrimental. Depending on your personality and tendencies, you might lean in one of these two directions. When we underemphasize the role of a teacher, it's possible we simply don't want to see certain things about ourselves that may be keeping us asleep. As was mentioned, a good teacher is like a mirror. They can often help you to see things that are hidden to you. At some level we might sense this and thus avoid particularly adept teachers so that we don't have to face something that we aren't ready for or are afraid to see. Additionally, we might want to maintain certain habits and/or belief systems that are largely ego driven, even if we have ourselves convinced that we are being "spiritual." It can be quite hard to maintain this illusion when you expose yourself to an authentic teacher who, without even trying, will help you dissolve ego structures, habits, and beliefs that continue to perpetuate the facade of separation.

When we overemphasize the role of a teacher, we take the responsibility of our own awakening off ourselves and put it on the teacher. Oddly, when we do this, the core issue is the same as when we underemphasize the role of a teacher; that is, we simply don't want to face certain things about ourselves. So when we project our drive for awakening onto our teacher, we convince ourselves that they are the enlightened one and that they have some magical quality we don't possess. We convince ourselves that if we wake up, it's by sheer luck or because the teacher has somehow "graced" it to us. What we don't want to see is that they are not superhuman or extraordinary. The truth is that they've simply done the work that we are avoiding and can continue to avoid as long as we convince ourselves that they have some special potential that we don't possess.

Social Proof

The teacher-student paradigm can reinforce a subconscious belief in you that they will always be the enlightened one and you will always be the one "on the path." This tendency is quite common and often not recognized. It occurs due to the social structures inherent to human group dynamics. Being social creatures, we automatically intuit the status of various members of a group we are part of. In large groups, we tend to assume hierarchies and then try to figure out who has higher and who has lower status. When someone in that group appears to have the highest status in the group, we might make assumptions that are untrue. One assumption is that because in the current setting they are the one imparting the knowledge, there is something fundamentally different and/or superior about them. I assure you there isn't. This belief can be quite insidious. In fact, with particularly charismatic, popular, or effective teachers, there is often a large following of people who reinforce this tendency to falsely elevate the teacher. This often comes in the form of students telling one another about special attention the teacher has given them through personal interaction and private audiences. These subtle or not-so-subtle validation-seeking and competitive tendencies can become quite a preoccupation in groups surrounding some teachers. This seemingly innocent pastime can really build an illusory sense of "specialness" around a given teacher. This, in turn, further reinforces the false belief that this teacher has something extraordinary that their followers don't have.

Depending on the teacher, this behavior might be discouraged, ignored, or even encouraged. A deeply realized or liberated teacher will certainly not encourage this, but they know that human tendencies make this behavior a side effect of group teaching. A dishonest teacher will use this tendency among their followers to manipulate them into giving the teacher what he or she secretly craves, such as validation, attention, and admiration. It's wise to always be a bit alert for a teacher that encourages students to compete for his or her attention.

Discounting Your Own Experience

It's easy to use a teacher's descriptions as a comparative standard of your own immediate experience. This can cause you to endlessly question yourself. I frequently reinforce in people that their immediate experience—whether it be a thought, belief, feeling, sensation, or sound—trumps anything any teacher or realized person has told them about how it's "supposed to be." I can't stress this enough because it is a pattern that sneaks in again and again. We carry so much self-doubt that it can be easy to disregard our immediate experience as "the wrong one." Then we recall a description we heard from a teacher or realized person and try to impose that onto our current experience or change our current experience into that description. This is a complete waste of time for two reasons. The first is that this is already secondhand knowledge. We can't directly know someone's experience through a description. Yes, it can be helpful to hear the description in certain settings, such as talks or guided meditations. Yet when we recall those descriptions outside of that teaching environment, we are often using the memory to discount our own immediate experience.

The second reason is that no matter what I seem to describe or point to, I'm actually pointing to what is already in your experience. It's just often overlooked, or "looked past." I frequently remind people that I'm not talking about something they haven't found yet. I'm always pointing to something that is already there, already the case, and immediately accessible. This is the whole point and why it works. This is why people wake up to their true nature; because it's already there.

❖ No matter what it sounds like they are doing, a realized teacher is always pointing to something that is already in your immediate experience.

❖ Never discount your current experience in favor of a description someone else has given you. Their description may help to clarify your own experience in the immediate, nothing more.

Choosing the Right Teacher

For any subject, there are good teachers, there are not-so-good teachers, and there are charlatans. Spirituality is no different. There are liberated teachers who are there to help you to wake up and can accelerate this process for you. Simply listening to them speak or reading their writings can have profound effects on you that are both obvious and subtle. Among these teachers there is considerable variation in the ways in which they teach/transmit. Some are highly effective through writing but may not be available to talk in person, nor do they appear in public teaching settings. Others will not provide written answers or correspondence to students but function best by interacting in a one-on-one arrangement or in group settings. Some liberated teachers are great at answering questions and having discourse with students. Others lecture in groups but prefer not to answer questions, or they tend to give very concise or brief answers. I would encourage you to explore these different styles and see what works best for you. Exposing yourself to a variety of teaching styles can help keep things alive and interesting and avoid stagnation by illuminating dark areas in your practice that otherwise could go unnoticed for decades.

There are many good teachers who have some degree of realization but who aren't yet liberated. They have experimental insight as well as practical knowledge and experience working with people in the process of awakening. They can impart practical knowledge to you and give you precise pointers on how to investigate your deeper nature. They also can transmit directly to various degrees. With that said, they will also tend to transmit their biases and views, so it's important to be aware of that.

I would be derelict in my duty if I didn't tell you that there are also charlatans in the world of spirituality. There are a lot of them, actually. I bring this up because I've seen many people fall into the trap of believing they have a true teacher when in reality they are being misled, taken advantage of, or even abused. This group of false teachers falls into to two general categories. The first category consists of those who don't realize they are charlatans. They don't know what they don't know (Dunning-Kruger effect). They also don't realize they aren't realized. The other category often overlaps the first one and consists of people who use the context of spirituality to knowingly manipulate, dupe, defraud, and/or abuse others. These are people with sociopathic tendencies. Be aware; this can and does happen. We will cover the signs of these types of non-teachers in detail so that you can avoid them.

Characteristics of a Good Teacher

➢ If you interact directly with them, they always work from an affirmation of your experience. Whereas a less adept teacher might invalidate your current view or experience "no it's not like that, it's like this," a liberated teacher will generally accommodate your experience effortlessly, then point from where you already are. This is teaching from non-separation. If someone tells or suggests to you that your current experience is "the wrong one" or the unenlightened view, they are still teaching from separation. In awake nature there is no separation, so how can your experience be wrong regardless of the viewpoint (yours or the teacher's)?

➢ They are radically authentic. They won't necessarily conform to stereotyped patterns of behavior, belief, or communication. This way of moving through the world is uncommon and has a distinct feel to it. You may get a very peaceful vibe listening to them speak or reading their writing. Interacting with them may cause "openings" in you in the immediate. Yet a true teacher is not there to simply make you feel good. They are not people pleasers. They know themselves well and they know you well, and they are not there to help you perpetuate any delusions. They are there to dispel delusions.

➤ They may say things that are hard to hear. Part of this type of teaching involves pointing to truths that are counter to a lot of the ways we think about ourselves and about reality. When our beliefs are challenged, we often have an internal defense response. Don't be surprised if a teacher's message triggers both enjoyable and not so enjoyable internal responses. While a good teacher shouldn't invalidate your current experience, they may well show you how that experience, if held too tightly or identified with (view), can cause you suffering. This may not always be comfortable to hear. This is not to be confused with abuse. I do not mean that a teacher has a right to directly or indirectly criticize or shame you as an individual.

➤ They are comfortable in their own skin. A liberated teacher will be extraordinarily present. They are comfortable and adaptable in the momentary flow of experience. They don't need anything from you or from their role as a teacher. They are at peace with their internal and external environment.

➤ Enlightenment/awakening/realization is not a big deal to them. This takes a bit of explaining because on one hand helping others to realize their deepest nature may be what they spend much of their time engaged in. A liberated teacher may spend most of their time writing, teaching, or holding retreats that revolve around helping others to wake up, and yet it should be clear that realization is not a big deal to them. I'll give you an analogy. Is the sky a big deal to you? Sure, sometimes you might gaze in wonder at its beauty, but in general you don't jump out of your shoes exclaiming how amazing it is that there is a sky above us. Why? Because you know it's always there. It's obvious and simply part of life. This is how a liberated teacher regards realization. It is not only obvious to them that this is just the way it is; it is also obvious to them that this is the way it is for you too. They know you couldn't miss your own true nature any more than you could miss the ground when you fall onto it.

➢ They should be approachable. They shouldn't come across as enlightened, distant, all-knowing, etc. In interactions they should be simple, relatable, human. They shouldn't have a "need" to talk about spirituality, realization, or always put the conversation into that context.

➢ They let you determine the pace. You shouldn't feel pressure from a teacher or feel judgement for not being awake enough, moving fast enough, or getting their descriptions immediately. This is true whether that judgement is overt or subtextual.

What to Avoid

Choosing the right teacher is as much a matter of recognizing what is not there as it is a matter of looking for specific qualities. You can consider this section a list of "red flags" that tell you to proceed with caution if you choose to engage a specific teacher with these qualities (or their teachings). There are enough great teachers out there that, in my opinion, the appearance of any of these red flags warrants dismissing someone as a teacher.

➢ They are abusive. This might be overt abuse, or it might be subtle. It might happen in the open, or it might happen behind closed doors with a select few students. This abuse may take the form of verbal or emotional abuse, physical abuse, or sexual abuse. A teacher who criticizes students and tells them the criticism is for their own good, plays certain students against one another, plays favorites, or ostracizes certain students is emotionally unhealthy and will be a waste of your time at best. These are individuals with toxic emotional tendencies, playing out their internal struggles in the guise of spiritual teaching. Some of them have extraordinarily manipulative personalities and have found that using spiritual language and concepts like unity, universal love, and enlightenment can be used to win a sensitive person's trust and manipulate them. Clearly these are people to avoid at all costs.

➤ They "act" a little too enlightened. I put act in quotes because I want to emphasize that this type of person will be putting on a front or an act to convince people he or she is enlightened or has superhuman powers. This might be partially unconscious on their part. This can take many forms, but the litmus test is they just don't feel deeply authentic. Here are some examples:

1. They allow or encourage their students to worship or deify them (even by not actively discouraging this behavior).

2. They say outright or suggest that they have spiritual or mystical powers that very few in the world have. In short, they want to convey to students that they are extraordinarily special in some way. I recommend avoiding this type of teacher completely. They will just slow down your progress.

➤ They appear to want or need something from you. It is important to keep in mind that a realized teacher won't want anything from you at all. They don't need your approval. They don't need your validation. They don't need you to worship them or believe they are enlightened. In fact, any of those intentions run counter to liberated realization. In the natural (liberated) reality there is no one who is more enlightened than someone else. The sense of individual separation in this way is gone. They also won't need you to believe any certain system or teaching style is superior to any other. They won't be threatened by anything you believe or practice. This may all sound obvious, but some teaching styles and personalities can sneakily hide these motivations. It's prudent and healthy to be open to the possibility that a teacher is hiding a need for validation or a need to convince you he or she is special. This can ironically manifest as exaggerated or projected confidence on their part.

➢ A teacher who feels threatened by other teachers or teachings is a red flag. I have known people whose teachers shamed, teased, or criticized them when they sought interactions with other teachers. While jealousy may be a human emotion, a teacher who has not matured enough to avoid compromising their teaching due to feeling jealous is not ready to teach in my opinion.

➢ They have a messiah complex. A teacher that believes they are some sort of god or God's messenger is a definite red flag. This person has the potential to cause tremendous harm in people's lives. These are the cult leaders and large-scale con artists of the spiritual world. They have the potential to leave people financially ruined and emotionally devastated.

Chapter 8:

Practices and Techniques

W hen it comes to the subject of awakening, it can be immensely valuable to investigate the most basic assumptions we have about ourselves, about life, and about reality. When it comes to utilizing various techniques and practices, it is similarly valuable to begin by clarifying why we are applying specific techniques, what we are expecting to get out of them, and whether we recognize their limitations and potential drawbacks. In this spirit, I'd like to begin this section by posing a basic question about techniques and practices when it comes to awakening:

*Do you need practices and techniques to awaken
to your true nature?*

Hopefully by now you won't be surprised when I tell you the answer is both yes and no.

No. Your true nature is your true nature. It has never gone anywhere. It never could go anywhere. You have never been one millimeter away from the living truth of what you are, of what everything is. True nature permeates your conscious experience at all times—that which is aware of what you're reading right now. It makes up everything you see, feel, hear, taste, and smell. It is the effortless fluctuation and movement of everything in your experience. It is the unassailable stillness right here and right now. It is not even an "it," because there is nothing apart from it to call it an it. It simply is. There is only this body-world-universe seamlessly self-expressing and dissolving with perfect clarity and precision. You can't lose it; thus, you can't regain it. How could it be possible that you need a tool or a method to regain something that could never be lost? Everything in immediate experience is on fire with the radiance of living truth at this very moment.

And also . . .

Yes. Everyone I know of that has woken up to their true nature has done a good amount of practice of one type or another. However, the timing and types of practices and how they are applied vary tremendously among practitioners.

The best way I can explain this seeming contradiction is to say that our nervous systems are particularly good at maintaining momentum. Without needing to "remind" them to do so, they will perpetuate ingrained patterns and neurological processes that make up our internal experience. This is especially true of the patterns of thought that create the ongoing experience of separation. Separation can never be found outside of thought, so we can't blame our perceptions of division, isolation, and thus struggle, on reality. It's not reality's fault we look at it through veils we constantly create with thoughts and preconceptions. So, what is a practice? Simply stated, it is the act of un-practicing these habituated tendencies that cause us to perceive reality as divided into subjects and objects, pasts and futures, and problems and solutions. When we slow down this momentum of the mind, we begin to remember (experientially) what it is to be unbound, vast, and intimate with all of existence. In short, to practice is to undo habituated mental patterns that cause us to suffer. As long as there is a sense of a self-apart, (the one struggling to get life right, to wake up, and to solve the problem of being a suffering human), then directing the effort that arises out of that sense, to an investigation of you true nature, is a valuable undertaking.

I find that a given individual's views of and approaches to practice will fall somewhere on a spectrum. On one end of this spectrum are people who feel that practices, methods, and techniques are the most important part of the process of self-realization. In fact, it would be difficult for such a person to conceive that realization comes any other way than through deliberate and sustained practice. On the other end of the spectrum are people who intuitively perceive practices and techniques as inauthentic, rigid, and cumbersome. People on this end of the spectrum say things like, "Isn't practicing denying the validity of what simply is?" or "If my true nature is already here, which I sense it is, then isn't practice just muddying the waters? It feels like control to me. If there is something I'm doing that contributes to a sense of separation from what is already here, isn't it more about acceptance and relaxing more into life than adding another activity in hopes of getting to a better state?"

Neither of these views is inherently wrong. Depending on a person's tendencies, beliefs, and experience, they will generally fall more to one end of this spectrum than the other. This is especially true early on in this process. Once there is some clarity and maturity of realization, then one will begin to see that both of these ways of viewing practice have their place and have some intrinsic truth to them. At some point these seemingly divergent views of practice are seen to be "not-two." This means that the yes and the no to the

132

original question posed in this section are seen to be exactly the same answer. At this stage of maturity, it would be accurate to say, "Practice practices, and when there is no practice, then there is no practice." Or "There is nothing apart from anything else, so practice is not separate from life."

In this section we will begin by investigating general approaches to techniques and practices. Then we will discuss various practices and learn some techniques. Here is a primer to start us off:

❖ Qualities of a good practice: A good practice puts attention on what is immediately happening (thoughts, emotions, sensory experiences).

❖ Qualities of less effective practice: A less than ideal practice puts attention onto something that's not immediately happening (the past, the future, ideals, plans, solutions).

❖ It is generally best to practice with no immediate goal; meaning, don't judge a practice or technique on the immediate experience or look for a result.

We all bring a certain misconception to practice—that we are practicing to cause something to happen. This is a perfectly natural perception, and it is not the only motivation we bring to practice. But if unrecognized, it can cause us unnecessary confusion. We might be expecting practice to cause relaxation, a peaceful or transcendent state, clarity, understanding, or even awakening. We may or may not be fully aware that we have these expectations. If we aren't fully aware of these expectations, we might notice we feel discouraged or frustrated with practice at times. If this occurs, then it can be helpful to ask ourselves, "What am I expecting from this practice?" If you ask and then get really quiet, you often find the answer. It is usually something like, "I've been feeling stressed. I was hoping meditation would make me relax." This simply means we are experiencing the emotion called disappointment. Once we recognize this, we have the opportunity to feel and accept the presence of that emotion.

That example shows how our unexamined beliefs about practice can really color our perceptions of practice. What we perceived to be a failed meditation experience, when examined more closely, turns out to be a successful meditation experience. Meditation allowed an emotion we weren't in contact with to come to the surface so we could accept it into our experience. Revealing that hidden expectation and then feeling the underlying emotion will often relax any struggle we are having with our practice. In these moments it can be helpful to remind yourself of the following:

Realization is uncaused and does not
need to be cultivated, learned, attained, or
achieved. It's already here.

Undivided, pristine reality is simply the case. It is
the case for you at every moment, and it is not a
state.

So there's no need to get attached to states, or
conclude that certain states occurring (or
imagined) during practice is the goal. No
experience is preferable.

No state is a mark of progress.
This is not about progress. This is about seeing
and feeling things as they are without the
distortions of preference and expectation.

Approach to Practices and Techniques

What is the value of practice? Realization is seeing things exactly as they are, without adding or subtracting. Practice is a way of undoing unconscious habits that lead us to see things as they are not. On this basis, practice is subtractive more than it is additive. Here are a few general approaches that will help to know when and how to apply practices most effectively:

Schedule

You have to find your own pace, approach, and balance when it comes to practice. You might find that scheduled daily practice feels natural to you. Even if it doesn't feel totally natural, consistent practice will be beneficial for most people. If you are the type of person who stays constantly busy and/or is easily distracted, then you might find great benefit in establishing a daily practice. On the contrary, you might find it feels most natural for you to surrender to practice when it comes forward spontaneously from the flow of life. This is a valid view of practice as well. Approaching practice in this way, you might find you enjoy practicing more than if you try to force yourself into a regimen.

Even if you currently tend toward one of these general approaches to practice, it's good to be aware that it can change as your experiential insight deepens. There may be times along this path when you need the consistency of daily practice. There may be other times when that begins to feel too regimented and rigid. I've utilized both of these approaches at various times. What I ultimately found was that practice practices itself, if and when it's needed. Sometimes it looks more regimented and sometimes it looks more intuitive, but there is a deep trust in the natural intelligence as to when and how it occurs.

Where Intention Meets Surrender

There is a part of us that wants to know the truth. It wants to live the truth. This is the part of us that wants to dig in and uproot delusions that keep us thinking and acting in ways that make us suffer. It wants to wake up from the illusion that we are separate, isolated beings who continually struggle, only to achieve occasional relief. I might call this our natural intention to live in truth and to dispel illusion. This intention is powerful, and when it is prevalent in our experience, it is truly a blessing. However, it's not the whole story. There is another side to things. There is a side to us that has no intention. It is always at rest. This side of us wants to open to the moment and let life permeate us. It wants to let life overtake us. It is naturally attuned to the mysterious and to the unknowable. It trusts surrender. It even trusts suffering. Most of us will tend toward one or the other of these instincts, but all of us can find both if we are willing to look. It might take some practice, patience, and contemplation, but it can be done. If you are able to find both of these aspects of your interface with reality, then you have found that "sweet spot" where practice becomes immensely powerful. Remaining in that place where intention meets surrender will set your practice (and your life) on fire.

Spirit

The specific technique you are applying is not nearly as important as the spirit with which you are applying it. While a technique may help unlock aspects of realization, it is realization itself we are concerned with. So, commitment to realization, not to any specific technique, will keep you on track. I've met people who are rigidly loyal to a certain technique, such as a specific type of meditation, and this attachment becomes a hindrance to them over time. This happened to me early on. I initially learned to meditate using a technique called a mantra. I was convinced that there was something special about this specific mantra that allowed me to access states of relaxation that I wouldn't have been able to access without it. The thought of using a different technique was extremely uncomfortable for me. In retrospect, I can see how much doubt in my intrinsic ability to access my true nature was built into that belief. While the mantra didn't cause this delusion, over time my attachment to it began to undermine my trust in my own inherent awakeness to some degree. At some point, it became clear that my intention and willingness to surrender mattered far more than that mantra, or any other technique. With that knowing, there was a great relaxing that occurred. From then on it was clear that no specific technique is required to access living truth, and that profound states of dissolution, interconnection, and peace were effortlessly accessed with many types of techniques, including no technique at all.

Evolution

Techniques and practices tend to naturally transform and evolve as long as we don't apply them too rigidly. If you're willing to allow a technique to change and evolve, it will teach you far more than if you hold a rigid view of how it has to be applied.

Come Up with Your Own

There's nothing magical about any one technique. Someone made up every one of them. I've come up with many while sitting in silence. I've also come up with them while interacting with others. Over time, you will likely come up with your own techniques or modifications of existing techniques as well. Trust your instincts and be willing to experiment.

A Technique Is Like a Catalyst or a Conduit

It can (but doesn't have to) open a portal of sorts. This isn't a portal you see visually, nor one that you can describe in concepts. This happens on its own timing. No one can make it happen. While I hesitate to say this because I don't want anyone to actively look for portals, I think it's important to point out so that this possibility is not overlooked. If this happens it can be subtle, and you can overlook it if you hold a technique too rigidly. What can happen is that the technique itself can fall away and the experiential insight will carry you onward. This is a natural process so if you sense it happening, you can just go with it. If suddenly the experience opens to something vast, beyond description, or just "beyond" in a way that cannot be put into words, then by all means let go of everything, including any technique you were using. This is the whole point of what we're engaged in here. It's okay if you aren't sure what I'm referring to here. This is the kind of thing that you'll know when it happens. When it does, you may remember this and then remember that it's okay to just let go. This is surrender.

Specific Techniques

There are many types and subtypes of techniques and practices that can help you investigate deeper truths. For simplicity, I've broken them down into the following four categories:

➤ Meditation Practices

➤ Mindfulness Practices

➤ Inquiry Practices

➤ Movement-Based Practices

This is not the only way to categorize all the different types of practices and techniques available. Nor is it an attempt to encapsulate all or even most of those available. It is simply a summary of the most common and effective practices that I've found useful for others and myself. In this section we will discuss these each of these categories in general terms. We will then look at specific techniques in each category. Feel free to try any of these techniques and modify them based on your own instincts and experiences.

1. Meditation Practices

There are numerous types of meditation practices. Here are some general categories. This is not intended to be an exhaustive list:

- ➤ Breath-Based meditations
- ➤ Mantra mediations
- ➤ Devotional meditations
- ➤ Compassion-Based meditations

Before we talk about the different types of meditation practices, I'd like to lay out a few pointers that can be helpful no matter which type of meditation you take up:

- ➤ Choose a quiet place with few distractions. Turn off your smartphone or leave it outside the room. This will help reduce the temptation to check it or distract yourself with it.

- ➤ Sit in a comfortable posture that feels supportive of being alert but without straining. Lying down is okay as well, but only if you don't have the tendency to fall immediately asleep (like I do). There are teachers and systems that teach you should never meditate lying down. I used to believe this based mostly on my own experience and teachings I had received. Now I see that this is too rigid an approach. I have met people who do almost all of their mediation lying down. I've seen people meditate lying down for almost every round during a weeklong retreat. They were able to stay alert and practice with great sincerity.

➤ You can close your eyes or keep them open. If you do keep them open, you might try to keep your eyelids relaxed and open just enough to see a few feet in front of you. Try it both ways and see what feels most natural to you.

➤ When beginning to meditate, it's helpful to develop a daily practice. Commit to a certain amount of time whether it's ten minutes or thirty minutes per day. Try to do one technique consistently for thirty days and then evaluate whether this type of meditation feels right for you.

➤ When we sit down to meditate, it is quite common that we notice there are a lot of thoughts. If you don't realize this is normal, you can quickly convince yourself that meditation isn't your cup of tea, or that it just doesn't work for you. It helps to remind yourself that those thoughts aren't caused by the meditation, nor do they indicate an error in the way you're meditating. You are simply becoming more aware of the thoughts that are already there. It's as if you are taking the role of the observer instead of becoming entangled in the thought stream as we often do throughout the day.

➤ As we become more aware of our thoughts, it is helpful to remember that there is no goal to reduce the number of thoughts. The presence, absence, quantity, and subject of thoughts say nothing about the quality of meditation. As concerns thoughts, it's best to have a hands-off approach. We don't need to push them away, wrestle with them, evaluate them, or indulge in them. Having a neutral relationship with thoughts will bring equanimity to your meditation practice. Regard thoughts like you would a beloved pet. If you're sitting in a room, your pet might come and sit on your lap, or it might lie next to you. It might run around the room in excitement, or it may leave the room altogether. If you just trust that it knows what to do and how to move naturally, then you will have a harmonious relationship with it. It's the same with thoughts. If you trust that they know how to move on their own accord, then you will have a harmonious relationship with them. As we start to cultivate this harmony, we often find that we are no longer entangled in thoughts. They become more like an old friend—the kind of friend that you know so well, you can sit comfortably in silence with them.

Natural Meditation

The first type of meditation I want to talk about is actually not a technique at all. I know that sounds strange; however, natural meditation is a very real phenomenon, and I find that most people who are sincere and experienced in meditation practice come across it at some point. The easiest way to illustrate what I'm talking about here is to tell you from my own personal experience how I came upon it. I had been meditating for several years when this clicked for me. Over that time, I had used various different meditation techniques. I really enjoyed meditation for the most part, as I found it relaxing and centering. At times there were more intense experiences. There were states of profound peace, dissolution, and insights that I couldn't begin to describe. There were also times of frustration, painful emotions, and challenging internal states. Regardless of what technique I was using and whether the experience was enjoyable or difficult, there was one thing I never questioned at the most fundamental level. That is whether or not I even needed a technique at all. There is a term in Zen called "shikantaza" that describes a meditative approach where one uses no specific technique. I had heard of this before, but even then, I

141

somehow still interpreted that as a technique. This sounds really funny to me now, but I can genuinely say that I just didn't get it until it came upon me naturally. I remember the exact moment it clicked. It was just an aha moment. I was sitting there, meditating in my bedroom, and the technique of meditation, as well as the sense of there being a practice, simply disappeared. It only took an instant, and from then on there was never a sense of needing a technique to meditate. Moreover, it felt like I was always sort of meditating. It was just a matter of how still the body and mind were as to whether it was obvious in any given moment. I still found various investigations and inquiries useful at times, but the basis of meditation for me became this natural, technique-less practice that is always here.

I will begin by doing my best to describe it, but please understand I'm not describing anything specific that you can do or make happen. This that I'm pointing to is already always happening. If you can sense into it in your own practice, then that's great. If it takes you a few years like it did me, then that's perfectly okay as well. It obviously doesn't have a name, so I'll call it "natural meditation." I also sometimes describe it as simple or basic meditation.

Natural meditation is best defined by what it is not:

➢ It's not a practice.

➢ It's not a technique.

➢ It's not something you can do wrong.

➢ It's not a means to an end.

➢ It's not focusing your attention in a certain way.

➢ It's not about trying to witness something.

- ➢ It's not about trying to label something.

- ➢ It's not trying to create a state.

- ➢ It's not trying to relax.

- ➢ It's not trying to heal the body, mind, or heart.

- ➢ It's not something you have to get better at.

- ➢ It's not something meant to cause enlightenment.

- ➢ It's not trying to make anything happen.

- ➢ It's not trying to stop something from happening.

- ➢ It's not trying to find out who you are.

- ➢ It's not trying to forget who you are.

- ➢ It's not trying to get rid of anything.

- ➢ It's not trying to gain anything.

Here's how you do it:

- ➢ Put away all distractions, including electronics, screens, etc. Sit or lie in a comfortable position. Sitting is better if you tend to easily fall asleep when lying down.

- ➢ Let go of all agendas.

- ➢ Don't try to do anything or make anything happen.

- ➢ Don't try to manage your experience.

➤ Don't judge. This means there is no such thing as "too many thoughts," or "an annoying sound." Let everything be as it is.

➤ Wherever your attention moves is right.

➤ There's no preference for alert versus distracted. If there is distraction, then that's just how it is.

➤ At some point, even the sense of monitoring your experience might fall away.

Natural meditation, by definition, doesn't have a how. We spend our entire day trying to do something, trying to be someone, trying to solve problems. Natural meditation is our opportunity to turn off all of those needs and agendas. It is our opportunity to experience this moment without filters, comparisons, or evaluations. It is a time when we can let life move exactly as it will with no influence on our part. It is a time to let life show us that it knows how to take care of everything inside and outside without our assistance.

This non-practice may be ironically difficult at first. However, over time it can become quite intuitive and pleasant. Since natural meditation is a subtle but valuable non-practice, it may help you to read this section each time before you meditate to remind yourself. After a while you will get the "feel" of it, and you won't need reminders of how to get into the groove of it. To summarize this in a remarkably simple way, I'll quote a Zen teacher I had many years ago:

"Just sit there and don't make anything."

Breath-Based Mediations

There are quite a few types of meditation that rely on observation or modulation of the breath. I will describe a simple breath-counting type of meditation.

➤ Choose a quiet environment, free of distractions.

➤ Sit in a stable posture.

➤ Close your eyes.

➤ Take about one or two minutes to become aware of your environment. Notice the sounds in the room. Feel your feet against the floor, or the cool air on your skin. Notice the sensations of the movement of your chest and belly as you breathe. Notice if there are any thoughts. Some common thoughts when we begin to meditate are:

  • "I'm too stressed to meditate right now."

  • "I wonder if I'm doing this right."

  • "I really need to get the laundry done."

  • "I hope this is relaxing. It's been a rough day."

    These are all normal thoughts; everyone has them. They don't mean you can't meditate. Just notice them as thoughts and you've done everything you need to do.

➤ Once you've taken a moment to become aware of your internal experience and your surroundings, you can gently turn your attention to your breathing.

➤ Don't try to change, modulate, or control your breathing. It's unnecessary and can be counterproductive. Instead, just observe the natural rhythm of the breath.

➤ Notice the sensation of the breath coming in and going back out. You needn't visualize anything, just feel in the same way as you feel your feet against the floor or the air against your skin.

➢ Once you're able to follow the sensation of breath for one or two in/out cycles, then count an out breath by internally verbalizing, One . . .

➢ Notice the following in-breath, but don't count it. Now count the out-breath again. Two . . .

➢ Count only the out-breaths in this way until you get to ten. At that point, start back at one. Continue in this way for the duration of your meditation session.

➢ If at any point you lose count, simply return to one and start over. If you find yourself at eleven, twelve, or twenty-six, start back at one. If you find yourself lost in thoughts, or distracted with the environment, return to one. Don't get upset with yourself when these distractions happen; they happen to everyone, and they will happen a lot at first.

➢ Even as you count, you want to rest your attention gently on the breathing. This means don't struggle with thoughts, sound, other sensations. If they are noticed, that's fine, we're not trying to keep anything out or cause absolute focus and quiet within the mind. If you make those your goals, you will become frustrated.

➢ The counting may become faint or may start to seem automatic, like you aren't consciously doing the counting, but rather the breath is counting itself. If this happens, simply let it be.

➢ If the counting disappears and there is still attention on the breathing, with very few to no thoughts, that's okay. There's no need to reintroduce the counting as long as attention is alert and remaining with the breath as opposed to getting lost in thoughts.

Mantra Meditation

Mantra meditation is a type of meditation that uses a word or sound internally spoken and repeated to cultivate a meditative state. The term mantra is a Sanskrit term meaning "instrument of thought" or "instrument of mind." In some traditions it is believed that the power of the mantra has to do with which specific mantra you use. Certain teachers lead their followers to believe that they have the best, most powerful mantra(s). You can see how this benefits the teacher, but in actuality, the power of mantra meditation is not in the mantra you use but in how you apply it. With that said, I suggest using a mantra that feels comfortable to you and is easy to repeat internally. You don't have to use a word or sound whose meaning you know, as the literal meaning of the word doesn't actually matter. More on this later. For now, just pick a word or sound that resonates with you and try it out. If it feels comfortable and accessible when you meditate, then use it. Here are some possible mantras:

I AM

AM

PEACE

UNITY

FREEDOM

ONE

ONENESS

NOT-TWO

COSMOS

WONDER

STILLNESS

AUM (pronounced "Aaaooohhhmmm")

HAM-SAH (a's are pronounced like the o in mom)

VAM   (the a pronounced like o in "mom")

RAM   (the a pronounced like o in "mom")

Here is the technique:

➤ Choose any of the mantras above, or come up with your own.

➤ Sit quietly without distraction.

- Close your eyes and take a moment to become aware of your internal and external environment.

- Speak the mantra internally into your mind.

- Listen intently to the effect of that spoken sound. Does it echo? Does it fade? Does it naturally repeat? There's no wrong answer, and you needn't contemplate these questions intellectually. It's more a matter of watching and feeling the effect of that sound in the mind.

- If the mantra fades or disappears, or you get lost in thought, then simply drop the mantra back into the mind by speaking it internally. This is sort of like letting go of a feather in the breeze. It might float to the ground, or it might swirl around you as it is carried on the currents of consciousness. It might change directions. It might get closer or more distant.

- You might find that repeating the mantra consistently feels most natural. If so, then gently repeat it at whatever frequency feels most natural to you. Don't try to force, control, or precisely pronounce the mantra. It's important to let it move in its own natural way in consciousness.

- When thoughts, mental images, sounds, or sensations come, don't push them away. There's plenty of room in consciousness for all experience. Just allow the mantra to be the priority of your attention. If you get lost in thought, then refocus your attention on the mantra.

- This may feel mechanical at first, but if you continue to return your attention to the mantra and allow it to change and alter itself as it repeats, you will start to feel like it takes on a cadence of its own. Once this is happening, the sound, pace, and quality of the mantra may change considerably. It may become completely different than the original sound. This is perfectly okay. If it feels natural, spontaneous, and effortless, let the mantra move as it will. The mantra might change in

149

the number of syllables it has. It might seem to get louder or fainter. It may seem internal or external. Your job is neither to direct any of this nor to analyze it. Your job is to allow it and go along for the ride.

➤ It may be subtle, or it may be obvious but at some point, there will be a transition. It might seem as if something else is voicing the mantra now. As if the Universe itself, consciousness, or Being is now voicing the mantra at its own pace. If this occurs, simply surrender to it. It may feel like a vibration or a wave. It may be quite energetic and loud, or it might be very subtle. It might be fast or slow. It might not even be pronounceable anymore; it may sound more like some otherworldly instrument or a cosmic symphony. No matter what qualities the mantra takes on, you can trust it as long as it feels natural and spontaneous.

➤ The key is to allow the mantra to begin to resonate with the natural movements of consciousness, which, in turn, reflect the cosmos.

➤ Here is a more advanced approach you may try once you feel comfortable with mantra meditation. Begin without a mantra. Become open, observant, and receptive. Do you sense an impulse? If not, then relax again and let attention move how it will. Remain receptive. Is there a subtle sound, vibration, or impulse somewhere in your experience? If so, then that's the natural mantra. This non-practice is a combination of natural meditation and mantra meditation. It can be quite powerful once you get the feel of it.

Devotional Meditation

Devotional meditation is a simple acknowledgment of the limitations of the human dimension. If we're sincere and humble, we will recognize at some point that our drive to awaken has certain innate self-limiting features. To attempt to utilize our personal will, with its built-in defense mechanisms and survival instincts, and to go beyond the individual human construct will ultimately end in futility. Yet in a very real sense, this is what is required for awakening to occur.

"To come to the knowledge you have not, you must go by a way in which you know not."

—Saint John of the Cross

Anyone who goes through this process will at some point come to a place where they instinctually know they are incapable of going any further relying on their own faculties. After countless hours, months, and years of desperation, practice, and exertion, we nevertheless arrive at a place where we are at a complete loss as to what to do or where to go next. Our own limited perspective, our own ego, and indeed our own self-interest will ultimately bring us to an insurmountable, self-imposed barrier. When we come to this place of devastation, surrender, and wonder, often the only thing left to do is to pray. Devotional meditation is prayer.

How you pray and who or what you pray to will depend on you. You might pray to God, you might pray to the Universe, you might pray to the intelligence of nature. You might pray to the unknown, or you might pray to life itself. It's a very personal thing, of course, but I can give you one piece of guidance: pray to that which you have the most reverence for.

For some of us it might be as simple as relinquishing control and saying, "I've done everything I possibly could. I'm at an existential impasse. I know I can't do this, but I remain open to it. It's up to you now, life; I give my will over to you." For others it might take the form of a prayer to a personal deity. It may be a prayer to Jesus. If you're Buddhist it might be a prayer to Kannon, the bodhisattva of compassion.

A powerful prayer is not a prayer
of acquisition but of acquiescence.

If you pray for what you want,
you are praying to your own ego.

If you pray for truth, for something
to carry you beyond yourself,
for unfiltered reality,
you are praying to an
immensely powerful force indeed.

Compassion-Based Meditation

There's a certain amount of relief in just admitting that you're a self-centered jerk. Of course, not all the time, but a lot of the time, right? Now I don't mean you should judge yourself for being self-interested or that you're wrong for having thousands of self-centered thoughts per day. I don't mean to say that you should feel shameful or that you are fundamentally flawed. I'm saying quite the opposite, in fact. If you think mostly about yourself and put your interests and beliefs ahead of those of others, that means that you are . . . completely normal. The point of this acknowledgement is to come into authenticity. How much energy do we waste trying to convince others through actions, words, and social media posts that we are kind and altruistic or a good partner, friend, and family member? A lot.

"Every man alone is sincere. At the entrance of a second person, hypocrisy begins. We parry and fend the approach of our fellow-man by compliments, by gossip, by amusements, by affairs. We cover up our thought from him under a hundred folds. I knew a man who under a certain religious frenzy cast off this drapery, and omitting all compliment and commonplace, spoke to the conscience of every person he encountered, and that with great insight and beauty. At first he was resisted, and all men agreed he was mad. But persisting—as indeed he could not help doing—for some time in this course, he attained to the advantage of bringing every man of his acquaintance into true relations with him. No man would think of speaking falsely with him . . . to most of us society shows not its face and eye, but its side and its back. To stand in true relations with men in a false age is worth a fit of insanity, is it not?"

—Ralph Waldo Emerson

Someone reading this might wonder if letting go of a positive, lofty, or idealized self-image could be harmful. Let me first be clear that I'm not saying we should act irresponsibly or selfishly. This is not an excuse to justify knowingly treating others poorly. It's simply a rectification of a tone of inauthenticity we have all developed as we learned to become adults. As we mature into adulthood, we all develop a persona, an artificial interface with which we engage the world. This acknowledgment is a call to let that persona rest. It is an experiment to see what happens when we disentangle ourselves from that projection of the one who has it all together, the one who is always positive, always working hard, always doing the right thing. It's a call to interface with the world in a simple, direct, and authentic way.

Ironically when we simply allow ourselves to be as we are instead of actively projecting something "better" (by societal standards) than we are, we often become a better person. We usually find that by admitting and accepting our natural self-centeredness, we don't become more self-centered as one might fear. Instead, by invoking our innate ability to see clearly and honestly, we are allowing a layer of inauthenticity to fall away. When we are able to do this, we begin to see those places where we become unconscious in our interactions with others. By unconscious here I mean the ability to overlook when and how we are acting in ways that are dishonest and/or harmful to others. You see, when we feel we have to uphold the guise of being a good person, there will be cognitive dissonance in circumstances where we are confronted with evidence to the contrary. Our minds don't like the feeling of cognitive dissonance, so our usual reaction to it is to overlook the evidence presented that is contrary to our "positive" self-image. So by actively trying to convince others and ourselves of what a great person we are, we set ourselves up to
totally overlook those moments when we are acting quite the opposite. Ultimately, this leads to patterns of unconsciousness where we then avoid looking more clearly at our behaviors, beliefs, and motivations. This, in turn, leads us to perpetuate self-centered behavior. In the end, it's seen that by acknowledging our self-centeredness, we are more apt to act in selfless ways.

What does all of this have to do with compassion-based mediation? Well, compassion-based mediation is a way to function outside this trap of projecting a persona and the inauthenticity that inevitably results. In truth, it is not you who are self-centered. In fact, that sense of the "you" that needs to defend itself by creating a persona is produced by the endless parade of self-centered and fear-based thoughts that run automatically through our minds, day in and day out. Those thoughts have never actually been about you. What you are cannot be defined by or contained within the narrow and dualistic view of a thought-structure. What you are cannot even make a distinction between self and other, between inside and outside, between good and bad. What you are, in the way I'm speaking now, is pure acceptance. Unconditional love. Compassion-based meditation is a practice of speaking, thinking, and moving from unconditional love.

I will describe two approaches to compassion-based meditation. The first is a solitary practice. This is for those times when you are free of distraction and are able to sit quietly and dedicate a period of time to meditation. The second can be practiced anywhere and at any time.

Solitary Practice

➢ Choose a time and place that feels natural and relaxing.

➢ Sit or lie in a comfortable posture, and put away any distracting elements.

➢ Take a few minutes to let your internal environment settle.

➢ Now put some attention into your body. Feel the sensations in the area of your chest. There's no need to label or think about them, just feel.

➢ Once you are feeling some sensation in the chest or heart area, then you know what love is. You know what compassion is. It's a sense. It's simple and direct. It doesn't judge and it doesn't say no. It's a direct beholding. In fact, it doesn't have to be just in the heart area. Any bodily sensation works.

➤ There might be thoughts that say, "This isn't love," or "This makes no sense." That's perfectly okay. Let them remain. You might even find a similar warm space of sensation somewhere in that thought space.

➤ Once you identify that direct contact, that sense of compassion and acceptance, you can begin to "find" it elsewhere in the body. Move attention to the hands or feet. Can you find a similar sensation? It may be tingly, warm, or feel like fullness or pressure. Once you notice it, just offer it simple acknowledgement.

➤ If you feel like you are struggling with this practice, be easy on yourself. Give it some time. It can also be helpful to communicate directly to the sensation. Just feel it, then say, "You are loved," or "You are accepted." Alternatively, you can say, "I love you."

➤ As you move your attention to various body spaces, keep inviting that sense of compassion, love, and acceptance. Stay as long as you want in any area. Do you notice an overall softening within your system? Do you feel like smiling? Even subtle differences mean this is working.

➤ Once you're beginning to feel this self-acceptance, or at least sense-acceptance, you can affirm (speaking directly to and from the sensations): "You deserve peace. You are accepted. You are loved exactly as you are."

➤ Sometimes it feels uncomfortable or silly to speak in this way to your body sensations. If that's the case, it can be helpful to acknowledge the awkwardness or discomfort in the same affirmative way. Find the sensations in the body corresponding to any awkward or uncomfortable feeling, and rest attention there. Even if it's tight, or there is a tendency to avoid the sensation, you are still in contact with it. That contact is called love. It's called acceptance.

➤ Once you get the hang of recognizing the natural acceptance and love that arises from directly feeling sensations with an open heart, you can begin to apply this contact, warmth, and acceptance to others.

➤ Bring anyone you are close to into your mind and heart. There's no need to form a precise image of them. It's more a matter of feeling the presence of them. Wherever you feel the sensation is right. Is it in your heart? It often is, but it doesn't have to be.

➤ Once you get the feel of your loved one, you can offer them warmth. This is as if you were to reach out and comfort them with a hug or a hand on the shoulder and a smile. You don't imagine that; you feel it in your own body. This contact is acceptance. It says, "You're okay, and I love you."

➤ You can offer words of affirmation as well: "I love you. I accept you. I am grateful to know you. The world is a better place with you in it. I love you unconditionally and want nothing from you other than to be fulfilled in whatever way feels most natural to you."

➤ You can expand this to friends, acquaintances, and strangers. You can even expand this to include those people who are the most difficult for you to be around. If you're able to do that with genuine warmth, maintaining contact with your own body sensations, then try the ultimate test. Try it with someone you have a grudge against, someone who has harmed you, or your least favorite public figure.

Anytime Practice

I'm going to paint this practice with broad brushstrokes. The reason for this is simple. What you are practicing here is a new way of living, and I can't tell you how that will look; I only know that it's possible for you. I want to empower you to develop compassion, acceptance, and a love-based way of moving through life. One that harmonizes with your personality and innermost promptings. In short, I want to offer a possibility that you, in the life you are living exactly as it is right now, will feel more natural, spontaneous, and fulfilled when you awaken your innate capacity for authenticity, acceptance, and altruism. I will make some suggestions for various situations. I encourage you to try them and see how they feel. See if you don't find powerful effects coming about from moving in these ways. Then I hope you'll modify and evolve these approaches in ways that make them fit your personality.

> As you see someone approaching, immediately smile, regardless of whether or not you know them. It doesn't matter if you are simply walking past them or are about to enter into a conversation with them. Just feel that smile of acceptance. This isn't a taking-smile, like an attempt to get acceptance from them. It is a giving-smile that says, "I already like you. I am human just like you are, and I accept you." You can even say these words internally to remind yourself. Even if you are too shy to make eye contact, you can smile with your body and heart, and they will feel it.

> When you are in nature, you can apply the solitary compassion-based meditation described above to the environment itself. Go through the steps and then once you feel that contact in your own sensations, begin to apply that acceptance, regard, and simple enjoyment of sensory contact to the sky, the trees, a rock, or the smell of the environment.

> When you are in a conversation with someone and notice the internal dialogue—How am I coming across? Do they like me? I don't know what to say. I'm anxious.—this is a good time to turn some attention to the sensations in the body. When you do that, you remind yourself of the acceptance and love that is intrinsic to that contact. Once you

can do this, (it may take some practice), you can then take the next step. The next step is to apply that contact you feel with your own sensations to the sense/feel of the other person, their body and presence. Feel the warmth, acceptance, and love in that sense of the presence of another. Once you have this down, see if you can find where the sensation in you and the sensation of their presence meet. Remember this is about feel not visualizing. If you are one of the many people out there who have severe social anxiety and find this too difficult to practice in live, spontaneous conversations, then consider practicing this with a friend who is easy to talk to. Better yet, practice with someone who wants to work on this along with you. This kind of practice can be challenging initially if you have social anxiety, but the rewards are endless if you keep at it.

➤ Take on a 30-day challenge to offer three compliments per day to any three people. The key is the compliments have to be honest, authentic, and come from a place of giving. This means you aren't doing it to people-please. You aren't doing it to get someone to like you. You're doing it to give. It can be a simple observation such as, "I like that pendant," or "Nice shoes." It can be an observation about their demeanor or character: "I like that you always seem calm and relaxed," or "You have good leadership skills." A particularly good way to turn a thought of jealousy or envy into an act of giving is to offer sincere appreciation. You might notice someone has a great relationship with their spouse, child, or parent, even if you have struggled in the same area. You could say, "Hey, I appreciate that you have such a good connection with your husband. It's inspiring to see two people who genuinely support one another and enjoy each other's company." If it's challenging to offer appreciation directly at first, you can do so internally. Ask yourself what you appreciate about so and so. Then say it to them internally until you feel more confident saying it to them verbally. It's important, however, to take that step at some point of actually saying it. By doing this daily, you start to be on the lookout for things to appreciate about the world and about people instead of internally ruminating over what you don't have or what's wrong with your life.

> Start to become interested in inanimate objects, mundane circumstances, and times when you would normally be bored or look for distraction. Regard the objects around you as living things, deserving of acceptance and love. Go through the steps in the solitary practice above and then when you feel the warmth and contact within your own body, start to feel for it in any object in your vicinity. It doesn't matter what the object is. It can be the carpet, a brick, a cloud, or the remote control. See if you can't find some contact there, some regard for mere existence. I understand that this part might sound a bit silly. Let me just say that the first time you experience yourself as both "you" and another object, whether that be a person, a tree, the sky, or a tombstone, there's no going back. Your life will have been changed forever. I can't tell you exactly what that's like because it's indescribable. But I will tell you that in my experience, it's what people are looking for, no matter what they think they're looking for. It's unconditioned intimacy. It's sublime.

"Working with plants, trees, fences and walls, if they practice sincerely they will attain enlightenment."

—Dogen

2. Mindfulness Practices

Mindfulness practices are a means of reorienting our attention to our immediate environment. This sounds simple enough, but anyone who has tried it for any length of time knows that you almost always find yourself lost in thought within a few minutes. The singular aim of this entire book is to break that spell which keeps us habituated to living in the dream world of imagined pasts and imagined futures, imagined problems, and imagined solutions. The point is to shatter the dream world of separation and seeking and then the true nature of presence will be naturally revealed. At that point you will realize that mindfulness isn't something that needs to be practiced. With that said, there are many varieties of mindfulness techniques you can learn. If you find one that you resonate with, then by all means use it.

3. Inquiry Practices

Inquiry is a powerful tool when it comes to awakening and realization. There is an entire chapter dedicated to inquiry later in this book. It is the most direct way to bypass and disrupt the filters that obscure your true nature on an ongoing basis. Inquiry effectively applied can make transformations possible in a very short time that would have taken decades through other means.

4. Movement-Based Practices

Movement-based practices, body practices, or energy practices include yoga, Tai Chi, Qigong, and others. These can be excellent adjuncts to the process of awakening and realization. These modalities can help to regulate and balance energy within your body. If you feel inclined to take on a movement-based practice, then by all means do so. It's not necessary, however. I am no expert on any specific movement modality, so I will just give a couple of pointers to augment any practice you might have. I defer teaching the techniques themselves to qualified teachers.

➤ Putting your attention into the sensations inside the body during movement practices can be quite powerful.

➤ If it seems too vague to try to find internal sensations in the body, or you find yourself visualizing the body areas instead of feeling them, you can start with contact points.

➤ Feel the contact point between your foot, your bottom, or you hand against the ground. Look for other contact points. Are the hands touching each other? What does it feel like at that point of contact?

➤ When you can keep attention in contact points for a period of time, you can start to move your attention from the contact point into the body part. Feel your way in. If the foot is contacting the floor, then slowly feel your way into the space one inch from the floor inside the foot. Then feel up into the ankle, and so on. Be sure you feel that continuity of sensation.

➤ Once you can access internal sensations easily, you can scan the body, resting attention in each area for a moment. Don't forget your face, tongue, jaw, eyes, and back of your head. How about the back of your neck, the tip of your nose, and your teeth? Can you feel your teeth?

➤ During slow movements, feel the sensations inside the body change, shift, and move. How do they move? Feel and find out.

➤ When you are in contact with the floor or earth, you might start to notice a subtle energy exchange between your body and the earth. This is subtle until you really start to have a strong sense of internal body sensations, so don't be frustrated if you don't feel it immediately. It will come.

➤ At some point you might even begin to perceive the exchange of energy between the body surfaces and the air and surrounding objects. This isn't something you visualize or imagine; it's a physical experience.

Intuitive Movement

One day I was making the schedule for an upcoming retreat, and I was trying to decide which movement-based practice to include for one round per day. In the past we had done yoga. Well, while I was contemplating what to do for this retreat, something just clicked. It was very much like when natural meditation clicked for me. This movement-based non-practice didn't have a name, but I knew exactly what it I was, and I was fairly sure people would find it accessible. I decided to call it "intuitive movement." It's best described as natural meditation in motion. When we began the round, I would give some suggestions about how this non-practice works, then people would move intuitively on their own for the rest of the session. People really enjoyed it, so I've incorporated it during every retreat since.

➤ Find a comfortable space free of distractions that you can move around in.

➤ Wear comfortable clothing that allows for flexibility and unhindered movement.

➤ Take a moment to let attention come into the present. Let some attention drift down into the body. Feel the contact points.

➤ Now what we're going to do is experiment with noticing that when we are not constantly thinking about what we want to do or how we want to move the body, the body has its own sense of how it wants to move. It's an experiment. See what happens when you give your body permission to move without trying to control how it moves. Just put your attention into any part of the body, then notice how it wants to move. It might be small movements or large movements. It might be repetitive movements or random movements. It might be fast movements, or it might be slow movements. It might be one part of the body moving, or it might be the entire body moving. The body might even stop moving. There are no rules to this other than to let the body lead the movement.

➢ You will probably feel conspicuous the first few times you do this, imagining that it would look silly from an outside observer. This is a great opportunity to recognize that we are so conditioned by the expectations of others that internal alarms go off when we start moving outside of socially expected and habituated patterns of movement.

➢ As you move intuitively, don't forget to give attention to your neck, jaw, fingers, toes, and eyes. How does it feel to let these body areas move in whatever way feels spontaneous to them?

Chapter 9:

Traditions

I t's common to believe that one's best chance for awakening is to get involved with some sort of group, system, or religion that is geared toward helping people realize their true nature. They must have it down by now, knowing all the steps and techniques, and can teach them to you, right? Many people assume this to be the case. I had definitely thought this way in the past. It makes perfect sense, doesn't it? Why reinvent the wheel when groups of people have been working on this for hundreds, even thousands of years? I wish I could give you an easy answer to these questions, but it's just not that cut-and-dried. There are many dynamics at play—both in the individual and in the various traditions and systems—that make it impossible to give a one-size-fits-all recommendation.

What I can say is there is a treasure trove of pointers hidden in books written by teachers of many lineages and traditions, going back thousands of years. Buddhism, Hinduism, Taoism, Christian Mysticism, Sikhism, and others have all had their share of exceptional writers, poets, and teachers who transmitted living truth through their writing. Furthermore, there are contemporary systems of inquiry, meditation, and other practices that don't claim roots in ancient traditions but are potent and effective if used wisely.

One chapter section would not be nearly sufficient to cover all the various traditions in any depth. So instead of describing specific systems and traditions, pointing out their strengths and weaknesses, I will give general guidance based on what I have encountered. I will discuss what I feel to be the strengths and weaknesses of engaging with groups and traditions in general, as well as what to look for and, more importantly, what to look out for.

The bottom line is that it's not necessary to become a member of any particular tradition or system, nor is it necessary to buy into the belief systems or dogma of any particular tradition. With that said, most realized people I know have had some degree of involvement at one point or another with a formal tradition. It is often relevant for a certain portion of your journey. Often people will gravitate away from groups at deeper stages of realization.

Potential Benefits of Traditions and Systems

Group Dynamics

There is potential value in joining a group of like-minded people (sometimes called a sangha). The group dynamic can help us focus our energy, concentration, and intention in ways that can be difficult on our own. This is especially true early in practice.

Knowledge and Practice

Many traditions have both doctrine and techniques/methods that support awakening and realization. The litmus test is this: Is it working? Do you see practitioners in that particular lineage, school, or tradition who have had authentic awakening or are liberated? I don't mean stories; I mean people you've actually met and interacted with.

Retreats

Retreats involving concentrated and extended meditation and inquiry are one of the most potent and transformative aspects of being involved with a tradition and system. This is especially true early in our practice. Many systems offer such retreats. These can be exceptionally helpful to you, especially if led by a deeply realized or liberated teacher. It's not that you couldn't go on a retreat on your own and sit in your house, forcing yourself to meditate ten hours per day for a week; it's just exceedingly unlikely that you actually will, especially when you're new to this type of thing. There are retreats associated with specific traditions, such as Zen. There are also retreats available led by liberated teachers that are not part of any specific lineage or system.

Potential Pitfalls of Traditions and Systems

Group Dynamics

Because of our tendency to take on the beliefs and habits of people around us, it's extremely easy to unknowingly adopt the beliefs, biases, and habits of the group you are involved in without realizing it. Oftentimes, this is innocent and just part of being a social mammal in a group of other individuals. Other times, it is quite deliberate within a group dynamic. Always be willing to examine the effect the group dynamic has on you and to question your beliefs and assumptions. If you ever feel pressured by a group to believe anything specific, adopt a certain doctrine, or take on any practice or activity that feels uncomfortable, you should at the very least question it. If you don't get a sufficient explanation, keep questioning or leave.

Variability

There is a tremendous amount of variability in the potency and effectiveness of various spiritual groups. You may have to do some searching to find one you really resonate with and that has no red flags. Always be willing to move on if you sense anything inauthentic or manipulative in a group.

You

Sometimes the distortions that can come out of being part of a group have little to do with the group or its members and a lot to do with you. Some good questions to ask yourself are: "What do I really want to get out of being part of a group?" or "What am I really expecting or hoping for by being part of this group?" It's important when asking these questions that you remind yourself there are no wrong answers. For instance, if the answer is, "I want to belong," or "I want to be liked," or "I want to find a romantic partner who is spiritual," then you have to acknowledge that motivation and be honest with yourself. If you tell yourself and others that you're there for spiritual awakening, but your real motivations are hidden even to you, then you will have cognitive dissonance. You will be frustrated on both accounts. So authenticity is key here.

Discernment

Even if you find a tradition or system that you resonate with, you'll have to use some discernment and judgement as to what you assimilate and what you don't. Even the best traditions consist of a mixture of valuable and not so valuable teachings. The same is true for smaller groups, centers, and temples.

Cult-Like Groups

The word cult may sound extreme, but it is not at all uncommon to find spiritual groups with some cult-like features. They might be subtle and reasonably harmless, but you should still be able to recognize the signs. On the other hand, they may be overt and predatory. Some groups purposely use the guise of spirituality, self-development, or self-actualization to defraud people. Never ignore red flags! Never mix up what you want something to be with what it actually is. I will go into what specifically constitutes a red flag below.

What to Look for in a Group, Community, Tradition, or System:

> A group led by a realized teacher that you resonate with.

> A group of people who feel authentic to you and share your interest in awakening.

> Opportunities for concentrated practice, retreats, and prolonged meditation.

> If there is doctrine involved, do you resonate with it?

> Transparency. It should be obvious that not only does the group have nothing to hide, but they also value purposeful transparency.

What to Watch Out For (Red Flags):

> If there is doctrine involved, be cautious if you feel pressured to adopt it, or if it's presented in a way that suggests, "This is the only true path."

➤ Any system, tradition, or group that requires you to contribute an unreasonable amount of money should be avoided.

➤ Any group where a central figure is deified, worshipped, or allows people to compete for their favor is a setup for disaster. Avoid it.

➤ Any group or tradition that pressures you to change your lifestyle, beliefs, or relationships is not interested in your awakening process; they are interested in controlling you. Don't mix these up.

➤ Any group where harsh criticism, favoritism, or punishment are used and justified as being necessary to wake you up will do you more harm than good. This kind of nonsense has nothing to do with awakening and everything to do with unresolved emotional issues of the leadership.

Chapter 10:

Stages of Awakening

Introduction

A handful of people, after having read this chapter, made suggestions along the lines of, "You might want to consider including a caution to the reader to proceed slowly at the beginning of this chapter. Much of the content is particularly potent and causes a lot of perceptual shifts and a sort of brain rewiring." So here it is: Some of the descriptions here, especially the ones pertaining to deeper stage realization, are quite direct. I usually calibrate very carefully how direct I am when talking with someone about this subject. I'm careful not to give someone too much too fast as it can be destabilizing, disorienting, and even scary. However, to accurately convey each insight and stage on its own terms and in its own light, I chose to use the communication style I would with someone at that stage. When discussing the deeper stages, I felt it was relevant to use direct language in a way I might with someone who has already had an awakening and has clarified their insight considerably. I recommend taking this chapter extra slowly, sitting with any experiential insights that may occur, writing about those insights if it feels relevant to do so, and rereading the various sections more than once.

It would be reasonable to conclude that processes as transformative as awakening and realization would proceed in an incremental manner—that they would occur in progressive stages. In one sense this is true. In another sense, it couldn't be further from the truth. If we interpret progression to mean that awakening and realization are linear processes with a definite point of departure and a definite destination, then we are mistaken. Yet there are reasonably predictable patterns that occur and certain key experiential insights that appear to be necessary for this unfolding to mature.

The awakening process is anything but linear. This is partly because as things clarify, we begin to experience timelessness more frequently and distinctly, and in timelessness the sense of linearity disappears. As our insights deepen, the belief that there is a destination becomes more obviously flawed. This is because we begin to experience natural interconnectedness. This indescribable insight could be called "self-everywhere" or "everywhere-here." From the direct experience of interconnectedness, it is clear there is no "other place." So, at some point the idea of there being a destination goes right down the drain. Nevertheless, there is clearly a subjective experience of progression, punctuated by certain key transformations or insights. As contradictory as all that might sound, hopefully by now you are prepared for a paradox. The following analogy will help to clarify this contradiction of there being progression and stages, without linearity or destination.

Imagine that you were the unwitting subject of a diabolical experiment. At a young age you were taken from your parents and placed into a chamber that was completely cut off from the world outside. At the same time, virtual reality goggles were placed on your head, covering your eyes and ears. As you grew, you were shown a story of a life somewhat like you might be living had you not been part of this experiment. You have no memory of anything except the virtual world that has been fed to you through the apparatus. The world as you know it consists of nothing but virtual sounds, images, people, and events. You don't know you are wearing VR goggles, nor are you aware of being in a small chamber cut off from the outside world. If this analogy sounds familiar, you might recall the plot of the blockbuster movie, The Matrix. In that movie all humans were electronically wired into a vast mainframe virtual reality world, while their bodies were used as batteries to power the computers that had imprisoned them.

As great as that movie was, it wasn't the first depiction of this metaphor for the human condition. The analogy of being bound in some way and forced to observe and interact with a narrow and limited virtual surrogate of what reality actually is, goes back a long way. In the seventeenth century René Descartes, the father of modern philosophy, described a similar scenario whereby a demon was carrying out an evil scheme by controlling someone's thoughts and sensory experiences, making them believe they were experiencing the "real world." This motif goes even further back. Plato, more than 2400 years ago, in perhaps the most famous passage in the history of Western philosophy, described the analogy of the cave, the fire, the shadows, and the sun. It's no mistake that this theme has recurred again and again throughout philosophy and literature. I would argue that this isn't just a motif or a story, but an archetype. In fact, this is the archetype. This pointer, this metaphor . . . this warning isn't just good storytelling, and it's not science fiction. It's absolutely true. Although there is no demon causing the trouble, and no one has been tied to a large stone in a cave. We aren't being used as human batteries by AI computers. The truth is more bizarre and surprising than all of those scenarios. We will get into that in detail in the chapter on mind-identification. Meanwhile, back to the involuntary human experiment.

"Behold! Human beings living in an underground den, which has a mouth open towards the light and reaching all along the den; here they have been from their childhood, and have their legs and necks chained so that they cannot move, and can only see before them, being prevented by the chains from turning round their heads. Above and behind them a fire is blazing at a distance, and between the fire and the prisoners there is a raised way; and you will see, if you look, a low wall built along the way, like the screen which marionette players have in front of them, over which they show the puppets.

I see.

And do you see, I said, men passing along the wall carrying all sorts of vessels, and statues and figures of animals made of wood and stone and various materials, which appear over the wall? Some of them are talking, others silent.

You have shown me a strange image, and they are strange prisoners.

Like ourselves, I replied . . . they see only their own shadows, or the shadows of one another, which the fire throws on the opposite wall of the cave?

How could they see anything but the shadows if they were never allowed to move their heads?"

—*Plato: The Republic*

So here you are in this chamber that you don't realize you're in. Your entire reality, in any way you can possibly know it, exists within this virtual world. For the moment, we won't concern ourselves with how you got in there or the nature of the VR goggles—that will come later. For now, let's talk about what happens when, for whatever reason, you are suddenly removed from that chamber and your VR goggles are removed from your face.

Let's suppose someone from outside the chamber found out you were an unwilling participant in this evil experiment. They decide to implement a rescue operation. Cutting a hole in the side of the chamber, they pull you from your unseen prison. Then they remove your VR goggles. Can you imagine how radically your experience of reality would change in that instant?

Two things would happen immediately. One is you would know experientially what the "real world" is. You may not be able to fully grasp its nature, and haven't really begun to explore it yet, but as you look around in wonder and astonishment, you darn well know this isn't the "dream" world you'd been living in all those years. The second thing that would happen is you would realize that those images, stories, and events that you had previously experienced to be so real are quite like ghosts. They have no more reality than a television show or a story in a book, which cease to exist as soon as you look away from the screen or close the book. The "problems" and "dramas" that had been consuming your energy and attention just a moment ago (when you still thought they were real) are suddenly vaporized. Could you ever really believe in that world again, even if you were to put the VR goggles back on? Could you ever convince yourself to believe in the problems, struggles, and stories of that world?

This abrupt and radical transition from the dream world that had been fed to you through the VR goggles, into the real world, is quite like what occurs with awakening. The shift in how we experience reality is truly this fundamental. Yet from the standpoint of the whole spectrum of what is possible with realization, this is just the first movement, the first step. There are many refinements beyond this.

However, from the perspective of reality itself, which you have just now glimpsed for the first time, it's pretty clear that things could not get any more "real" than this. I mean once you are out of the box, can you get any more out? Of course not. When you experience the real, it is clear, obvious, and self-validating. When you see that what you'd been taking to be reality is and has always been an illusion, then everything else by default, is reality. From this perspective, there aren't stages; you're either in the dream or you've woken up out of it. There's reality, which doesn't have degrees, it just is, and then there's illusion, which does have degrees. Reality is undivided, pristine, clear and marvelous; it doesn't wonder what is real and what is unreal. You now recognize the reality that was obscured by the dream stories and images as the natural reality. It feels instinctually right in a way that the virtual world never quite did. Can it get any more "real" than this? Well no . . . and yes.

Here's the thing. Once you're rescued from that virtual world, you're so overwhelmed by the vastness, freedom, and vividness of the real that you don't immediately consider the implications of going through such a radical and fundamental change. You don't initially realize that in many ways it can be uncomfortable to be outside the protections of the predictable and "safe" virtual world before you fully adjust to it. Once the magnitude of the transition you've just gone through begins to settle in, you'll occasionally find yourself looking for comfort in the familiar. You might try on your goggles again here and there when things get too intense, too unpredictable, or too unfamiliar in the world of the real. In fact, you might even crawl back in the

176

chamber for a time. The funny thing is that when you do this, you can never really forget what happened. You can't "un-know" what was discovered, can you? And yet it's still sometimes comforting to go back to the known. For a time, we will still take refuge in the false, simply because it's familiar and predictable, both of which can be comforting.

Here's where things get really bizarre. Are you ready? Have you thought about what happens when you put those VR goggles back on? Have you considered how the dream story you're being shown might have changed? Well, if you guessed that now the dream story will incorporate the awakening, you're exactly right! When you try those goggles back on, you have the new storyline of "the one that had an awakening." You will be shown a replay of getting out of the box and removing the goggles and discovering the "real world" with the goggles still on! What's more, the VR feed will now incorporate the awakening story and what follows it, in the context of the virtual world. You will be shown the epic journey of the spiritual seeker going through all of their trials and tribulations to "get back" to the real world that was discovered during the awakening. Of course, now it's the illusory seeker (the story of you) that is trying to get back to the virtual awakening, because you've never left the real world that was discovered during the actual awakening, nor could you. So, the seeking can go on and on as long as you have those VR goggles back on.

This is exactly what happens. After awakening, there is often a honeymoon period of exploration of the "real" world. This is typically followed by periods of voluntarily putting those trusty VR goggles back on (going voluntarily unconscious for the familiarity of it). We imagine ourselves as an "awakened being" or, conversely, "the one that lost the awakening." In either case, some part of us now knows that these stories are just that—stories. Can you convince yourself that the VR version of the awakening is the actual awakening? Yes, you can for a while, but only in the moments you're wearing the goggles.

At other times when they are removed it will be blatantly obvious that the VR world including the VR awakening is simply a story.

As you become more comfortable in the world of the real, you stop depending on the VR goggles and chamber for comfort, and ultimately you abandon them completely. This means that at some point after awakening, you will lose the desire and the ability to purposely go unconscious, even for comfort or familiarity. This marks a significant shift in maturity described by the sixth oxherding picture in Zen literature:

"Mounting the ox, slowly I return homeward. The voice of my flute intones through the evening. Measuring with hand-beats the pulsating harmony, I direct the endless rhythm. Whoever hears this melody will join me.

This struggle is over; gain and loss are assimilated. I sing the song of the village woodsman, and play the tunes of the children. Astride the ox, I observe the clouds above. Onward I go, no matter who may wish to call me back.

-Sixth Oxherding Picture

After we've accepted that this process of unbinding ourselves from illusion in all its facets is the only way this can ultimately go, there will still be a lot of clarification and deepening that will have to take place. If we proceed with earnestness, willingness, and an orientation to truth, then these natural processes will be reasonably smooth. If we fight the process . . . well, let's just say I don't recommend doing that. These ongoing refinements represent a deeper and more intimate experiential understanding of the nature of the world outside the VR dream. What follows is an investigation and integration of the nature of unfiltered reality and its eternal (always now/not in time) and intimate (interconnected/not in space) nature. This continues ongoing in a more and more refined way. A simple way of saying this is that the progression and refinements that occur after initial awakening don't mean you have more reality or are more awake (you can't be more out of the chamber). They represent the process of clarifying the nature of the relationship between the personal and the radically impersonal, clarifying the moment-to-moment experiential insight, and merging seamlessly into natural reality, which there could never be more or less of.

Why This Matters

You might be wondering why it's important to be aware of this paradoxical truth about the progression and stages of realization. Is there a value to talking in terms of progression and stages at all? Can't talking this way confuse the matter unnecessarily? Yes, and yes. What I've found is that a given individual at a given time can either overemphasize or underemphasize the progression and "stages" aspects of awakening. A certain person might generally tend toward one or the other of these extremes, but most of us will lean in each of these directions at various times throughout this process.

Both of these tendencies can lead to distortions that hinder further clarification and deepening of realization. In situations where someone is tending toward either of these extremes, I've found it helpful to ease the fixation by guiding them toward the opposite polarity. Let's look at each of these tendencies, how it typically presents, and the implications of not recognizing when we are leaning toward one or the other extreme.

Overemphasis

It's quite common that when we get a taste of unfiltered reality, or vivid presence, we get quite excited about it. We usually conclude, "Whatever I have to do to get some more of that, I'm going to do." The logical next step is to find a path. So we start to read all the information we can find about awakening and enlightenment. We believe that if we can find the most efficient path, the best path, the highest path, we will surely accomplish our goal. We compare teachers. We compare systems and traditions. We compare descriptions written by enlightened people. We might even engage in ongoing discussions and arguments with others about which path is the right path, which map is the most accurate map, and so on.

I acknowledge that it's normal to have a natural curiosity about something that we care a lot about, especially something as remarkable as awakening. However, this preoccupation with information and data gathering about awakening that I'm referring to can go far beyond curiosity. It can become almost an obsession for the right person and in the right circumstances. When we're engaged in this obsessive data gathering and analysis activity, we usually have ourselves convinced that this is the best way of waking up. "If I can just know more about this subject than anyone else, then I will surely wake up!" It makes sense from the standpoint of the intellect, which sees and understands the world through analysis and comparison. Unfortunately, this conclusion is about as wrong as it gets. This is because the first major shift or transition (awakening) is largely defined by going beyond the intellect, beyond conceptuality. Furthermore, subsequent refinements and integration of this important insight largely deal with seeing through increasingly subtler beliefs and identities that reside in the realm of thought and concept.

If you have strong tendencies to collect data, analyze and compare in this way, it's imperative that you get real with yourself at some point and abandon the belief that if you just learn enough about awakening, it will cause it to happen for you. If you are able to clearly see that the conceptual world itself is the barrier, then you have a chance to abandon the data collection and seeking of the perfect understanding, system, or map so that you can go fully beyond the conceptual. To help you do this, it can be fruitful to examine the beliefs you hold surrounding this intellectual approach to awakening (or anything else). The following set of questions and discussions is designed to help you investigate these tendencies:

> ➤ "What is more important to me: being right and knowing everything about awakening or actually waking up? If I could only have one or the other, which would I choose?"

> ➤ "If I could wake up but awakening meant that no one would ever know that it had happened to me, and I couldn't relate it to anyone, would I still want it?"

> ➤ "Would I prefer a life where I knew everything about awakening, and people thought I was enlightened and smart, but I never actually experienced true awakening?"

It is critical that you are honest with yourself about the answers to these questions, even if it is uncomfortable to ask. If the answers to any of these questions reveal a tendency toward a preference for being viewed as smart or enlightened, over actually going through the process of awakening, that's perfectly alright. Even if it seems like a tough decision, or a toss-up, that's okay, but it is imperative to acknowledge your beliefs and preferences; otherwise, you'll only be fooling yourself. Having these competing drives or agendas doesn't mean that there is no authentic drive to awaken. However, if competing drives go unnoticed, they can become problematic.

If you find that you feel strongly that understanding (knowing all the best maps and most advanced teachings) is as important or more important than awakening itself (or you can see that you act as if this is true by endlessly reading and discussing), then it's helpful to investigate what you think you will get out of being the smartest and most well informed, the one who knows the most powerful maps and the clearest teachings. This question can be helpful to get at hidden motivations:

> ➤ "What do I think it will provide me to know the best strategies, maps, and teachings about enlightenment?"

For one thing, you might find that you crave the respect of others with this same value system. You get validation from those who similarly place a high value on understanding, describing, and knowing the most about something. Also consider the competitive aspect. We never want to see that we're competitive, do we? Well, if we find ourselves sparring with others about the best paths, highest teachings, and most effective techniques, we might consider the possibility that we're secretly competitive. We get little validation hits by one-upping someone or suggesting we know the highest path, way, or teaching, and they don't. This is all human stuff. Sooner or later, each of us will have to work through these unconscious habits that keep us in the validation game. It's natural to desire validation, but if we don't see this about ourselves, we will be acting out of unconscious motivations in various areas of our lives.

It can also be helpful to look at things in the opposite sense. We can do this by investigating which fears drive us to remain in the tendency to intellectualize, rather than immersing ourselves in the experience of the immediate. The following questions can give us some insight here:

> ➤ "What do I fear will happen if I stop collecting data about awakening and realization?"

> ➤ "What would it feel like to let go of all of my accumulated knowledge about spirituality and awakening?"

> ➢ "How would I be perceived if I didn't know anything about awakening or spirituality by those who know a lot about it?"

> ➢ "How would that feel?"

If you look into these questions, you may uncover a fear of not knowing or a fear of looking dumb or simple. You might find fear of humiliation. You might find fear of losing the validation of others who base their validation on knowledge. We as a society place tremendous value on knowledge. Of course, in and of itself, knowledge is a wonderful tool, yet it is still a tool. And when it comes to waking up, all the knowledge in the world will get us exactly nowhere. Since society values knowledge, there is a built-in disregard or devaluation of those who lack knowledge. Have you ever criticized someone for not knowing, looked down on someone for being "ignorant," or judged someone for their overall lack of intellectual prowess? Of course you have, we all have. What effect does that have on us when we come up against a situation where we sense we will have to become intellectually disarmed? How does it make us feel to let go into a place where all of our knowledge and understanding is completely useless? It makes us feel vulnerable. It makes us feel unprepared. We might feel we are opening ourselves up for criticism, or to look the fool.

Summary: Overemphasis on maps, stages, patterns, and knowledge about awakening and realization can be (and often is) used to actually avoid awakening. This can be hard to see in ourselves and can take some digging and inquiry into our motivations to uncover, but it is well worth looking into.

Underemphasis

It is also possible to underemphasize the importance of progression and stages of realization. This can take a few different forms. One common form is mistaking a spiritual lifestyle for awakening. We might adopt a spiritual lifestyle that may include an individual spiritual identity, and/or an identity tied into a specific spiritual group or community. We then mistake that lifestyle for the drive to awaken. There is nothing wrong with the spiritual lifestyle, but do not fool yourself that it is equivalent to awakening; it is not. Having a spiritual lifestyle and identity do not cause or bring about awakening. An intention to wake up to the deepest truths of reality—even if it means you'll be stripped of all identities, spiritual and otherwise—is what brings about awakening.

The other way we underemphasize the progression aspect of awakening is by spiritual bypassing. To directly explore this phenomenon, consider the following statements:

➢ "Enlightenment is life exactly as it is."

➢ "There's nowhere to go and nothing to attain."

➢ "When there is no seeking, reality is naturally revealed."

➢ "There's no such thing as awakening; there is only life."

➢ "Integration is what matters, not awakening."

➢ "You should embrace your personal story, not abandon it."

➢ "Trying to transcend anything is spiritual bypassing."

Any one of these statements, taken in the right context and by the right person, can purvey a lot of truth. It may be exactly what that person needs to hear in that moment. On the contrary, if you find yourself holding these types of beliefs, genuinely believing that a profound and fundamental transformation defined by a shift in identity doesn't exist or that by orienting yourself to awakening you would be abandoning the immediate truth of your life, you are selling yourself a bill of goods.

My Zen teacher said the following years ago:

"Ultimately, spiritual realization is about living out of the innermost promptings of your tender and loving heart. However, without awakening you will think you are living out of the innermost promptings of your tender and loving heart, when in fact you will be living out of the outermost promptings of your deluded ego."

This is exactly what I'm pointing to here. We can conveniently use teachings such as the ones listed above to convince ourselves that we don't really have to face our willing unconsciousness and the fact that we perpetuate self-centeredness, greed, and ignorance at various levels. It's a way of avoiding the discomfort, fear, and grief that is inherent in thoroughgoing realization.

This can manifest as a person building a "spiritual persona" consisting of spiritual beliefs, communication patterns, and interests. While the heart of this interest in spirituality may be genuine, there is an unconscious but persistent part of us that is using this persona to project a more peaceful version of ourselves that is less than authentic. It can be a hard pill to swallow to see that we are doing this to manipulate others for complicity, sympathy, attention, and/or validation. We do this using guilt manipulation, projection, and blame. If you consider yourself a spiritual, righteous, or evolved person, you might want to look into this possibility. Those exact spiritual identities may well be preventing you from waking up. Furthermore, if others around you have suggested or outright informed you that you don't act in accord with the persona you project, it is imperative that you look into this.

While the spiritual persona might give us a certain sense of control over our image, it also undermines our ability to be deeply authentic and willing to let go into the mystery of realization. The game of trying to control others' perception of us is a game we can never win. So it's best not to play. When we give everyone permission to hold whatever view of us they see fit, we free ourselves from the bondage of attaching our happiness to the perceptions of others.

There is a third setting in which a failure to realize that there are stages and refinements to awakening can lead to some serious problems. This one is reasonably uncommon, but it can and does happen to a small number of people. This occurs when, after an initial awakening, the practitioner becomes thoroughly convinced that they are enlightened. They mistake the first movement of this process to be the completion of the process. This is a fairly big mistake. This is often accompanied by the person appointing themselves to the role of spiritual teacher or guru. They can have a surprising amount of success at this, and some will gather quite a large following. While I have no problem with anyone pursuing any vocation they feel inclined to pursue, this writing comes from an intention to give you the best possibility of liberation, so in good conscience I have to warn you about this. Let's look at how this can happen.

Many people I have worked with find that immediately after awakening, others will gravitate toward them, sometimes asking them for spiritual advice. They usually don't feel inclined to try to fill the role of spiritual adviser, but sometimes they ask me what to do because they want to help others. I tell them I can't direct how they should respond, but I do caution them that it is a common pitfall at this stage to start giving others advice and direction. Out of compassion, a few will try to offer advice, but without exception they find they truly aren't ready and quickly come to the limit of what they can do for someone as far as realization is concerned. Furthermore, they usually find that these types of interactions can get sticky pretty fast; it can even distort their own clarity regarding their recent shift. I know this because they tell me. The bottom line is that you're far better off directing your energy toward deepening and clarifying your own realization than trying to help others wake up to what you've realized at this stage. The former will lead to liberation, the latter to your own confusion and the confusion of whomever you're trying to help.

There is the occasional case of someone who takes this tendency to the extreme. This can become a true messiah complex. Although it's pretty uncommon in this extreme form, it happens frequently enough that it's worth mentioning.

If you have the tendency to become a teacher or guru immediately after awakening, ignoring the advice of those who have come before you, putting on a front to convince people that you are the enlightened teacher and they are the unenlightened students, you are starting down a path that it can be pretty hard to get off of. Often this doesn't end by the teacher's choice, because the same fear of truly letting go of control is still driving this whole charade. It often ends when the students finally realize the teacher is projecting an image of being enlightened beyond his or her ability to transmit it. So instead of helping people wake up to their true nature, you're transmitting your unaddressed emotional dysfunction. Several well-known and popular teachers have gone down this path. I don't recommend it.

I'd like to lay out a few simple principles that can help to avoid these pitfalls and keep you on track to your own liberation from suffering:

➢ After awakening, it is important to remain humble. You are just starting the process of realization, not completing it.

➢ Being open to pointers and teachings from those who have come before you can help clarify the refinements necessary to mature to later stages of realization, including liberation.

➤ If you find that others (including students) tend to suggest you are not as awake (usually based on your behaviors) as you seem to believe you are, it's particularly important to be open and receptive to these communications. While communications like this can be hard to hear, they truly are a blessing in disguise. Ignore them to your peril.

Summary: Underemphasis of the possibility of genuine, thoroughgoing awakening and the refinements required to achieve it can lead you into a world of self-deception. Similarly, "using" a spiritual persona or lifestyle to try to get unmet emotional needs addressed can cause ongoing confusion. You're far better off addressing those needs directly and authentically, returning to spirituality when the drive to awaken is authentic and clear.

What's interesting is that both overemphasizing and underemphasizing the progression and stages aspect of awakening are ultimately rooted in the same tendency: a deep-seated and unrecognized tendency to distance ourselves from life. In the first case (overemphasis), we distance ourselves by using concepts and intellect to hide in the "safe" domain of thought where we maintain control by endlessly rearranging and comparing concepts. In the second case (underemphasis), we distance ourselves from life by failing to acknowledge that to truly get under our self-centered and unconscious tendencies, we have to be willing to let go, which includes letting go of control of what others think about us. We have to face the truth of dissolution—that everything will go in time, including all ideas we have about ourselves, our story, and the body we inhabit.

By recognizing these tendencies in their extremes, we may be alert to times when we drift one way or the other. We will all touch into these fixations sooner or later, so it is valuable to get acquainted with them early on.

Before We Go On

In the following sections, we will explore two different descriptions (maps) of the stages of realization. The first is quite simple, and the second is more complex and detailed. Before we get to them, I wanted to make a few statements about the use of these types of descriptions and how to avoid misusing them.

Benefits

The benefit of reading about the stages of realization is that these descriptions may trigger a stirring and recognition in deeper parts of your being. They have the power to awaken innate wisdom that lies dormant in unseen places. Earlier in my life, I began reading a famous set of Zen passages called the "ten oxherding pictures." These are collectively an ancient map that utilizes woodblock pictures and short poetic descriptions to delineate the process of realization. For a long time, I had no idea what most of it meant. Yet I could sense there was something important being depicted. As I read, there was a nearly imperceptible echo in some ancient place inside me, and that was enough. I returned to these writings periodically. This wasn't to analyze or try to understand; it was to continue to awaken the ancient mystery that had seemed to lie dormant during most of my early life. Over time, the oxherding pictures began to illuminate different aspects of living truth that were observable in my moment-to-moment experience. I could see what they were pointing to now, and not in a conceptual way. I could see it in my own immediate experience of reality.

Cautions

When it comes to maps and stages, the cautions are more important than the potential benefits. There is absolutely no need to understand, read, or know anything about maps and stages to wake up. Many people have woken up with no knowledge of this material. In fact, if I were to make a generalization about this topic, it would be that people who are overly concerned with maps and stages, on average, wake up slower than those who are able to approach realization with a "beginners mind."

I've made many mistakes and taken many wrong turns along this path. However, in this area, for whatever reason, I lucked out. As fascinated as I was with these types of writings, I knew better than to try to understand them intellectually. I didn't go read analysis about the oxherding pictures, or other maps, or ask anyone else's opinion about what they meant. I trusted that in time things would clarify, and they did. If you are able to approach these maps in a similar regard, I think they can be helpful and won't necessarily lead to conceptualization or added self-doubt. The following guidelines summarize how best to utilize maps without falling into common pitfalls:

> Never use someone else's description of an insight or a stage of realization as the litmus test for what you should be experiencing. When we do this we knowingly or unknowingly discount our immediate experience as the wrong one and their description as the right one. This is an error. All things being equal, your immediate experience, just how it is, is "best practice."

> These types of pointers can be obscure and confusing at first. That's okay. Don't try to dispel the confusion with conceptual understanding. It's much more profitable to remain in the mystery. Return from time to time and just "feel into" what is being described.

> Hold all descriptions of maps and stages lightly. Even the clearest and most succinct descriptions I've seen are still

"flavored" by the personality, experience, writing style, and background of the person who wrote them.

➤ It's often the case that you begin to recognize the truth of various descriptions after your own insights have matured. So, these descriptions are more like a fine-tuning than a map or a recipe.

➤ Avoid the tendency to compare maps, believing there is one perfect map out there and that all the others are inferior. You can find truth in various types of maps and non-map pointers. Sometimes the most obscure and/or overlooked of life's pointers ends up being the one that launches you directly into the unknown. If you keep an innocent and receptive mindset, you might be quite surprised that even the most unspiritual of situations and circumstances can be potent catalysts.

A Simple Map

Continuing with the VR goggle analogy, we can delineate a simple map of the awakening process. I find this map to be reasonably consistent among those who have traversed this path. If you were to ask anyone who is going through the awakening process, they would likely tell you that it is a topsy-turvy, unpredictable path, often without any discernible direction. Even so, there are a few important stages that are generally the most clearly demarcated no matter how convoluted the path seems to be. The first stage is what I usually call "first awakening," or just "awakening." Sometimes I use the term "kensho" because I've had some experience with Zen Buddhism and that's the term often used in that tradition. This profound transformation, marked by a fundamental shift in your identity (what you take yourself to be), was discussed in the chapter, What Is Awakening? We are not finished exploring it, as a handful of upcoming chapters will address it as well. This transition is so profound that you realize that your life (and reality itself) is not what you thought it was. Your life (reality) is more real, more intimate, more natural, and more satisfying than anything that can be imagined. This is, of course, analogous to the moment you are rescued from your virtual prison and remove the VR goggles. You stand in utter wonderment, looking upon the brilliance and vibrant aliveness of the real world for the first time.

Once this shift occurs, you have a fundamentally different relationship with both internal and external experiences. You find yourself with a vastly more inclusive and fluidly adaptive perspective that was simply not available before awakening. Even the word "perspective" is not right here, because you are often so merged with momentary experience that there's nothing that can stand apart and watch it all happen. Your journey into the innermost mysteries of existence has begun. Even so, the implications of this first shift in identity are not yet known to you. You still have no idea how deep this rabbit hole actually goes.

Following this initial awakening, there is generally a honeymoon period. During this time, it seems as if all the doubt, worry, longing, and hesitation that had plagued you for so long have been completely obliterated. A weight you had forgotten you'd been carrying for so many years is suddenly lifted. Like a fish slipping effortlessly through water, there is a fluidity that is freeing beyond description. A profound peace pervades most or all of your experience. The most marvelous part is that you realize that this is actually how life is! You'd simply been unknowingly living in an artificial internal reality that had been sapping all of your energy and binding you with the pervasive sense of isolation and lack. During this period, it often seems as if there never was, nor ever could be, any obstruction anywhere in your field of experience. In short, this feels like liberation. In reality, it is the first authentic step toward liberation.

There is a lot of variation in depth and duration to this honeymoon period among practitioners. Regardless, the honeymoon period often lasts weeks or even months. Following this honeymoon phase, the true work of realization begins. Through habit-force, the tendencies to resist experience, conceptualize, and distance ourselves from life begin to sneak back in. This often happens slowly at first, and we are strangely aware of it yet welcoming of it. There is a part of us that knows this has to happen for the insight to mature. As we are reacquainted with old patterns, doubts, and fears, there remains an underlying okayness and understanding that this is simply the way of things. We know that what was realized during the initial awakening is not gone (nor could it be), and because of this we are now able to face and accept these old patterns and habits in a much more direct and authentic way. Whereas before awakening we might have wanted these difficult or confusing parts of ourselves to be removed, healed, or transcended, now we see it's actually a process of exploration, understanding, acceptance, and integration. Throughout this integration process, the presence of awake nature is still very much in play. However, it now has a different job than to enable us to sit around in blissful clarity. Now its job is to induce us to examine all of our resistance patterns, repressed emotions, and divisive belief structures. This exploration will necessarily include all those unconscious places we've been avoiding for years. As this occurs, we will be compelled to look closer and closer . . . and closer.

Sometimes this looking will be enjoyable, and other times it will be particularly unenjoyable. When it is unenjoyable it is because of our ingrained (but not natural) tendency to avoid looking at certain beliefs, emotions, and behavior patterns. Reversing those tendencies can be quite uncomfortable at times, but it is necessary and lawful. These are unconscious places that before awakening we were somehow able avoid experiencing. Indeed, we were able to avoid acknowledging their very existence. Now we find we cannot help but look, listen, and feel directly into these places. We find now that our attention naturally gravitates into these unconscious spaces regardless of how we feel about that happening. We will resist this at times, but as things progress, resistance becomes more uncomfortable and less of a viable option. In fact, a good prayer can be something like the following: "Universe, I pray that it becomes increasingly uncomfortable for me to avoid or resist anything in my immediate experience."

Another way of describing this phase is to say that once the initial elation of awakening subsides, we begin to settle into a different way of living and experiencing reality. We enter a phase where we feel rather unenlightened. This is analogous to having been removed from the isolation chamber and having the VR headset removed. As we take up the endeavor of beginning to explore the actual world, we will occasionally encounter something quite uncomfortable, surprising, or difficult to understand and integrate. Can you imagine how vivid, raw, and unfiltered the sense world must appear after all those years engaging a facsimile of reality? As was previously mentioned, we occasionally find ourselves regressing to old habits of avoidance and hiding by putting the VR goggles back on and even crawling back inside the chamber. This is the second phase; it usually takes a few years but can take ten or more. I've seen it happen in less than a couple of years, but I have no doubt it could occur even faster.

Over time and with proper guidance and practice, another major shift takes place. In many respects it is similar in quality to the initial awakening, but it is far clearer and now experienced to be simple moment-to-moment reality. It is not a phenomenon that comes and goes; it is simply "how this is" and couldn't be other. In this moment-to-moment experience of reality, the illusion of separation has dropped. In fact, you find it hard to even remember what separation felt like or how you used to construct it with the mind. Furthermore, there is a freeing from all need to hold onto, push away, control, manage, or even understand any aspect of life. You're too busy being immersed in the flow of life to concern yourself with such trivialities. You could call this an intrinsic trust in life itself. However, this isn't an intellectual trust; this is a trust that you feel in your marrow. The combination of non-separation and freedom from holding, resistance, need, lack, and doubt gives rise to a profound peace.

This third phase I'll call "liberation." This is the end of individual suffering in this lifetime. In the VR analogy, this is equivalent to the point where we've become so comfortable in the unpredictable, immediate, and vivid world of the actual that we completely abandon the isolation chamber and the VR goggles. We set fire to them so that we have no chance of running back into that false reality again.

Liberation is when we lose the ability to live in the illusory thought world of "me, my problems, my past, and my future." While there can still be thoughts and even resistance patterns, there is no ability to inhabit the illusory world of the self apart from the rest of life. This moment of realization sometimes comes with a wave of fear, dread, or terror as we realize that unfiltered, actual reality is now our only moment-to-moment choice. This is the death cry of the ego. The wave of terror (if it comes) is quickly replaced by a profound and pervasive sense of peace that permeates all experience. This is the biblical "peace that passes all understanding."

"When the angel of death approaches you, he is horrific; when he reaches you it is bliss."

—The Thousand and One Nights

An Unnecessarily Complicated Map: The Pond Revisited

The pond analogy that we touched on in an earlier chapter is a good metaphor to expand upon to describe the stages of awakening in greater detail.

Stage 1: "A Shard of Light"

If you recall, in chapter two I described a person standing in a clearing, viewing a pond at night. There is a full moon, and the light of the moon is being reflected upon the surface of the water. To appreciate this analogy, you have to assume that the person viewing the pond has no memory of any other experience. As far as they know they've always been viewing the pond surface. Furthermore, they don't even realize it is a pond, or a reflective surface. They are fixated on one area of the pond, watching the various shards of light dance and scatter in a chaotic fashion. It might sound like a pleasant scene, but we have to further assume that this person has identified with being a single shard of light. Their identity feels fractured, chaotic, confusing, and short-lived. There is a strong sense of clinging because these shards of light come and go so quickly and unpredictably. Further, all of those other shards seem so foreign and similarly chaotic and confusing in their movement. You could call this the first stage. We find ourselves disillusioned in life. We feel like we inhabit a body and mind that is limited, discreet, isolated, and always struggling—most of the time against itself. What's worse, all of the advice on how to be a successful human and navigate life's challenges seems to amplify the sense of angst. This is because the advice is always reinforcing the sense of being an isolated shard of light acting in opposition to other shards of light, endlessly trying to navigate a chaotic environment. Acting on advice that reinforces the sense of isolation and confusion is like throwing gas on the fire of our confusion and pain.

We look at others and most seem to be getting along fine. What is wrong with us? Why are we so different, so isolated, so miserable? It might seem odd to call this predicament a "stage," but the mere recognition that we suffer is usually essential to set the process of realization in motion. To be unaware of our own suffering and the suffering of others around us is true unconsciousness. This initial movement in the awakening process is defined by our becoming conscious of our own suffering. This often includes

196

becoming aware of the mass of human suffering and how it affects all of humanity as well as everything we come into contact with.

"Following unnamed rivers, lost upon the interpenetrating paths of distant mountains, My strength failing and my vitality exhausted, I cannot find the ox . . . Far from home, I see many cross- roads, but which way is the right one I know not. Greed and fear, good and bad, entangle me."

—First Oxherding Picture

Stage 2: "The Nature of Light"

One day you're observing your little shard of light as usual. You're feeling that familiar angst, isolation, and fear associated with the fleeting nature of existence. You begin to ponder what this is all about.

Isn't there anything more than suffering to this feeble existence? you wonder.

You instantly become curious about the nature of the light that the shard is made up of. Somehow, you'd never really gotten curious in this way.

What is this? What is the nature of the light that I am made of? you wonder.

As you observe with innocent curiosity, you notice that it has somewhat of an indescribable nature, a certain undefinable beauty. There is an almost imperceptible shift in perception, and now you see the fluctuating nature of light in a different way. It feels more intimate than it did a moment ago. It has a certain purity to it—some potential you hadn't recognized before. You might notice that even though they are composed of varying shapes and seem separate from yours, the other shards around you seem to be made up of a similar light.

Could this all be the same light somehow? you wonder.

Then you ask yourself a funny question,

Well, if they appear to be made of the same mysterious substance, how can I know they are actually separate?

That question seems to stop time. In that gap between life and death, between never and forever, you get a "taste" of something fully beyond all the ways you'd perceived reality up to this point. There's an expansion, an openness to possibility, and a mysterious "something" that you can't put your finger on. For a few moments, those other shards near you don't seem foreign. Everything is familiar here. In this sacred gap, the isolation that had become so familiar subsides for a period of time.

This second stage I will call "recognition." This is that moment you get a taste of something clearly more real than the usual paradigms through which we typically experience the world and ourselves. This taste is so compelling, so real, that it cannot be denied. It's the discernment of a path or a possibility. It's that little nudge in a different instinctual direction than we ever thought our life would take. Once we experience this glimmer, we know that we're going to have to investigate further. This is the only thing we remember encountering in our life that hadn't felt like "more of the same."

The investigation of the nature of light as described in this analogy correlates to our own investigation of our thoughts and beliefs and their relation to consciousness. Along with this comes a natural curiosity about our own identity, as at this stage our identity is very much intertwined with thoughts and consciousness. When we peer into consciousness in the right way, something opens; we perceive that the "stuff" of me and what I call my life (and even the lives of others) is quite mysterious indeed! What is its nature? Does it come and go when thoughts form, or does it remain? If it remains, am I the thoughts or the one perceiving the thoughts, or am I consciousness? Or perhaps I am all of them. This is the entry point.

This little taste or glimpse is often short-lived and followed by a disappointing notice of its fleeting nature: "I can't deny that I've experienced something special, and I clearly remember the feeling, but where the heck did it go? How can I get it to come back?" It's almost worse to know there is a possibility outside of this suffering, but then have no way to access it. You know now that something more is possible; however, you are not aware of the ramifications of that knowing.

"Along the riverbank under the trees, I discover footprints! Even under the fragrant grass I see his prints. Deep in remote mountains they are found. These traces no more can be hidden than one's nose, looking heavenward . . . Not yet having entered the gate, nevertheless I have discerned the path."

—Second Oxherding Picture

Stage 3: One Luminous Body

Now that you've had that taste, you can't help but keep on with the investigation. You are still fascinated by the question, "What is the nature of light?" You find yourself spending more time looking deeply into that light, concerning yourself less with its immediate shape or relationship to other shards of light. You still feel angst, isolation, and confusion, but there are occasional moments where you are just consumed by this fascination with light. In these moments of consumption, there is sometimes a passing experience of only light. You're never sure how you caused that to happen or whether you caused it at all, but those moments are unquestionably real and profound. They have a timeless quality.

During one of these pure-light moments, when you happen to be particularly absorbed into and infused with light-stuff, the air suddenly becomes still and calm. The ripples on the surface of the pond begin to settle. As you watch the light, you suddenly lose track of which shard of light you are; you just seem to see light everywhere and it seems to be consuming all of your experience. You have no interest in looking away as this is the most natural and fascinating thing you've ever experienced. Then the most unexpected thing occurs. The water becomes still, and all shards of light merge into one luminous globe! You immediately know at every level of your being that there never were distinct shards of light. They had always been one! There has always been nothing but light, and it has never been in parts. As you stare in wonder and awe at that luminous globe of light, you recognize that all the concerns and problems that had arisen out of the perception that there were various pieces of light competing and opposing one another are, and always were, completely unfounded.

You find yourself laughing and crying simultaneously as you realize that the whole world of problems, solutions, selves, and others was always an illusion. It was simply a side effect of misperceiving the nature of light. Now you see that all there is is light, and that it could never be divided, tainted, fractured, or lose its nature. This comes with a tremendous emotional release and a feeling of being truly reborn. It is clear now that suffering is not intrinsic to being human. Although you still don't fully know the nature of the light, you have a profound and pervasive trust in it. You have a love for this light and still enjoy investigating it closer and more intimately. You no longer feel threatened in any way, so this investigation arises from a place of innocence, curiosity, and trust, rather than from desperation and anguish.

This corresponds to one's first awakening. The deepening of the interest in stage two becomes almost an obsession with the nature of identity. We start to pour more and more of our energy into asking, "Who am I?" or "What is consciousness?" or "What was my face before my parents were born?" or "Where does suffering end?" At some point, we become so absorbed in the inquiry that we lose the sense of being the one who is inquiring. We even forget what we were originally looking for. There is just that pure wordless inquiry, penetrating deeper and deeper and deeper. Then, unexpectedly, everything stops. There is clarity, quietude, and peace. All thought-waves have subsided, and all that is left is the ocean of consciousness. Pure consciousness. Unbound consciousness. All that remains is the sense of pure Being. Some people will experience this as the pure sense of I or I AM. It's undeniable and self-validating. Most notably, all of that seeking, self-doubt, confusion, and angst is nowhere to be found. The fracturing of identity that seemed to have plagued you up to this point is seen to have been an illusion. You had been searching inside consciousness and thus were actively forgetting that you are consciousness! There has always just been this whole of unbound (not bound to any thought object) consciousness that comprises everything. There is an obvious naturalness and completeness in this place you have never been away from. You feel light and fluid, and life flows effortlessly along with you.

Returning to the pond analogy, the light represents consciousness, and the luminous globe (moon) represents the

201

wholeness of unbound consciousness, or the experience of pure Being.

This is spiritual birth. This backward step into the root of identity in consciousness is the first true step on the path to liberation. This is the beginning of a wondrous and mysterious unfolding. This experience, this shift, is so profound that many take it to be final. This is a misperception. Although you've experienced pure, unbound consciousness, you haven't realized its nature or the nature of realization itself. You haven't sorted out the nature of identity. To put it in Zen terms, you haven't yet solved the problem of birth and death. Nevertheless, life has changed in a fundamental way, and for some time (several days to several months usually), there is fluidity, peace, spontaneity, and various degrees of interconnectedness.

"I hear the song of the nightingale. The sun is warm, the wind is mild, willows are green along the shore,

Here no bull can hide! What artist can draw that massive head, those majestic horns? As soon as the six senses merge, the gate is entered. Wherever one enters one sees the head of the bull! This unity is like salt in water, like color in dyestuff. The slightest thing is not apart from self."

—Third Oxherding Picture

You enjoy the wholeness of that luminous body for a time, often basking in its light. All of life is now infused with this radiance.

This feels like a rebirth or a second childhood of sorts. Then one day you notice the disk has shattered again. The wind has picked up, or something has disturbed the surface and some of those old chaotic patterns have returned. This can be disconcerting because we see that there are forces at work here that are out of our control. We no more caused the shards to merge into one wholeness than we caused them to scatter again into thousands of pieces. While this can be unnerving, there is still an underlying peace in the knowing that the nature of light is wholeness. No matter how things appear moment to moment, there is an undeniable unity to all the dancing shards of light; therefore no shard is ever truly isolated.

Our curiosity and interest in this mysterious process continues to deepen. We've freed up a lot of energy by no longer being in a constant state of struggle with the world and ourselves. We find it enjoyable and fulfilling to turn that freed-up energy toward further investigation. While we are still fascinated with the nature of light and the "wholeness" aspect that is naturally revealed when conditions are ripe, we suspect that there is something even more fundamental going on. If the luminous disk can so suddenly be shattered and then reassemble itself, then perhaps there is something even more fundamental that can be realized about reality. We also begin to notice that when we don't struggle so much with ourselves and with life, we don't add to the ripples on the water's surface. This relinquishing of struggle cultivates more calmness on the surface, and a more frequent sense of clarity and wholeness.

Similarly, when the honeymoon period starts to subside, we enter a new phase of this process. There are times when it seems we have returned to the old ways of suffering. In a certain sense it's worse because now we have less ability to distance ourselves from our own pain. Our ability to run off into thoughts and stories that used to offer us false comfort in the form of distraction is now waning. At other times, there is peace, timelessness, and flow. It becomes obvious that we are not in control of when we feel peace and clarity, and when we feel resistance patterns and disorientation. With this recognition, a certain wisdom begins to emerge. We now see that while the bliss of pure consciousness is indeed a wondrous, profoundly "real" experience when it is present, holding onto it is not in alignment with the deeper truths of reality. We can see that deriving identity from pure consciousness or even pure Being is unreliable and unsatisfying in some fundamental way. We begin to recognize that the conditions which bring it about or obscure it are not in our immediate control. We learn that we can inquire, meditate, and dissolve many of the fixations and ego structures that cause us to habitually disturb the surface, resulting in a calmer internal environment, and less of a threatened identity. Yet we are still tying identity to something that we don't fully grasp, and which comes and goes at the whim of momentary conditions. So, our interest now penetrates even beyond the nature of light! The light is undeniably unified in a certain way, and yet its unity still seems to come and go in experience. So, the question naturally arises,

"What in the world is that light, that unity, coming and going in? What allows it to unify and seemingly shatter again? What is the vessel for lightness and darkness?"

"His great will and power are inexhaustible. He charges to the high plateau far above the cloud-mists, or in an impenetrable ravine he stands.

He dwelt in the forest a long time . . . infatuation for scenery interferes with his direction. Longing for sweeter grass, he wanders away."

—Fourth Oxherding Picture

Stage 4: The Nature of Reflection

As you ponder the nature of light more deeply, recognizing that there must be something that allows that wholeness of light to be and to not be at various times, something dawns on you. It's the strangest thing. Suddenly you are able to look through the light somehow. Whether there is a whole luminous globe or an erratic dance of shards of light, there is still something that makes it possible for there to be light, shape, and movement. Indeed, there is something that even allows you to perceive the absence of light—a potentiality perhaps. Furthermore, you realize you've been looking right at it the whole time. Even in the darkest of dark spaces, this potential is there. It's such a subtle realization that you second-guess yourself at times, but it becomes clearer the more you explore this reflective nature. You start to perceive that you are not only the pure Being of that magnificent luminous globe, but you are also each shard of light across the surface when that globe has been shattered into thousands of pieces. What's more bizarre and compelling is that you are equally the places where there is no light on the dark surface. Then it hits you . . . you are the reflective nature of the surface! You never were the shard of light, nor were you the wholeness of the sense of the luminous globe. Well, you were, but those conformations of light were not the limits of what you are. Those were expressions of your true identity, but your true identity was not bound by those. Now there is a far more complete but fluid and subtle sense of identity. You can now clearly see the entire pond surface as well as its reflective nature and all that it is reflecting.

This stage represents a maturing of the realization that occurred at the previous stage. It has various features to it, but a couple of the most important ones are the following. First of all, it's clear that the undeniable sense of pure Being or pure "I" is not conditional upon experience, location, or time. This means that the essence of that realization of pure Being exists in each shard even when the wholeness is not apparent due to disturbances on the surface of the water. Each shard is not a part of the whole; each shard is the entirety of the whole. This is sometimes experienced as universality, oneness, or a sense of being everywhere/everything. You might even experience moments of being in two places, people, or objects at once. This will not be a steady perception until the next stage, but it will be quite undeniable and marvelous when it occurs. The other aspect of this insight into reflective nature is that it becomes clear that identity is not limited to experience. This means that this most basic experience of Being or sense of "I" is not the limit of what is going on. There is something even more fundamental at work. There is still "something" there even when that experience is absent or indeed when there is no experience at all. There is a deeper, although more subtle and indefinable, peace that arises with this realization.

Things begin to get paradoxical here, as there starts to be an appreciation that there is still okayness even when the pristine sense of pure existence isn't currently available. A funny way of saying this is that just as much as the undeniable experience of pure consciousness is seamless with natural reality, so, too, is the complete lack of that sense seamless with reality. It's as if pure Being and non-Being are fused together, and that point of fusion brings with it another degree of freedom. Or you could say that unbound consciousness and what's there when there is fractured consciousness, or even no consciousness at all, are equally the essential nature of reality.

I should mention that these perceptions are not always this clear to someone who is at this stage, but it will be intuited to some degree or another. Also, there is often a good amount of struggle still occurring because our tendency to identify with and thus hold onto the universality of consciousness, or pure sense of "I," is strong and very deeply rooted in our psyche. It's usually in retrospect that we fully appreciate the nature of these shifts and insights.

While this adjustment can be a confusing and disorienting time, it is laying the groundwork for something very unexpected and wondrous. If you think it's strange to live in a world where you identify as universal consciousness and everything contained therein, as well as nothing at all, just wait, we're going to redefine strange . . . but in a good way. You could say that this phase is a sort of a staging area. Reality is simply setting up the conditions to launch you into world of mystery beyond comprehension.

Just as with the previous stage, there is a potential trap here. In my experience, it is common that we will get stuck in this trap for a time. Because identity has become so thin at this stage, it is often not obvious at all that we are fixating. There can be an overemphasis on the darkness or formless aspect here. This makes sense from this level of realization because this reflective nature (regardless of what it's reflecting or not reflecting) is the most fundamental aspect of identity. The problem and trap here are that we are still holding onto the paradigm of identity itself! It can be extremely easy to overlook this assumption that identity is an actual thing because the sense of identity has been with us for so long and feels quite familiar. This assumption is not just a conceptual fixation; it is deeply felt and is so intrinsic to the experience of being a someone that it is easily overlooked. The seeming selfless self or I without an I is being taken as an identity. It's as if we have become so tired of inhabiting a positive identity that we unknowingly adopt a negative identity. We identify as what is not there but overlook the reality that the underlying mechanism of identity is still functioning.

Still, there is a deepening natural enjoyment with practice and with life. There becomes a lot of crossover between what you previously considered "spiritual" life and regular day-to-day living. The investigation is ongoing. The commitment to furthering realization is usually, but not always, quite strong by this point.

"Mounting the bull, slowly I return homeward.
The voice of my flute intones through the evening.
Measuring with hand-beats the pulsating harmony,
I direct the endless rhythm.

Whoever hears this melody will join me. This
struggle is over; gain and loss are assimilated. I
sing the song of the village woodsman and play
the tunes of the children. Astride the bull, I
observe the clouds above. Onward I go, no matter
who may wish to call me back."

—Sixth Oxherding Picture

Stage 5: The Actual

One day while you are pondering the depths of the reflective surface (still not realizing that this is a pond), it hits you . . , the fundamental question! "If all of this is reflective nature, what in the world is it that is being reflected?" The very possibility that there might be something more than this reflection, which contains all possible conformations of light, while perfectly accommodating darkness, shakes you to your very core. You sense things stirring in places far beyond your limits of perception and even beyond your physical incarnation in this lifetime. You know instinctually that your experience of reality is about to change in fundamental and mysterious ways. A sublime, paradoxical, and radical shift is at hand.

The moment you recognize that with a reflection there must also be that which is being reflected, you turn your gaze away from the surface of the pond for the first time. You had never before had the capacity to recognize that the reflective surface—with all of its mystery, profundity, and splendor—was still only an exceedingly small and fleeting part of what is actually occurring. Now as you gaze upon the actual world for the first time, there is a quantum leap in depth and realness of all textures and experiences. Everything is radiantly alive and interconnected, and there is a paradoxical immediate and complete dissolution of distance, time, and experiencer/experience split. This vivid, experience-less reality goes far beyond anything you'd encountered when you believed the universe was contained in that reflection. The radiant brilliance and radical intimacy of all phenomena is dazzling beyond compare.

This "new" world functions quite differently than the reflective surface and all of its expressions of light and darkness. When the reflective surface was perceived to be the whole of reality, there was clearly a continuity of some sort, a set of natural laws that seemed to govern all experience. The sense that there was a world or a container of experience, sort of like a substratum, and a perceiving entity navigating that world, seemed like just the way things had to be. Now it's clear that the seeming substratum that contained the dark and the light doesn't exist on its own in this reality. It is seen to have always been part of the intimate textures of zero-distance experience. With that recognition, the phenomena themselves take on a new degree of integrity, clarity, and perfection. When there is no relational matrix, every discreet phenomenon is naturally expanded to infinite significance.

In this world of the actual, there is also a notable absence of another characteristic that seemed quite inherent to the reflective world. Even though the reflective world seemed to offer tremendous variation in experiences, events, and objects, it carried with it a certain intrinsic weight that had gone unnoticed. This unnoticed burden, somewhat like a tether or an anchor, was impossible to appreciate until it was finally released by looking away from the reflection. This tether, this weight, was the sense that this was all somehow happening to, or for a central character (earlier) or a universal awareness (later), called, "me." All the time that that sense of a discreet self was there, it had felt like something that needed to be upheld and defended. Now it becomes exquisitely obvious that it was never an actual thing, and that trying to constantly reconstruct, define, and defend that artificial construct had caused a nearly constant sense of isolation, doubt, and lack. Now that has all come to an end. The restraints of doubt are nowhere to be found. Reality moves, creates, and dissolves effortlessly, displaying the full spectrum of its potential.

"Astride the bull, I reach home. I am serene. The bull too can rest. The dawn has come.

Within my thatched dwelling I have abandoned the whip and rope. All is one law, not two. We only make the bull a temporary subject. It is as the relation of rabbit and trap, of fish and net. It is as gold and dross, or the moon emerging from a cloud. One path of clear light travels on throughout endless time."

—Seventh Oxherding Picture

As you gaze upon the trees, the stars, and the moon, it's exquisitely clear that there are only the trees, the stars, and the moon. The profundity of this cannot be described, even to yourself. This gets exceedingly difficult to talk about, and even the pond analogy really begins to break down here. This is because when we start to ask, "Then what is it that is being reflected?" it is like asking, "What is reality like when the paradigm of identity that interfaces with reality has completely disappeared?" or "What is actually here when we don't take reference from reflective consciousness as to how reality is experienced?" The salient feature that occurs at this stage is a dissolving of the paradigm of identity altogether. It is dissolved at the intellectual, emotional, and instinctual level.

Let's investigate exactly how and why the pond analogy breaks down here. This will help to make the transition into describing how this stage of realization plays out for the individual. In the pond analogy, it would seem that the moment we turn away from the pond, we see a vast world of objects arranged in three-dimensional space, and the person who turned away from the pond can now go navigate that world. In the actuality of realization, it's not like that. It's more like the moment the person standing on the shore turns to the world of the actual, that person ceases to exist. The whole experience of being a someone looking at this and looking at that, trying to figure it all out and having the experience of being someone experiencing an evolution of insight and understanding (awakening) was fundamentally in error. Now when they turn to the world of the real, they were simply never there to begin with. Now there is only the real with nothing standing apart from it to observe it. There was only ever the real! You could say that now you experience yourself as everything, but importantly there is no "yourself" so there is just everything. That everything is crisp, vivid, undeniable, and has no apart-ness to it. The reflective nature of consciousness (self-referencing) made things appear as if there was a noticer and that which was noticed, a person and a life that person was living, objects out there and a subject here, navigating those objects. This ranges in scale from the macro (life events, beliefs, time, and space) down to the discrete (a single sound, sensation, shape, taste, or smell).

In realization this is what I refer to as liberation. It can happen suddenly, and it can happen gradually, but the relational (reflective) framework of experience we perceive that creates the illusion of separation subsides. Technically, this is the end of the entanglement with consciousness that was creating the sense of a discrete self apart from the world. Now when there is sound, there is only sound— pristine, complete, and all-pervasive. When there is a color or a shape, there is only that color, only that shape—impossibly vivid and not apart from anything. There are only trees, with no observer. There are only stars, with no one watching them. There is only the moon, with no one gazing upon it.

The awareness of the dazzling dance of color has collapsed into the colors themselves. Color does the seeing. Sound does the hearing. Sensation does the feeling; sensation is the feeling. With this collapse of the seeing into the colors, the feeler into the sensations, and the thinker into the thought, there is also a collapse of the individual into everything. This is somewhat like a self-propagating and self-dissolving cloud of radiant and pure (no experiencer) experience. Whether it's a car, the hum of a fan, or a voice, there is no one hearing it; the hearing is intrinsic to the sound. The experiencer has fully collapsed onto the experience, and it is seen that this is the natural way. There is no longer the possibility to "stand apart and observe" as seemed to be happening before. Instead, the sense of observing is seen to have been a simple misreading of the nature of reflective consciousness. Consciousness doesn't have to go away; it is simply experienced as another vivid no-distance sense. There is no inside and there is no outside. There is no other possibility, as every possibility is playing out effortlessly as the Universe coming into being and dissolving as each discreet quanta of sense phenomena, each movement, each expression of radiance. That sound is completeness itself and it is not apart from, or essentially different from, all of existence. Those colors and shapes are not other than the observer, and their radiance and clarity are exquisite and without equal. That one bodily sensation fills up the Universe and dissolves instantaneously.

There is no substratum here. There is no background or foreground. Nothing is held; everything is just on time, and also not in time. There is no timeline. Nothing is moving from moment to moment. There aren't even moments. This is the only moment and thus there is no need to call it a moment. It is not a point in time; it is every point in time, always right here. Timelessness is intuited to be simply the way it is. Eternity is no big deal because it simply and obviously is. There is nothing acting against anything else. This struggle is over. There is wholeness in discrete experiences, yet nothing is carried out of those experiences.

There is one more "aspect" to this realization that is probably the most bizarre of all and inherently impossible to fully relate, but it is intrinsic to this world of the actual. It can be related in one simple statement:

There is no exact way that things actually are.

I have no idea how that comes across as you read it. I can imagine it could trigger some sense of confusion, fear, or helplessness. However, in actual experience, it is just obvious and wonderful beyond compare. It may also sound impossible or somewhat like an oxymoron. Yet in this bizarre world of no self apart from anything, there is also no view or frame of reference inherent to reality. A different way of saying this is that reality, as self-experiencing, radiant phenomena, has no location or boundary, and also no absolute or essential nature. Still another way of saying this is that there is infinite degree freedom. Reality is like a magician that can do anything, including being nothing at all. It can do seemingly contradictory things simultaneously. It can stop being any certain way and effortlessly transition in marvelous and profoundly mysterious ways. Indeed, there is not even a thing called "reality." This could sound dizzying, confusing, or disorienting, but when there is no distance "between" anything, and nothing trying to stand apart and manage experience, or hold a reference frame, then it is just simply so. Nothing apart— nothing to offend or disrupt. Just everything-ness, and/or one-thingness expressed out of nothingness, and at the same time never leaving nothingness, moment to moment. Spontaneous, free, intimate, and void of any essential nature.

An analogy I sometimes use is this. Imagine you are walking down a hallway. Only the portion of the hallway you occupy is illuminated at any given time. So as you pass a certain area, the lights behind you go out. Similarly, as you enter a new area of the hallway, the lights begin to turn on. Ahead and behind there is darkness. Now further imagine there is no body, no "you," and no sense of continuous consciousness. The lights illuminating down the hallway are vivid zero-distance sense phenomena (sounds, colors, shapes, sensations, tastes, smells, and consciousness). Instead of lighting the way for "you," they are simply coming into being (or at least their radiant nature is apparent) moment to moment. If viewed a certain way (by looking through the distorting lens of reflective consciousness), it could appear as if this creates movement down a hallway, or a sense of someone or some consciousness moving and aware of the lights. In actuality, consciousness is itself simply one of the vividly illuminated yet empty phenomena appearing and disappearing. In reality there is no body, mind, or world. There is only illumination, and nothing apart from that illumination to know or to observe it. There is just a magnificent display of impossibly vivid and essence-less textures creating the illusion of movement and solidity. It is self-illuminating and radically intimate. Here and gone, here and gone.

Stage 6: Empty Illumination

From this point forward, it remains clear that the real world, the world of the actual that was realized upon turning from the reflective surface, is reality in its natural state. Although we still can feel a pull and tendency to gaze upon the pond from time to time, we know its nature and we are instinctually aware of the simple and non-conditional truth that there is a reality that is intrinsically free of the distortions of reflection. The trees, objects, and celestial bodies in this world are pristine, alive, radiant, and intimate in a way they simply could not be when reflected off the surface. There is a great relaxation

214

that comes with this realization that all hindrance, isolation, and struggle was brought about by habituated entanglements with the nature of the reflective surface. Now you begin a deeper exploration of the details of this world of the actual. What is the underlying essence of the stars and the moon that cannot be experienced as objects? What is this interconnected nature that is intuited in all radiant experience? What is the nature of this "here and gone without a trace" aspect of everything? What causes the tendency to entangle attention with conscious reflection in a way that distorts this pristine, natural reality? You could say you've lost interest in the lifelong pursuit to understand and realize the truth of you and how you fit in to everything. It's seen that that was never an issue in the first place; it was only a misperception based on the illusion of separation and a view of a self in time that never actually was. So now out of true enjoyment and spontaneity, you investigate the nature of the fabric of reality itself. What is the substance and mechanism of radiant experience? How does it function? How can everything be eternally here and nowhere at all simultaneously, yet feel instinctually exactly right?

We now take up the investigation of the most fundamental quanta of existence, zero-distance experience, and reality. This isn't out of a need or desire to wake up. That concern is no longer found except in an occasional fluctuation in consciousness that briefly catches our attention. No, this is a spontaneous movement of pure fascination. It is fueled by an unconditional love for truth and all of existence and nonexistence. To be perfectly honest, it is because there is nothing else left to do.

Just when it seemed things couldn't get more difficult to talk about, we arrive at a place that is so primordial, so instinctual, so subtle, and paradoxical that I almost don't want to say anything about it. It is extremely easy to miscommunicate, but here goes. At some point it becomes clear that the nature of the most fundamental building blocks of experience—let's call them vivid sense phenomena —come out of nothingness, return to nothingness, are never separate from nothingness, and yet somehow create all possibility of experience. The word experience here means nothing like the usual sense of the word. Also, the word nothingness means nothing like the usual sense of the word. The most fundamental movement of nondualistic experience and nothingness or emptiness are one intertwined here. This is the urge of the Universe to experience itself, or of a single color to come forth as the entire Universe. This experience is immediate, immaculate, without doubt, without distance, and not subject to time.

"I have heard what the talkers were talking, the talk of the
beginning and the end,
But I do not talk of the beginning or the end.

There was never any more inception than there is now,
Nor any more youth or age than there is now,
And will never be any more perfection than there is now,
Nor any more heaven or hell than there is now.

Urge and urge and urge,
Always the procreant urge of the world.

Out of the dimness opposite equals advance,
always substance and
increase, always sex,
Always a knit of identity, always distinction,
always a breed of life.
To elaborate is no avail, learn'd and unlearn'd feel
that it is so.

Sure as the most certain sure, plumb in the
uprights, well
entretied, braced in the beams,
Stout as a horse, affectionate, haughty, electrical,
I and this mystery here we stand.

Clear and sweet is my soul, and clear and sweet is
all that is not my soul."

—*Walt Whitman, "Song of Myself"*

You could say this quantum fluctuation between nothingness and somethingness is the fabric or most fundamental identity of reality itself. This is not the same as personal identity or universal identity/consciousness. Here there is no self, and there is no other. There is no distance, knowing, understanding, or doing. Yet there is an awareness that is intrinsic to radiant phenomena. There is no desire here, nor is there aversion. There are no preferences, and nothing is left out or missing. There is no longer any need to wake up nor any perception of an unenlightened state. There is no suffering here, and there is no avoidance of suffering. Nothing moves, and yet all movement is effortless. Nothing is excluded, and nothing is included. Everything is, and that i-ness doesn't stick; it's gone before it can even register anywhere. Nothing is grasped for. Nothing can be lost so nothing can be gained. There is richness and wonderment everywhere. There are no more questions, and there is no need for answers. It is not that you have arrived, because arrival is seen to be a false paradigm. You can no more arrive anywhere than you could leave anywhere.

*"Whip, rope, person, and bull—all merge in No-
Thing. This heaven is so vast no message can stain
it. How may a snowflake exist in a raging fire?*

*Mediocrity is gone. Mind is clear of limitation. I
seek no state of enlightenment. Neither do I remain
where no enlightenment exists. Since I linger in
neither condition, eyes cannot see me. If hundreds
of birds strew my path with flowers, such praise
would be meaningless."*

—*Eighth Oxherding Picture*

None of this is an escape from being human; indeed, humanness is infused with these moment-to-moment experiential truths. Now life can play out perfectly naturally with its ups and downs, heartbreaks and accomplishments, twists and turns. None of this disturbs the underlying peace and fascination with the empty nature of experience/reality. This empty nature is not even bound by the dichotomy of real or unreal, manifest or unmanifest.

This is infinite degree freedom. Not freedom for anyone, but freedom for freedom itself. It would be inaccurate to say that realization ends here, but I must say that it proceeds now not from any sense of need, lack, seeking, or wanting to know. It proceeds now as a refinement of itself. Empty, radiant nature now moves endlessly into itself. It does so with innocent fascination. The full gets fuller and the empty gets emptier. The full gets more non-full and the empty gets more non-empty. The most subtle natural laws are dissolved here. The most enlightened is the least enlightened. The conventional is none other than the fluctuating empty nature of all phenomena.

The relationship between the two is perfectly managed, and also there needn't be any relationship at all. Discreetness is perfectly accommodated, and interconnectedness is never lost. The most profound loss is the most exquisite gain. One after another or co-arising, equally supported. Birth and death and death and birth are dancing like butterflies around the flower of indeterminacy.

"Dwelling in one's true abode, unconcerned with that without. The river flows tranquilly on and the flowers are red.

From the beginning, truth is clear. Poised in silence, I observe the forms of integration and disintegration. One who is not attached to "form" need not be "reformed." The water is emerald, the mountain is indigo, and I see that which is creating and that which is destroying."

—*Ninth Oxherding Picture*

Chapter 11:

Mind-Identification

Introduction

*Avi: He's all up here [pointing to his head],
pretending to be you. You're in a game, Jake.
You're in "the" game. Everyone's in his game, and
nobody knows it. And all of this, this is his world.
He owns it. He controls it.*

*Jake's internal voice: I've had enough of this shit.
Tell him you've had enough . . . .*

Avi: He tells you what to do . . .

Jake: Look, that's enough . . .

Avi: . . . and when to do it.

Jake's internal voice: Tell him!

Jake [yelling]: I said that's enough, Avi!

Avi: He's behind all the pain there ever was.
Behind every crime ever committed.

Jake's internal voice: How can I be behind all the
pain, all the crime, if I don't even exist?

Avi: And right now, he's telling you that he doesn't
even exist. We just put you to war with the only
enemy that ever existed, and you, you think he's
your best friend.

—Roof scene from the movie *Revolver*

I n the previous chapter we discussed some of the later stages of realization. When those insights are realized, unobstructed flow, intimacy, spontaneity, and unbroken peace are not only experienced, but it becomes clear that they are natural qualities of unfiltered reality. These natural qualities no longer have to be discovered or cultivated; they shine radiantly in and as the momentary expression of life force.

Someone making a reasonable assessment of their inner life might wonder after hearing that, Well, then why in the heck do I not experience that kind of peace and flow moment to moment? If it is my birthright, why does it seem to be so elusive? That's a very good and very relevant question. This chapter will answer that question. At least it will answer it conceptually and give you a framework for the undertaking that will eventually help you to understand it directly, through realization. The simple answer to the question of what obscures natural reality, that is by nature free of suffering, is mind-identification.

"The Way is basically perfect and all-pervading. How could it be contingent upon practice and realization? Indeed, the whole body is far beyond the world's dust. Who could believe in a means to brush it clean? It is never apart from one, right where one is. What is the use of going off here and there to practice?

And yet, if there is the slightest discrepancy, the Way is as distant as heaven from earth."

—Dogen

Mind-identification is the mode of experiencing reality where our identity is derived from and intertwined with thoughts, concepts, and beliefs. This isn't merely a paradigm or a specific way of thinking about ourselves and our relation to the various aspects of our lives. It is a pervasive pattern of perceptive distortions that, on an ongoing basis, affects how it feels to be a human inhabiting a body and navigating the seeming external world. Specifically, it creates the ongoing illusions that we are:

➢ Separate from our own thoughts, emotions, and bodies.

➢ Separate from others, even those who are closest to us.

➢ Separate from our environment.

➢ Separate from the cosmos.

➢ Something discrete and short-lived, such that we feel we are always at risk and need to constantly protect ourselves.

> Living in a prison of time. It feels like there are never enough hours in the day, and we must negotiate and sacrifice to best "use" the precious little time we have. This leads to impatience, urgency, and restlessness.

> Endlessly seeking.

> Experiencing some degree of angst most or all of the time.

> Never fully satisfied.

> Never truly at peace.

> Experiencing life in a way that often feels inauthentic.

In this chapter we will break mind-identification down into its causes, mechanisms, implications, and effects. Before we proceed, I want to make a disclaimer. This topic can be uncomfortable to explore. At times it might seem like a lot of bad news. We can feel discouraged when we realize the magnitude of what is already in place that keeps the illusion of suffering operating. We might conclude that it would be just too much work to disentangle all of this. It might seem like ten lifetimes wouldn't be enough to navigate and integrate all of this unseen material that we carry around inside us.

"Disturbance comes only from within—from our own perceptions."

—Marcus Aurelius

Well, the good news is that we don't need to understand anything about mind-identification to wake up. The techniques and inquiries that lead to awakening and realization are actually quite simple and don't require nuanced understanding of the material in this chapter. So, the purpose of this chapter is not to urge you to make an intellectual study of mind-identification or ego structures. Rather, it is to give you the whole picture. Its purpose is to relate to you that as uncomfortable as it might feel to realize that all the mechanisms that keep us suffering are ones that we are carrying around with us all the time, it is equally empowering to recognize that we hold literally every key necessary to wake ourselves up.

Things Might Get a Little Weird

Learning about mind-identification can set off certain internal alarms. The mechanism of mind-identification is by nature a hidden one. It's not supposed to be obvious. It's not designed to be revealed. It's supposed to remain hidden. We will look deeply into the hows and whys of its hidden nature, but at the outset I feel obligated to warn you. When we start dissecting it and digging in, things can get . . . strange. When the mind-identification apparatus senses it is being probed and brought into the light, it can set defense mechanisms into motion to prevent further investigation.

"The most strongly enforced of all known taboos is the taboo against knowing who or what you really are behind the mask of your apparently separate, independent, and isolated ego."

—Alan Watts

These defense mechanisms can take several forms. A common one is an old magician's trick: distraction and redirection. You might find yourself suddenly not interested in this topic, even if you were previously curious about it. You might find your mind wandering to other subjects or interests. You might feel compelled to take up a new activity. This is a surprisingly effective strategy because it flies under the radar. You may not even recognize the defensive nature of the distraction; it just feels like, "Oh, I changed my mind."

Another common defense mechanism is to raise a strong cognitive objection. You might want to argue with the material or argue with me. You might find yourself wanting to discount this subject matter outright. The third and probably most potent mechanism is the use of intense emotions. These intense emotions can come with or without a context. Sometimes fear can come out of nowhere. Sometimes anger will show up. You might suddenly find yourself afraid to read on, or angry at the content, or even angry at me. Alternatively, you might feel these raw emotions with no particular target of blame.

"Toto, I've a feeling we're not in Kansas anymore."

—Dorothy

If any of these experiences materialize it's completely okay. In fact, it's expected. These are simply alarm bells indicating we are delving into places that have been kept hidden, and for good reason. The mechanisms of mind-identification have to remain hidden to function properly. So if you experience any of these, my advice is to just relax. You can remind yourself that this is supposed to happen. This will help you to see the defense mechanisms for what they are. Give them some time. Give yourself some time, and whatever mind-state or emotion-state that has arisen will pass, just as everything passes with time. The arrival of these defense mechanisms is an indicator that things are moving and shifting. The light is starting to shine through the cracks. Obstructions are dissolving; portals to deeper truths are opening.

I can't predict when, to whom, or to what degree these experiences will occur. My intent is to merely state the possibilities ahead of time to prevent an unnecessary overreaction, such as abandoning this endeavor altogether because you didn't realize these were normal (expected) experiences. That happens more frequently than you might think.

Virtual Non-Reality

Just when you thought you'd put those VR goggles on for the last time, here I am taking them out, dusting them off, and handing them to you again. I promise this time you won't have them on long, but there is still one thing we haven't discussed about this virtual world. Do you remember how I said that we would address what causes this virtual world to come into being, keeping the story running? Well, here we are. Go ahead, put those goggles back on for a moment. What do you see? It looks a lot like the room you were in right before you put them on, doesn't it? Yes, that virtual reality simulator is particularly good at making the virtual story seamless with your previous experiences. It doesn't miss a beat.

It feels like one ongoing story, and you can recall various portions of that story at a moment's notice. You can even influence the story as you go along, can't you? In fact, there are other characters that come along in this virtual world and teach you how to do just that. They tell you that if you imagine something in this virtual world, you will create that reality. Then you try it, and it works! Everything you think seems to be happening. Well, it hasn't happened yet, but there is comfort in those thoughts, isn't there?

You're creating your own story minute by minute. How fun, how hypnotic. Here, you don't have to feel painful emotions because you can immediately imagine something more pleasant. Wait! When did you decide that it wasn't okay to feel emotions? Never mind . . . let's go explore.

Morpheus: "It is the world that has been pulled over your eyes to blind you from the truth".

Neo: "What truth?"

Morpheus: "That you are a slave, Neo. Like everyone else you were born into bondage. Into a prison that you cannot taste or see or touch. A prison for your mind."

—The Matrix

This is how it goes. The VR world, as you may have guessed, is the world of thought and imagination. The VR world isn't being imposed upon us; we are creating it ourselves moment to moment. But are we? Do we specifically remember the point in time when we decided to forego actual life for this internal reflection of reality?

"Hmm, I can't actually remember, because as I remember I'm no longer clear on whether that memory is a thought I'm creating right now or if that actually happened. Wow, it's kind of scary if I think about it. Wait! Fear, that's another "negative" emotion. I've learned what to do when those come. I simply imagine a better reality, a "future" where things feel better. Ahh . . ."

"Now I notice another layer of thoughts has replaced the previous layer that was uncomfortable. This starts to make me feel uneasy, like there's something wrong with this story, but I can't remember how it started. I really want to stop for a moment and see what's happening."

Then a trusted person comes along, and then another, and they tell you, "Don't look too close at what's happening or how you got here. Don't ruminate. You have to keep looking forward, imagining a better life, then chase that life to make it happen."

"Oh, that's right. I have to keep the thoughts going and changing this world into what I want it to be. That's the key. Something still just doesn't feel right about all of this . . ."

The last piece of the puzzle with regard to the VR goggles is that we are not kept prisoner by force; we are kept prisoner by choice. We willingly interact with and engage the VR world. Well, we do at first, but very quickly that world swallows us up. At some point we get confused about whether it is me that is choosing these thoughts, or whether they are just coming automatically. After a time, we even forget that we ever actually entered this virtual world. By the time we start to recognize that it feels uncomfortable to be in here, we've already learned how to avoid that very discomfort using the thought system to purposely push ourselves farther into the house of mirrors. So ultimately, we learn to use the virtual reality system to avoid the truth that it's fundamentally uncomfortable to be inside that system. We are now becoming an active supporter of the system that is imprisoning us.

A further trick we play on ourselves is forgetting that it is a choice to be in the house of mirrors in the first place. We've become identified with the thought system itself, meaning we feel compelled to defend its integrity and thus walk deeper and deeper into the house of mirrors that is made up of thought and belief. Each layer of delusional identity we add requires another layer of distorting beliefs to help us forget what it is to live in and as unfiltered reality. This in turn creates further reinforcement and defense of the lie we keep telling ourselves. This requires more and more effort and more and more thought, which ultimately becomes exhausting. Yet as long as we keep pushing ourselves further into this delusion, the "alarm" bells going off in the emotion body get more and more distant.

"What you know you can't explain, but you feel it. You've felt it your entire life, that there's something wrong with the world. You don't know what it is, but it's there, like a splinter in your mind, driving you mad."

—*Morpheus, The Matrix*

This is the human condition, and it's a problem defined by thought-identification and entanglement. If this goes on long enough, we become like automatons, numb beings carrying out stereotyped scripts. We become disconnected from our deeper selves and our deeper truths. Deeply rooted resistance patterns and repressed emotions create a perfect storm for unconscious, self-centered, and callous behaviors. If our circumstances and conditioning are unfavorable enough, this will inevitably lead to violence at some level. In the right set of local conditions, groups of people can begin to act in concert in unconscious ways, perpetrating violence on larger scales. This can happen in families, communities, even entire nations.

A Taboo Subject

When you were a child you spent a lot of your time in presence. You were so immersed in play, exploration, and wonder, that most of the time you didn't even reflect internally on what was happening. You had thoughts here and there, and the older you got the more frequent they were. At some point thoughts became your near-constant companion. Since this happened gradually as you grew, it likely didn't seem intrusive most of the time.

By adulthood we often have trains of thought that go on for hours at a time. By some estimates we have as many as 70,000 thoughts per day. Now considering thoughts become our constant companion by early adulthood, do you find it odd that we rarely talk about our thoughts in the immediate? More accurately, there are some thoughts we talk about, but there are a heck of a lot more thoughts we avoid talking about. In fact, there are certain types of thoughts that we avoid revealing like we would avoid the plague. For example, how likely are you to communicate these types of thoughts:

➤ "I'm not good enough."

➤ "I'm full of shame."

➤ "I'm pretty certain that I'm deeply flawed."

➤ "I'm rehearsing an argument with my partner before it happens."

➤ "I doubt my partner is the right person for me."

➤ "I'm imagining myself having sex with a random person."

➤ "A thought just came into my mind of me punching someone in the face."

Just reading those makes you uncomfortable, doesn't it? Yet every single person walking the face of the Earth has had these exact thoughts. What are we hiding from? The reality is that we are far more alike in our inner worlds than we realize. There is a cultural taboo about discussing our innermost thoughts, or even our immediate thoughts, without heavily filtering them. There are also taboos surrounding asking others about their thoughts unless it stays within certain socially acceptable contexts. The central point I want to make is that there is a lot of avoidance and shame tied around certain categories of thoughts. We tend to hide most of our thoughts (and the fact that we are constantly paying attention to thoughts) not only from others, but even from ourselves. It's as if we believe that if others knew what some of our thoughts were, we'd be humiliated, ostracized, or worse. This avoidance/hiding mechanism is necessary to create and maintain the landscape in which mind-identification operates.

"Every man alone is sincere. At the entrance of a second person, hypocrisy begins. We parry and fend the approach of our fellow-man by compliments, by gossip, by amusements, by affairs. We cover up our thought from him under a hundred folds."

—Ralph Waldo Emerson

I can recall a conversation with a friend that stands out as a salient example of this phenomenon. I was talking to her about mindfulness. I asked her, "When you know you are going to see someone in a few minutes, do you imagine what you are going to say to them?" I wasn't trying to pry or reveal something embarrassing. I was simply using this common thought pattern as an example to demonstrate how we are often less present and mindful than we realize. Her reaction surprised me, partly because she is a particularly honest and open person, and partly because I thought the question was obviously referring to something that happens to all of us. Anyways, she turned beet red and giggled, shyly answering, "Yes." She looked as if she'd just gotten caught with her hand in the cookie jar. This event reinforced something I had observed many times before. That is that there are certain types of thoughts that we feel very compelled to hide from those around us. In fact, we often don't even realize we're doing it. What's more, there seems to be a set of hidden rules that govern the contexts in which it is or isn't acceptable to share certain types of thoughts with certain people. We even feel guilty or shameful when certain thoughts occur, don't we?

There are some thoughts that are on the extreme end of this spectrum; thoughts that feel shameful or even scary. Yet they keep coming, almost as if the fact that we are scared of them is what gives them energy. In the extreme, this can become obsessive and lead to dysfunction, such as with obsessive-compulsive disorder. We can also become so afraid and avoidant of a single thought, image, or memory, that we use all of our will to try to push and keep it out of our consciousness. This can evolve into post-traumatic stress disorder, wherein we spend so much energy trying to force a thought or memory out of our experience that it begins invade our dreams and our daily activities, causing us to avoid circumstances that may trigger that thought or memory.

As we further dissect the phenomenon of mind-identification, it will become clear how these tendencies to hide and avoid acknowledging thoughts are necessary to keep the process going. This is especially true of thoughts associated with certain emotions such as helplessness, resentment, and guilt.

How Does Mind-Identification Start?

Quite simply, we're wired for it. The complexity of the human nervous system is such that rudimentary thoughts begin to form at a young age and develop in complexity as we mature. By young adulthood, we have built a complex thought-based identity in which we have taken up residence.

The most fundamental form of self-reflective thought begins around eighteen months of age. This is when we begin to perceive ourselves as an entity that is distinct from other entities. We become aware that our mom and dad are "not-me" and that the cat and dog are also not-me. A twenty-month-old child can look into the mirror and recognize that the image in the mirror is "me." It can recognize its own movements and identity as distinct from those of other people and objects. Simultaneously, it recognizes that there are "others." This child quickly learns that the "other" called "Mom" or "Dad" has the job of providing nourishment, comfort, and protection.

By the age of two we are aware that others may have preferences about what we should be doing that we don't necessarily share. This is marked by behaviors that some parents refer to as "the terrible twos." The child recognizes that she may not always want to do what Mom or Dad wants her to do and learns that she has her own volition.

By the age of three a child has a clear understanding that there is a difference between a thought object and an actual object. The child can play make-believe. He can pretend that a plastic bottle is a rocket ship that can fly through space. He learns that by using imagination, he can turn that bottle from a rocket ship into a penguin. This is a rudimentary understanding of the symbolic nature of thought. This child is already learning to manipulate his experience of the world by superimposing thoughts upon it.

By the age of four, the complexity of our thought has become far more developed. A four-year-old child is aware of something that a three-year-old child is not aware of. The four-year-old is clearly aware that other people are thinking beings. That means that the four-year-old not only recognizes that she has an inner world of thoughts and can manipulate her experience through the use of thought, but she is also aware that you have an inner world of thoughts and that she can influence your experience through the use of communication. Developmental psychologists would say that this child has developed "theory of mind."

*"When childhood dies, its corpses are called
adults and they enter society, one of the politer
names of Hell. That is why we dread children, even
if we love them. They show us the state of our
decay."*

—*Brian Aldiss*

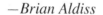

A classic test used to demonstrate this milestone in cognitive development is the following. Joshua is shown a box of candy. He is told he can open the box and have some candy. When he opens the box, he sees that the box has no candy in it, but is instead full of rocks. Joshua might laugh or he might be disappointed. Either way, once the box is closed again, Joshua will remember that even though this is a candy box, it is indeed full of rocks.

Here's the interesting part. Joshua is taken out of the room and watches on a monitor as Sarah is brought into the room with the candy box sitting on the table. Before Sarah is told that she can take some candy from the box, Joshua is asked, "What does Sarah think is in that box?" If Joshua is three, he'll say, "Rocks." However, if he is four, he will most likely laugh and say, "Candy!" He's in on the joke and is aware of Sarah's inner world, her expectations, and her worldview with respect to the box.

These examples demonstrate how complex our inner world of thought becomes, even at a young age. As we grow older thoughts become far more frequent and far more abstract. We spend more and more time in our internal worlds thinking about ourselves, our lives, our ideas, our problems, and our solutions in increasingly complex ways. This complex and abstract nature of self-reflective thought makes it possible to construct the apparatus of mind-identification. The question remains, "Who or what facilitates and maintains this process?"

Enter the Ego

Ego is deeply paradoxical in nature. For instance, there is no actual thing called an ego. You will never find an ego or directly perceive it. To conceptually solidify a thing called ego can just add one more layer of delusion to our already crowded minds. Believing that there is some "extra" aspect to us that is causing trouble can give us a project, something to root out. It can add one more facet of complexity to our already overly complex inner world of thought.

"The finest trick of the devil is to persuade you that he does not exist."

—Charles Baudelaire XXIX

On that basis, I have to caution you at the outset. Talking about ego in the way I'm going to in this chapter is not intended to convince you to adopt a whole bunch of beliefs about ego, or even to convince you that you have one. It's simply a convenient way of pointing out certain thought-based mechanisms that keep us absorbed in the inner world of mind in ways that cause us to suffer. It is a teaching paradigm, nothing more. With that said, it behooves you to have a certain level of respect for the power of the ego. As I've said to people many times:

The only bigger mistake than believing that there is an ego is believing that there is no such thing as an ego. This is because it will be the ego that holds that belief.

The following section will examine ego mechanisms in detail. After reading it you will have a good understanding of the various "tricks" the ego uses to keep us transfixed on and identified with our thoughts.

Ego Mechanisms

If mind-identification is the mental prison that prevents us from immediately realizing our unbound, undivided nature, then self-referential thoughts are the prison bars, and the ego is the warden. The ego is there not only to assure we don't find our way out of prison, but also to make sure we keep constructing new walls. As we constantly construct these walls (identities), we actively forget that there is even a possibility of being outside this prison. This section will point out some of the tricks the ego uses to ensure that we continue to hold ourselves hostage in our own internal world of self-reflection.

"The first rule of poker is that there is always a sucker. When you sit down at the poker table, look around and identify the sucker. If you can't identify the sucker, just get up and leave, because you're the sucker."

—*Unknown*

The Ego Has Rules That You Don't Know and Can't Look Up

Ego mechanisms are somewhat like software that runs inside the hardware of the human mind. They have evolved right along with the human race. These programs pass readily from human to human and do so without our notice. They have self-protective instincts and survival mechanisms. They are quite adaptable. You could say that the ego has a few thousand years on you. It's an ancient force. It knows far more about how your mind operates than you do. It knows exactly how to get and keep your attention. It knows how to convince you to argue and even fight for your right to make yourself suffer. It operates by rules you can't see. It causes you to adopt beliefs that serve its purpose, not yours. You're never given a list of these beliefs so you can consciously decide which ones you want to adopt and which ones you don't. Playing the game of life living with an ego is like playing a game of chess against a world-class chess master when you have never even seen a chessboard.

Ego Speaks in the First-Person

This is the ego's sneakiest trick. It's ingenious, really. Ego always speaks in the first person. The ego doesn't tell you what it thinks. It doesn't tell you what it wants you to think. In fact, it doesn't even tell you what you think.

Ego does the thinking for you.

Take a moment to let that sink in. The ego convinces you that its view is your view. It does this by speaking as if you are the one speaking. It structures thoughts in such a way that it sounds and feels like they are your voice, your thoughts. Because it's happening inside your mind, you immediately assume that the ego's voice and its view are your voice and your view!

"We have met the enemy and he is us."

—Walt Kelley

Here is an illustrative example. Imagine you are sitting in a chair not doing anything in particular. Out of nowhere a thought says, I'm really disappointed in myself. I could have done that better. Now first of all, notice I didn't say, "You think to yourself, I'm really disappointed . . ." I stated it the first way so that you can see that there isn't volition in thought. You don't create it, you don't think it, it simply occurs to you. It arises in your mind. However, the way it's stated makes it sound like you did the thinking. It seems as if you have already chosen to believe the assertion of that thought. Since the thought is stated in the first person, we usually don't recognize that we have the choice to decide whether this thought is true or not.

Let's clarify this a bit more. If someone said to you, "You're really disappointed in yourself right now," it might not feel good to hear, and you'd probably wonder why someone else is telling you what you believe or feel. However, you could critically evaluate whether or not it was a true statement about yourself. Before we evaluate someone else's statement, even if it seems to be about us, it's clearly not our view, it's their view, right? Now what if that person's voice wasn't "out there" somewhere but was being transmitted into your mind? I know this is getting weird, but stick with me and it will become much clearer. If the statement were, "You're really disappointed in yourself right now . . . ," you'd probably wonder, Who the heck is speaking to me inside my mind? The ego knows better than to out itself like this, as it would immediately alert you to its presence. So instead, it says, "I'm really disappointed in myself . . ." Naturally, there is no perception that the thought was placed there by some voice that was not ours, so it sounds like, "I am the one that thought that." This point is so important that I strongly encourage you to stop reading and spend a few minutes noticing every thought you have. See if you can identify what I'm referring to. The moment you choose to stop and become the watcher of those thoughts, then it's not you creating them, is it?

Self-Aware Thoughts Always Have Built-In Assumptions

Let's consider a common thought/belief that might come up about awakening:

Until I get more consistent with meditation, I'll never wake up.

Now let's look at all of the assumptions and beliefs that are implicit in that one thought. By doing this we will see that if we believe this is our thought, like we are the thinker of that thought, we automatically make several assumptions about other things we believe. Here are some assumptions or hidden beliefs I see here:

> That the "I" thought represents what I actually am.

> That this thought-person is moving through time.

> That this thought-person is not awake.

> That this thought-person is seeking and wants to awaken.

> That this thought-person is in control and can decide what to do.

> That awakening is an event.

> That awakening is something that happens later.

> That awakening needs to be earned.

> That the mental me can decide when awakening occurs.

> That there are forces acting against me that are causing me not to meditate as much as I want to.

"It is the mark of an educated mind to be able to entertain a thought without accepting it."

—Aristotle

If you have the inclination, listing hidden beliefs associated with any thought you have is a very potent practice. Just as we did above, take any thought that occurs to you (the more fundamentally true it feels, the better) and write it down. Then take some time to list all the assumptions built into that thought.

The Ego Uses Images That Perpetuate the Inner World

The thought we examined above was a conceptual or language thought. The other common type of thought is an image thought. This is any visual image that is not happening right now in your actual environment, yet you can perceive it in your mind. For example, take a moment to think of a pig. Now when you imagined that pig you clearly were aware that it didn't suddenly appear in the room you're sitting in, right? Yet if you focus attention on the mental image, you can probably see it almost as clearly as if it had. That is a visual image thought. It is an internal reflection of the outside world, as perceived through the senses.

Ego uses this sort of internal imagery rather consistently to keep us transfixed on our internal world. Whereas conceptual thoughts tend to come and go quickly (unless we really contemplate them), images tend to stay fixed and slowly morph into different images as our thought stream continues. The key insight I want you to take away from this is that this inner visual world is dimensional in nature. For example, when we are remembering a recent event in our lives, it really looks like we're there, doesn't it? This is due to this sense of being in a dimensional space reliving the event. Because it "looks" a lot like the actual world, our bodies and minds respond accordingly. We get physiological stress responses, and our attention is fixed onto these imaginary spaces. I don't have to tell you how uncomfortable it can be to keep reliving experiences you'd rather forget. It makes us feel like we are at the mercy of those thoughts. We start to pay them more attention than our actual senses. Image thoughts are largely the fixative "glue" that keeps this happening.

Subjectification

Subjectification is a hidden dualistic mechanism that makes us "feel" separate as we navigate our lives, with our attention remaining largely in thoughts. This is tied into the dimensional nature of image-based thoughts we just discussed, but is more subtle in operation. It's easier to feel than to see. Don't sweat it if this is not immediately clear; it's the kind of thing that can just dawn on you in a moment of clarity when you are directly examining the nature of thought.

When we imagine a scene such as talking to someone we know, we usually picture their face and the scene from a first-person point of view, right? In these instances, the thoughts make it appear as if we are looking from our own frame of reference. This makes sense because this is how memories are stored based on sensory input. The thing is that when we engage a thought in this way, we are subtly reinforcing the sense of being a subject and whatever we are thinking about as being the object. This ongoing reinforcement of a sense of subjectivity becomes quite solidified over time. We start to feel like a thought-subject, and even begin to identify with that subjectified though structure. We start to apply this tendency to subjectify (unknowingly) to the actual world. We feel more and more like a subject "back here," engaging a world "out there," even when we're not engaging a specific mental image or memory.

This contributes to and reinforces the sense of being separate from our immediate environment. It can make it feel like there is a veil or barrier between you and life. It may be experienced as a kind of uncomfortable numbness. This tendency to subjectify carries with it a charge that builds over time and culminates in a deep sense of isolation. It is usually not obvious that this sense of isolation and associated loneliness is causally related to subjectification in thought and the distancing sense that results. We just find ourselves feeling lost and isolated and have no idea how we got there or how to get out of it. What's worse, since we are unknowingly applying this subjectification to our perception of the actual world, we find little comfort in things that are supposed to make us feel better when we feel isolated and lonely. Even human contact can lose its ability to comfort and soothe us. If this experience of subjectification, being distanced from life, and isolation gets intense enough, we may begin to experience depersonalization or derealization.

The Ego Binds You in Time

Here is a common scenario I encounter when talking with people about realization. I will be pointing in a very direct way to the immediate experience of natural reality; this place where unenlightenment has never tread. I can do this because it is already in their experience in that very moment, just as it is in yours right now. I know through the exchange that they get what I'm pointing to; more importantly, they feel the truth of their immediate experience. I can see and feel them relax and become more present. Then a moment later they will say something like, "Wow, I can't wait until that's true for me too." Usually, I just look at them and smile, waiting to see if they catch what just happened. Sometimes they do and sometimes they don't. If they don't, I'll usually point it out to them.

"The sword of time will pierce our skins,
It doesn't hurt when it begins,
But as it works its way on in,
The pain grows stronger watch it grin."

Song lyrics from "Suicide Is Painless" by Mike Altman

244

What happened in that instance is that they were experientially aware of unfiltered reality as it was unfolding in the immediate. This is an immersive experience that is not contingent upon thought. It is also not time based because reality can only happen now. Then a thought formed in their mind that essentially said, "Wow, that sounds nice, but too bad I don't have it. Well, at least I can seek for it and maybe someday I'll realize it." This is a common lure the ego will use to pull our attention back into thought.

I'm sure you can see how many assumptions were baked into that thought/belief. First and foremost, there is an assumption being made in that thought that "I" am a distinct entity moving through time, one that experiences external events. Further, there is an assumption that one event that I can experience is presence. Still another assumption is that the realization of presence will be "not now." You see can see that these assumed beliefs are contrary to the person's immediate experience of presence. Yet the "pull" of the thought stream can be strong. In believing that one thought, believing that it's my thought, and believing that we can find this omnipresent truth somewhere in the imaginary (thought-based) timeline called "the future," we have totally distanced ourselves experientially from this immediate truth of unassailable presence and peace.

As long as realization, truth, connection, and
surrender are put in time, we will be using the illusion
of time to put off claiming what we have always
searched for but had never accepted as already here.

The ego has many other ways of using the illusion of time to hold you captive, but I will keep the discussion brief in this section. Here are some words and phrases that are dead giveaways that you are dealing with a thought or belief that is using time to convince you that you are captive in the prison of time:

245

➤ Always: As in, "I always get stuck in my thoughts in _____ (situation)."

➤ Never: As in, "I can never stay in presence when I'm not meditating or on retreat." Or, "This will never happen for me."

➤ Still: As in, "I'm still _____ (not awake, not there yet, confused, doing xyz behavior, etc.)."

➤ Later, when . . .

➤ As soon as . . .

I'm sure you get the sense of what a time-based thought is. It can be a fruitful endeavor to sit and recognize one thought at a time. When you see any of these motifs that suggest time, you can ask, "What happens in my experience right now when I recognize that this time-based story is one single thought occurring right now?" Doing this consistently will bring your attention more into the present. The sense of struggling with time will dissolve with some practice.

It Disguises Fear as Empowerment

The ubiquitous feelings of lack and isolation among humans are rooted in the misperception that we are apart from everything—that we are small, discrete, and short-lived. This is based in subjectification and reinforced by various beliefs and tendencies that we pick up along the way. The ego offers you a "solution" in the form of imagining and seeking conditions that will finally make these feelings subside. Unfortunately, the imagining and seeking are only mental processes and as such will only reinforce the sense that we are a subject endlessly seeking or avoiding internal or external objects and circumstances. To assure this process of reinforcing separate self by seeking mental objects goes on unnoticed and unabated, the ego takes on an "empowerment" persona. More precisely, it makes sure that you take on the empowerment persona. It tells you that you take pride in and identify with being the empowered one, the one who can make anything happen, the one who is always in control. The problem here is that the underlying mechanism of trying to find the perceived missing piece is what is actually driving this identity of empowerment. So now we add a layer of inauthenticity to the whole script.

As a side note, I'm not referring here to practical plan-making and simple goal-setting. These activities are valuable and are performed with clarity and ease when we are not listening to the stories of the ego.

It Makes Something Impersonal Feel Extremely Personal

In a previous section we discussed how mind-identification causes us to hide things, even from ourselves. Well, one of the best ways to do that is to wrap it in an emotion and then tell us that we fear that emotion and want to avoid it at all costs.

"You're protecting him [ego], Mr. Green, but with what? Where's the best place an opponent should hide? In the very last place you'd ever look. He's hiding behind your pain, Jake. You're protecting him with your pain. Embrace the pain and you will win this game."

—Avi, from the movie Revolver

One of the salient features of shame is that it feels incredibly personal. It also seems to say, "Don't look here!" In actuality, it's not shame that says that, it's our beliefs about shame. These beliefs are brought to us by our old friend the ego. What a brilliant way to hide the truth of what fuels the ego engine (a false sense of separation). The ego hides it under a shame barrier. This causes us to never look close enough to see that the mechanisms of ego are all a farce. It also keeps us from talking to others about these deeper places in our emotion-body. If we did so, we'd pretty quickly see that these ego structures, false beliefs, and shame are shared among all humans. Recognizing that, we could start to arrive at the insight that none of this is personal at all. It's a software program running in every member of the human race. We are simply made to feel as if it's exquisitely personal so that we don't look closely enough to see and dispel the whole illusion.

Binding of Attention

In the preceding sections we discussed the nature of mind-identification. We explored the ego mechanisms that reinforce the sense of separation, keep us seeking, and hide the whole operation from our notice. As was described, the "bars" of the prison of mind-identification are thoughts. More precisely, it is our entanglement with thoughts that keeps us imprisoned. There is an entire chapter dedicated to thoughts coming later in the book, so we won't go into great detail about them here. However, it is important to look into how our attention becomes and remains bound in thoughts on an ongoing basis. This binding is required for the illusions of mind-identification and ego to continue operating.

If we were able to simply let our attention rest in the senses all the time, then this book wouldn't be necessary. The illusion of separation would be dispelled in a short time, and individual suffering would come to an end. Anyone who has tried to meditate for five minutes knows that it is not nearly that simple. Thoughts bombard us almost constantly until we cultivate some degree of clarity in meditative practice, and even then, they are frequent visitors. When I said "bombard," that was a little misleading. In truth, our attention is directed into thought on a nearly constant basis. The thoughts are innocent; it is our addiction to them and entanglement with them that causes us trouble. This section will address how that ongoing binding of attention happens in real time.

Thoughts Are Like Magicians

A thought can't know reality directly because a thought is a reflection of reality. So, the "world" portrayed inside a single thought is not actually there. It's a snapshot of the actual world. You cannot go further into that thought's reality any more than you can walk into the reflected world of a mirror. If this isn't clear, you can test it by remembering a recent moment you experienced in your life. Can you walk into that memory? Of course not. So, if it's so obvious that a thought is just a reflection with no reality to it, how is it that we remain so transfixed? Well for one thing, a thought is a master of misdirection. It is like a magician manipulating your attention.

The first trick is to get your attention. The thought has to make you believe it's important. There are many ways this happens, but the salient point is that it always uses what works on you. Our nervous systems are wired such that anything (including a thought) that causes a shift in our attention, especially accompanied by an emotional response, will be reinforced through strengthening of neural pathways. This means that thoughts that get our attention and cause emotional reactions will be repeated preferentially over thoughts that don't. So the more attention we give a certain thought, the more likely that thought is to recur to get our attention! This is why we can all relate to uncomfortable, repetitive thought mechanisms such as rumination, thinking about events we'd be prefer to forget, and the like.

The second trick the magician of the mind uses is to redirect your attention to the next thought. As we discussed, a single thought has no real internal substance, and seeing that clearly, we would lose interest pretty quickly. So our mind-magician uses the trick of redirection to redirect our attention to the next thought. This redirection mechanism is a bit complex in the way it functions, but I'll simplify here by saying that it utilizes the illusion of time to seamlessly move our attention from one thought to another. Let's look at an example of how this might work.

Suppose that you are at home in your garden. You're feeling present and enjoying the colors and textures of the plants and flowers as you tend to them. Suddenly a thought comes into your mind. It is a memory of a conversation you'd had at work a few days before. A coworker had criticized your work unfairly. You feel a bit of tightness in your chest as you recall this tense moment. By this time the magician has already played the first trick on you, it has called your attention to this "important" thought. It was an emotionally charged moment, and any situation where our competency has been called into question will get our attention. So the magician has used its two common tricks to convince you of the importance of shifting your attention from the present into the shadow world of thought. Now you've all but forgotten those vivid colors and textures of the flowers in the garden. You're no longer aware of the fragrances or the sensations of your hands on the plants. Instead, you are reliving an uncomfortable moment. Well, you aren't actually reliving it, but the brain sure hasn't gotten that message, has it?

If the mind only had that one trick up its sleeve, then you would realize pretty quickly how uncomfortable it is to distance yourself from the enjoyment and immediacy of presence, just to relive an uncomfortable situation in your imagination. Within a few moments, those feelings of inadequacy would pass, and the thought/ memory of the event would fade. You would just melt back into presence. That's not what happens, though, is it? No, the magician has another trick up its sleeve. It immediately redirects your attention from the memory thought (false past) to a solution thought (false future). Do you see how the mind has to invoke time to keep your attention from naturally returning to presence? This redirection uses the illusion of control to redirect our attention to the future thought where you can defend yourself and your work the next time you see the overly critical coworker. In that thought of an imaginary future, you are standing up for yourself and telling that coworker that you indeed do good work, and that it is actually their work that is subpar. You tell them that they are projecting their own sense of inadequacy onto you.

Do you see how the magician of the mind has plucked you out of the peace and connection with your environment (that is always available in the present) and shot you experientially into the past and then experientially into the future? This pattern of attention redirection is a common way to bind ourselves into thought and thus into the illusion of time. If you take some time to investigate this directly, you'll find that it happens all day long. To the degree that we are being led by this magician through our minds like a dog on a leash, we suffer the experience of being distanced from presence, from ourselves, and from life.

A thought has two jobs: to get your attention,
then to redirect your attention to the next thought.

When the Gloves Come Off

Even though some of the previous sections may have been a bit uncomfortable to read, we have largely been discussing the "normal" day-to-day functioning of the human mind. All we have really done is looked at this subject in a topical way, using a few direct investigations to clarify certain points. Understanding and knowing how these mechanisms function is not the same as disentangling our identity from them. Knowledge can be a helpful start, but the true disentanglement is experiential.

*"Fortunately, some are born with spiritual
immune systems that sooner or later give rejection
to the illusory worldview grafted upon them from
birth through social conditioning. They begin
sensing that something is amiss, and start looking
for answers. Inner knowledge and anomalous
outer experiences show them a side of reality
others are oblivious to, and so begins the journey
of awakening."*

—Henri Bergson

When we do begin to earnestly disentangle identity from these mechanisms, the alarms that have gone off so far will seem like child's play. You see, even the poking around we've done thus far has really not threatened the ego defenses on any significant level. The ego is sitting in a hammock right now with a mojito in its hand and a bemused smile on its face watching you poke around. It's honestly not concerned. If it had a voice it might say, "Spirituality? Sure, we can do that. I've done it for thousands of years. No problem! Let's get started. In fact, I can help you."

When we really start digging into the false thought-based identity, the ego defenses will begin to ramp up their game. If you're not scared yet, you will be. If you're not confused yet, you will be. If you're not disillusioned yet, you will be. It's just a matter of time. Later chapters thoroughly address how to navigate once the ego begins to be truly threatened and identity starts unraveling. Doesn't that sound like fun?

For now, I just want to point out some of the motifs you can expect from more serious ego defense mechanisms. These can occur before initial awakening but are more likely and more intense after awakening. My hope is that by being aware of their nature ahead of time, you will realize that it's okay when they occur. It's normal during this process, and while they can be quite unsettling at times, they are only there to show you exactly where to go. They are some of the best pointers there are.

Disturbing Thoughts

One of the most common ego defenses is the use of unsettling, disturbing, and occasionally terrifying thoughts. Here are some examples:

➤ "If I keep on this path, I might lose my mind and become psychotic."

➤ "To go any further, I will have to abandon my family, children, partner, etc."

➤ "What if I lose my ability to work, provide for myself, and provide for my family?"

➤ "I'm losing control over my life."

➤ "I'm suffering unbearably."

➤ "I'm dying."

➤ "I can't handle this."

➤ "I will become completely helpless and unable to feed myself."

➤ "I can't handle these emotions, they're destroying me."

Obviously, these can be particularly uncomfortable thoughts. Here's the thing to remember: they're just thoughts. None of them has any more truth value than any other thought. If one of these thoughts occurs, I recommend you just observe it: "Oh, hello there unsettling thought. Welcome. I'd heard you might be coming around." There is no need to evaluate it, reject it, or believe it. It is simply mental activity. It causes no more harm than a thought suddenly occurring to you that says, "I'm the Queen of England." Also recognize that if these types of thoughts are coming, you are in good territory. Give them some time. Like any thought, these disturbing thoughts will pass away to be replaced by other thoughts in the thought stream.

Intense Emotions

The second type of ego defense that is common when we start to dig into our identity structures is intense emotions. Technically it's not the emotions that are so triggering; it is our resistance patterns and identities that are in place to prevent us from feeling certain emotions. Indeed, there is nothing fundamentally problematic about any emotion. The chapter on emotions will clarify this. For now, we will discuss some of the more intense emotions that are likely to surface during this process. Even the word "intense" can imply that there is something about the emotion that is difficult to handle. I am only using that word because people will often associate that descriptor with certain emotions in this setting. Here are some of the visitors you can expect:

➤ Guilt

➤ Confusion

➤ Resentment

➤ Grief

- ➤ Shame

- ➤ Helplessness

- ➤ Hopelessness

- ➤ Doubt

- ➤ Fear

- ➤ Anger

If and when any of these surfaces, it's best to remind yourself that it's okay to feel whatever emotion is present at that moment. See if you can find where you feel it in your body. Give it some time and watch as it fades. Every emotion will fade if you don't struggle with it or try to run from it. Let it run its natural course. It's perfectly okay.

Intense Physical Reactions

Physical reactions in the body are also possible. For some people they are common, for others they are rare. If you experience these, it's okay. There's nothing you need to do to get rid of them. Just let these reactions run their course:

- ➤ Sweating

- ➤ Shaking

- ➤ Increased heart rate

- ➤ Unfamiliar sensations moving through the body

- ➤ Involuntary movement of parts of the body, such as hands, arms, legs, or head

It's always wise to keep in mind the possibility that new physical symptoms are related to a medical issue. If you are concerned, get yourself examined by a medical professional.

Closing Comments

The most important takeaway from this chapter is to not take anything you've read here too seriously.

> ➤ There is no evil entity lurking inside you called the ego. It is simply a collection of thought patterns and mental tendencies to use those thought patterns to filter perceptions. This filtering obscures the undivided and pristine nature of reality available at all times. These tendencies to tie our experiences and identity into thought will subside more and more as we wake up and further refine our insights.

> ➤ It is useless and often counterproductive to go to war with an imaginary ego. If you do this, it will be the ego that is going to war with the imaginary ego. It is far more fruitful to utilize the techniques and inquiries provided in later chapters to directly investigate your immediate experience, which will open to your undivided nature. In doing so, the egoic mechanisms will naturally relax and fall away. At some point, the spell of mind-identification will be broken.

> ➤ While the mechanisms of mind identification and ego do operate at fundamental levels of our perceptual experience, there is something that is always fundamental to them. This unnamable living truth is always with you and can never be touched, marred, or threatened by the machinery of the human thought process.

Chapter 12:

Thoughts

Introduction

Many years ago, I was reading a book about Zen Buddhism and one line of text seemed to jump right off the page. It struck me like a bolt of lightning. It wasn't the literal meaning of the statement that struck me. This statement had power beyond the words that conveyed it. It reached deep inside me, beyond the limits of my cognitive faculties. It resonated in a part of my being that I hadn't been consciously in touch with for some time. It illuminated and awoke something primal, something instinctual, something that quite honestly felt ancient. There was an intimate knowing that a profound truth was being illuminated in this one simple sentence. It was a living truth, a living thing. The sentence was:

Thinking is the disease of the human mind.

I had always known that certain thoughts felt uncomfortable. I knew that overthinking caused me to feel frustrated, anxious, and even helpless at times. In my teen years, I remember thinking over and over, What's wrong with me? It felt extremely uncomfortable. Yet it didn't occur to me that the thoughts themselves, and how I was taking them to be "about me," were what was causing the discomfort. I assumed the suffering was because I couldn't find the elusive solution to problem of "what's wrong with me?" I believed that thought. Rather, I believed the assumption that it made, that there was something wrong with me in the first place. Worse, I believed I had to use thought to solve this "big problem." In actuality, putting so much effort into the thinking is what was causing and then reinforcing the sense of there being a problem in the first place. It's sort of like your hair being on fire and then you try to put it out by pouring gasoline on your head. Of course, that just makes the fire worse, but if you don't realize the gas is causing the fire and believe it can put the fire out, you will just repeat that cycle.

"Someone who wants to attain enlightenment must be brave. He must rush into the crowd of enemies with a dagger. In the practice of Zen, enemies are our delusive thoughts and passions."

—Koun Yamada

Because thoughts felt so integral to who I was, I couldn't quite elucidate that the nature of thought itself had to be investigated if I ever wanted to address the pervasive sense of self-doubt and isolation in my life. This one sentence and the effect it had on me in that moment changed all that. The suffering caused by thought didn't immediately abate, but I knew where to look and that I had to find ways to investigate this matter in earnest. My heart told me that this was an important piece of the puzzle.

It took me quite some time to realize the full implications of what I had glimpsed. There are nuances to this statement that take some experience and realization to appreciate and integrate. I want to make a few points of clarity along these lines. First, it is important to know that this statement is not referring to all types of thought. It is referring to a specific type of thought that just so happens to constitute the majority of our thinking. This statement is specifically referring to discursive, or self-referential thought. Self-referential thoughts are the endless thoughts about "me." This "me" in the way discursive thoughts function is a very distorted version of what you are. It is also largely hidden, in that it is typically assumed or presupposed inside the content of the various thoughts. It's sort of like joining a television program after it's already begun, and it is assumed that you already know the characters. The content of these self-referential thoughts revolves around "my past and my future, my problems and potential solutions." What we don't realize is that these types of thoughts constantly assume and reinforce two views. The first is: "I am separate from everything and everyone else." This view brings with it a pervasive sense of isolation and loneliness. The second view is: "There is a big problem to solve, and only when I have solved that can I be happy, relaxed, and at peace." Together these lead to a deepening sense of shame that says, "I'm not good enough," helplessness that says, "No matter how much I do I can never seem to solve the problem of me," and exhaustion.

The second point I want to make is that this statement is not suggesting that the mere presence of thoughts is what is causing our unhappiness and pain. The presence of thoughts is, in and of itself, harmless. It is our relationship with thoughts that is the core issue. It is the way we interact with thoughts that causes all the confusion, doubt, chronic distraction, and that gnawing sense of isolation—in short, suffering. Understanding this, we see that there is no need to try to stop thinking or go to battle with our thoughts. Doing either of these would be counterproductive. As was mentioned, it is our relationship with thought, not the presence of thought, that is at the root of the issue. Thus, it is most profitable to investigate the nature of this relationship.

Lastly, I want to emphasize that this disease of the human mind we are talking about does not refer to planning, creativity, intelligence, problem solving, logical reasoning, or empirical scientific methods. Indeed, once the distortions in our relationship with thought are sorted out, these cognitive functions become far more accessible, efficient, and precise.

So how do we go about sorting this out? This is done through a direct investigation of the nature of thought and our relationship to it. We will look into how our relationship with thought obscures the wonder, intimacy, and freedom that is immediately available to us in all circumstances. This chapter—along with the chapters on beliefs, inquiry, and mind-identification—will address this issue from various angles. You will be given tools to allow you to investigate this matter on your own. We will discuss how and when to use them, and how to adapt them to your life and practice in ways that feel natural to you.

Before we jump in, I'd like to pose a few questions that will help to turn some of our attention onto the thought process itself. These aren't meant to stimulate intense analysis. They are more to cultivate a simple curiosity about that which is so close that we rarely look directly and clearly at it. You will get the most out of these questions if you try to directly reference your own immediate experience and then answer them in as clear a statement as possible. This can be done verbally or by writing down your answer. It can also be helpful to do this exercise along with someone else so that you can assure you are clearly describing your experience. You might want to note how it makes you feel to ponder and answer these questions.

- What is a thought? If someone who had never experienced a thought asked you this question, how would you respond if you were trying to be as accurate as possible?

- Is thought productive and useful all of the time, some of the time, or none of the time?

- When you recall times in your life when things seemed the most spontaneous, enjoyable, and wondrous, were there a lot of thoughts or few thoughts?

- Do thoughts define who and what you are? If not, in what ways do they describe or capture who and what you are?

- Have you ever had a time when it was uncomfortable to think?

- Have you ever had the experience of trying to "push away" a thought?

- Have you ever had the experience of holding onto a thought?

- How do thoughts, such as, I don't feel like a good person make you feel?

- When you have a thought that suggests you are good person, have done something right, or have gotten approval from someone, how do you feel?

- If the answer to the previous question was "good," are there any other feelings mixed in?

How did contemplating or answering those questions make you feel? Was it an emotional experience? Did you have feelings of curiosity, frustration, discomfort, curiosity, or peace? Did you find it challenging or easy? Did you find yourself referring to thoughts you remember having, or were you able to notice a thought in real time to observe? You might consider returning periodically to this question set just to see if your experience of thoughts evolves. Spoiler alert: it almost certainly will.

A Simple Definition

What is a thought? What is its nature? Considering thoughts are our constant companion, it would seem reasonable to know something about them, wouldn't it? There are many ways to describe what a thought is. We could describe thoughts as ideas with power that can lead to innovation, invention, and improvement of our environment. We can talk about thoughts as occasional nuisances that keep poking us awake at night when we are trying to sleep. We can talk about thought as a faculty of self-reflection that differentiates us from plants and most animals, and which allows us to plan, communicate our plans, and work in large groups to execute those plans. We could take a more scientific approach and describe thoughts as neurochemical processes that involve neurotransmitters being released in vast networks of neurons in a coordinated fashion to formulate an internal experience that is remarkably flexible and adaptable.

All of these ways of talking about thoughts are useful in certain contexts. However, for purposes of awakening, I have found that a direct experiential definition of thought is the most accurate and useful. I would like to offer a simple and succinct definition that will serve as a foundational reference as we proceed on. I'm not suggesting that this definition is the only one or the right one, but in my experience, it is the most helpful way of understanding what a thought is and how it functions when it comes to the realization process. Even as your experience of thought evolves along your path to liberation, I think you will find that this definition lends itself to facilitating and adapting to that evolution.

A thought is a simple reflection of one of the five
senses or of another thought.

Thoughts can seem quite varied and complex, but if you look at the immediate experience of a thought "right now," it is always made up of a reflection of a basic sense and/or another thought. I'm not interested in you adopting this definition and believing it on a theoretical basis. I'm only interested in what you can directly experience, so let's test this out straightaway. Take a moment to recall a short exchange (a couple of sentences) that you had with someone recently. It may be easiest to close your eyes for a moment to tune into that memory. This might be the most recent conversation you've had, or it might be one that stands out in your memory for some reason.

Now spend a few moments "thinking" that thought, viewing it, and replaying it in your mind. Did you do it? Great, now what was that thought made out of? There were voices (sound/auditory), as well as faces, bodies, surroundings (images/visual), weren't there? There might have even been some physical sensations, especially if it was an emotionally charged exchange. While it is possible to imagine tastes and smells, it is far more common for thoughts to consist of visual images, sounds, and sensations. That's it, isn't it? Clearly the actual faces and voices weren't there, but the visual and auditory reflections of them were. To drive that point home, those people in the thought (the person you were talking to and the past "copy" of yourself) didn't physically appear in the room you are in right now as you performed this exercise, did they? Now if they did, then please get ahold of me, I'd love to talk to you. I've yet to see evidence of time travel, but if you are able to do it, let's sit down and chat about it. I'll even buy dinner. No, only images and sounds representing the people that were the subjects of the thought appeared. So aside from those reflections of visual images, sound reflections, and maybe sensations, was there anything else to that thought? Most of us would say no, there were only those reflections of the senses.

A particularly observant person might say something like, "The awareness of those sense reflections, or the capacity to reflect was also there." This is a good point, and it is true. If you were to walk up to a mirror hanging on a wall, you would see a reflected image of your face, right? You would also be looking at the reflective capacity of the mirror itself, the "reflectivity." To illustrate this, imagine that after looking in the mirror, you took a few steps to the side and looked at the wall next to the mirror. You wouldn't see that reflected image because the wall does not have the reflective capacity that the mirror does. So there is something important about the mirror that is more primary or fundamental than the images it seems to produce that the wall does not have. The images in the mirror could change a hundred times per day, but the reflective nature never changes and is always necessary for those images to appear. This is the reflective capacity of the mirror.

In the same way, a thought is possible because of the reflective capacity of the mind. Similar to looking into a mirror, you can become directly aware of the reflective nature (mirrorness or reflectivity) of thought. This reflective nature is experienced and described differently by different people. It is sometimes experienced as the pure sense of "I" or the pure sense of knowing that requires no specific object. If when observing a thought, you can perceive that reflective nature as such, then great. The next step is to notice that because that reflective nature is fundamental to everything you've ever thought, perceived, or known about the world and about yourself, and is simultaneously indiscernible from you as the perceiver, then you are immediately perceiving everything that is perceivable. Your whole world, your self, your past and future, your beliefs and doubts, even your potential to experience things you haven't yet experienced are none other than the consciousness that is aware of these words right now—the one seeing through those eyes and hearing through those ears. This is experience of unbound consciousness! If this is immediately obvious to you and you don't have to think about it, then just rest in that infinite reflection that makes up you, your perceptions, the world, and anything you could ever think. If not, it's perfectly okay; it will clarify over time. For now, I just wanted to point this out as an appetizer for what's to come.

"It is beyond a doubt that all our knowledge begins with experience."

—Immanuel Kant

Here is another variation on the exercise above that can help clarify what is meant by the reflective nature of thought. You can randomly grab any one thought from the thought stream, or you can choose one that seems to be particularly charged for you. Once you've clarified what the thought is, then you can perform this simple experiment. Take a few moments to "think" the thought, meaning observe each sense involved. What are the colors and shapes of the visual images? What are the sounds and words in the thought? You can ask other questions, such as, "How does this thought make me feel?" or "Do I like or dislike this thought?" You can also make up your own questions. Once you've looked and listened closely to that thought, you can remind yourself that everything that was experienced in that thought was a reflection. For comparison, you can listen to the sounds in your environment and look at the colors and forms in your surroundings. In this way, you can compare the "flavor" of actual sensory experience with that of reflected (thought-based) sensory experience. If you do this with curiosity and an intention to clearly see the difference, it can be quite a powerful way to investigate and de-identify from thoughts.

What about a more complex or abstract example of thought? This was a simple and concrete "event" we were thinking about (a person and a simple few word exchanges). Thoughts can be much more abstract than that simple example. Some might argue that their power is largely derived from their ability to abstract. Let's address this. Consider this quote by Immanuel Kant. It seemed appropriate to choose a quote by one of the most renowned rationalist philosophers.

Morality is not properly the doctrine of how we may make ourselves happy, but how we may make ourselves worthy of happiness.

Let's subject this statement to the above experiment. Read this statement and then contemplate or "think" it in your mind. As you do so, what is the nature of that thought? It is a voice, is it not? It is an internal dialogue. That dialogue is made out of words, isn't it? It's probably your own voice, but it is definitely auditory. Perhaps there is an image or two as well. So, although this is a complex sort of thought, what the thought is actually made out of is a reflection of a sense: the auditory sense. If you're still skeptical, then try to contemplate that statement without an internal voice. How did that go for you?

I want to make a distinction now between this simple experience of the Kant statement as a singular thought, and thinking about the meaning of that statement. This is where thoughts begin to reflect other thoughts. Clearly the statement has a lot of complexity built into it based on the concepts it represents. To "unpack" or further contemplate the assertion, we need a string of other thoughts. So as our mind produces one thought after another relating to the original statement, it can seem like there is something going on aside from simple sensory reflection. Well, the only difference is that the additional thoughts are now reflecting the previous thoughts. Yet it's important to recognize that each thought still maintains its nature as a simple sensory reflection. Any time you are lost in a long string of thoughts, you can prove this to yourself. Just take the most recent thought that you were aware of and clarify it in your mind. Consider just that one thought. What is it made of? As with the examples we discussed above, you will find it is made up of auditory and visual thought-stuff.

Now that you have a sense of what it means that thoughts can reflect other thoughts, I'm going to point out something that may or may not be obvious. The vast majority of our thoughts are of this nature. They are reflections of reflections. Have you ever looked into a mirror where there was also a mirror positioned behind you in such a way that the mirrors reflected one another multiple times inwardly, creating a bizarre and distorted version of reality? The capacity of a thought to reflect another thought is quite like this. When thoughts start reflecting one another, it can very quickly become a house of mirrors.

What does this house of mirrors of thought look like for a human being? In short, it looks like human suffering. It looks like the pervasive feelings of isolation and separation that plague humanity. It looks like constant seeking, distraction, and repression of our inner truths, our authenticity. It is a lot like being in a prison inside of our own minds. Only this prison is far more effective at keeping us incarcerated than a prison made out of cement and steel and staffed with armed guards. In this prison we think ourselves into solitary confinement. Whoever built this prison realized something ingenious about humans. They realized that we love to seek and are easily addicted to promises of future happiness. The problem is that those promises are always thoughts. So instead of directly realizing the spontaneity, peace, and freedom that is here right now, we follow thought after thought into a future that can never be.

You may have noticed that the house of mirrors analogy and my description of unbound consciousness sound similar. While they

267

could sound similar conceptually, experientially the difference between them is the difference between heaven and hell. The key insight that differentiates them is a matter of identity. As long as you take yourself to be a single reflection, you will feel like a thought chasing a thought and then chasing another thought. The more this happens, the more distant you get from the senses or the physical experience of being alive. As we touched on above, the more thoughts start reflecting other thoughts, the less clear it becomes that an individual thought is nothing but a direct sensory reflection. So, the more identified we get with the thought stream, which is made up of reflections of reflections, the more distant from life and isolated from our senses and our bodies we feel. This is the analogy of mirrors endlessly reflecting one another. You feel like an isolated mirror image somewhere deep inside that reflection stream. Everything looks the same. It's all scripted. Nothing seems very real, and there is a gnawing numbness and desperation that you can't fully identify.

In contrast, the moment we recognize the reflective nature of mind and that it encompasses all experience, including the experience of being a conscious being, then everything expands out to infinity. We suddenly see thoughts as the ghosts they are, and only vivid reflection remains. The sense world is intimate and inseparable from immediate experience. There's no more chasing, seeking, trying to find the way out of the house of mirrors. It's clear that every mirror (thought) in that accursed house was always just a reflection of what you are. The beauty of this is that it doesn't matter how far into that reflection stream you appear to be; the moment you recognize your identity as the capacity to reflect and the purely conscious "stuff" that makes up everything, the whole struggle instantly vanishes.

The takeaway in this section is that the definition above, while not the only way of defining thought, is experientially accurate. If it's still not clear, or you have doubts about this definition, the best way to proceed is to do the thought experiments described above with various thoughts until things become clearer.

Litmus Test

When working with people at various stages of realization, I find myself frequently repeating one simple but particularly important statement concerning thought. It will sound so simple that it might seem absurd at first. Its potency isn't in its profundity as a statement, but in its power when applied directly to one's immediate experience. Interestingly, its potency and importance grow the further along people are in the realization process. Specifically, it is a sort of litmus test. Because of the slippery nature of thought and identity, and the evolution of one's relationship with thought throughout the awakening process, it can be immensely helpful to have a simple litmus test to determine if something you are experiencing is a thought or if it's something in present experience. This is particularly useful when we find ourselves ruminating. Here is the litmus test:

Can you write it down in words?
If you can, then it's a thought.

Because of its simplicity and because it's easy to overlook the importance of this litmus test, I will illustrate with an example. Imagine you and I are sitting in a room together. Then you say, "My partner is going to come home in ten minutes, and I know he's going to be in a bad mood." Depending on the situation, I might respond in one of several ways. In the context we are speaking about here, I might point out that what you just said is a thought. The image of your partner walking through the door and the look on his face betraying his foul mood are not real in the same way that the couch you are sitting on in that moment is real. The argument that you imagine you might get into after he arrives, and the harsh words exchanged between the two of you are not in immediate experience in the same way that the color of your shoes and the sound of the birds outside are.

It is imperative that I point out that I am not invalidating the mere fact that you are having that internal experience. I'm not suggesting that those thoughts aren't relevant, nor am I suggesting we try to avoid the experience of the thought. I'm also not discounting that the thought might have some importance or relevance. Perhaps you are in an abusive relationship and that thought is a pointer to a deeper part of you. It might be pointing to an emotion such as fear that is trying to tell you something isn't right with the situation. We will talk about all of this in later chapters. What I am saying here is that it's important to recognize that what you are experiencing is indeed a thought. In that moment, your partner is not in the room. In that moment, the future you are imagining is not occurring, not in the same way that the events in the room you and I are sitting in are occurring, right?

I'm pointing out that what is being experienced is a thought and not the content of the thought. A thought is in your direct experience, just as the sensations in your hands and the feeling of breath entering and leaving the body are. You see everything in the Universe simply wants to be seen as what it is. When a thought is recognized as what it is, we are honoring its nature, and thus its presence becomes a gateway to our immediate and direct experience. In the scenario described above, you had me sitting with you, annoying you, pointing out that the narrative about your partner coming home was a thought. But what about when you are alone, lost in thought, ruminating, etc.? Well in those moments it can be quite helpful to have a simple tool you can apply to determine whether what you are experiencing is a thought or if it is a direct sensory experience. So if you find yourself ruminating, or feel that a certain loop of thought is playing out over and over in your mind, you can use this litmus test.

*"We are powerfully imprisoned in these Dark Ages
simply by the terms in which we have been
conditioned to think."*

—*Buckminster Fuller*

I'll give you an example of how this might play out. Imagine you are at home on a Saturday morning. The week's responsibilities are behind you, and now you just want to relax. What seems to be getting in your way of relaxation is a memory of a short exchange with your boss that occurred on Friday afternoon. She had called your attention to a mistake you had made. While you weren't averse to admitting the mistake, you were taken aback by her harsh tone and her proclamation that "this is unacceptable." You pride yourself on doing good work, and you can't remember the last time your boss brought an error to your attention. You wish you could just let this go, but the memory of her harsh words keeps replaying in your mind. As well, you keep recalling the image of her face and her apparent upset, which seemed overblown for the issue at hand. As you sit in your house on Saturday morning drinking coffee and this memory stirs in your mind, you realize this may be a good time to apply the litmus test. You decide to do so. You recall the harsh words, This is unacceptable. You remind yourself that these are internal words you are repeating. You could write them down. Okay, so now you recognize this is a thought. You notice a slight bit of relief. You start to come back a bit into the present. It's Saturday, and you are in your kitchen drinking delicious coffee. It's not Friday, and you are not staring into the upset face of your boss. You give a giggle and feel a bit more relaxed.

Then the next thought comes, But that was unfair. I didn't deserve it! This is followed by another thought, Oh no, the thoughts are back, and they are ruining my Saturday. I wanted to relax. Then you remember, Oh! If I can write it down, then it's a thought. You realize that these last two statements were actually thoughts. Oh, another thought, then another. Now you start to look around. You feel your feet against the floor. You notice your breath moving gently in and out. Then the coffee again! You look toward the window and see a robin hopping across the ground. For a moment that robin felt so close. Had you ever seen such bright colors on a robin's chest? Then a thought comes, Wait a minute, it's not this easy. If I just stay present and ignore my thoughts, then how will I deal with the problems of life? How will I make sure I'm not being taken advantage of? For a second your attention is jerked back to work and your boss. Then you remember, Oh, if I can write that out, then it is another thought! Then you acknowledge, This is a thought right here, right now. The thought is here; this table is here. This coffee and the beautiful robin are here.

In this way you are seeing things as they are. Sounds, colors, shapes, and sensations are always immediate and clearly present. They don't need descriptions to be what they are. A thought, when recognized as a thought, is this way as well. Everything just wants to be experienced as what it is.

Observing Thoughts in Real Time

In the last section we did a bit of inquiry. We explored how becoming aware of thoughts as such can quickly lead us into presence. In the example above, presence was the flavor of the coffee, the feeling of the breath, the colors of the robin. This section will focus specifically on the practice of observing thoughts. We will go in-depth on the dynamics of this practice, discuss pointers on how to apply it, and explore examples of how this application might look.

Of the many contemplations and inquiries offered in this book, this one is one of the most potent, especially as a stand-alone practice. If you did nothing but apply this technique with sincerity and ruthless willingness to see the truth of your immediate experience, it alone could take you all the way to liberation. I know this because I have known people for whom this has been the case.

You can apply this practice anytime. During silent sitting or meditation is a wonderful time to practice in this way. You can also take up this investigation whenever you have some idle time, even a few moments. Perhaps you'll think of this when you are sitting around with some free time and out of habit reach for your smartphone. Instead of thumb-jockeying through social media or the internet, you might decide to put down the phone and spend a few minutes observing thoughts. Many other times throughout the day can be opportune for observing thoughts. Here are a few examples:

➤ While waiting on hold on the phone: This is such a waste of time. You can recognize "Oh! That is a thought!" Then you realize that this wasn't so much a waste of time. Indeed, it was an opportunity to identify thought and thus bring a bit more presence into your experience.

➤ While waiting in traffic: I can't wait to get home and see my kids. I'm also hungry. In that moment you might recognize, "Oh, those are thoughts." The focus is shifted a bit from the thought world of "later" to the senses in your immediate experience, such as the sound of the radio, or the feeling of your hands on the steering wheel. Now you might not have quite as much FOMO (fear of missing out). You begin to recognize this moment isn't so bad after all once you've turned your attention to it.

➤ When you are ruminating: Here I am again thinking about the same problem that I have been thinking about for months. What am I going to do to finally solve it? You might recognize "Aha! That's another thought I'm paying attention to there. Here I am in this room, with these sensations, sounds, and sights. There is also the sense of this thought. But seeing that it is a thought, I recognize that the long history of ruminating on this issue isn't here in the same way that my immediate sensory experience is. The thought is here, but the content of the thought is not." You might now feel a little more presence and a little bit more relaxation in the body.

➤ When you're remembering a painful or traumatic event: If someone spoke harshly to you or insulted you, you might feel like it's happening to you again in this moment. You might then remember, "Oh, this is a thought." In that recognition, you realize the harsh treatment is not happening to you right now in the same way that the feeling of sitting on the couch and the hearing sounds in the room are happening. I will add that this shouldn't be taken to mean that the sensations in the body such as the belly, chest, or neck aren't happening in this moment, because if they are felt, then they are in present experience. So if the next thought says, That didn't work because I still feel the pain in my body, you can recognize again: "Oh, that is also a thought!" Now your attention is back in your current experience with the sounds, sights, and sensations in the body immediately available to you.

As these examples illustrate, there are many instances in which a moment of recognition will cause a shift from being dragged along by a thought or stream of thoughts to being back in your current experience. The technique of observing thoughts in real time is quite simple. If you follow these steps you can't fail:

1. Take a moment to become aware of your surroundings. Listen to the noises. Feel the body sensations in the feet, hands, and face. Feel the breath moving in and out.

2. Tell yourself that for these few minutes, the only thing you are interested in is observing thoughts.

3. Now turn your attention to the thought-space, wherever that is.

4. Peer into that thought-space like you're peering into a fishpond to get a glimpse of a beautiful fish. This is an analogy; you needn't picture an actual pond.

5. Stop actively thinking and watch for the next discernable thought.

6. It can help to simultaneously notice the quietude between the thoughts or in the waiting period before a thought begins. Often a thought is noticed in contrast to that quietude.

7. As soon as the thought starts to form or is fully formed, give it your attention. If it is an auditory or language thought, try to clarify what it is saying.

8. If the thought is an image thought, try to clarify or sharpen that image for a moment so that it is clear and obvious what it is.

9. Now let the thought go and immediately return to step number four.

Simple, right? How did it go for you? Let's look at an example of how this might play out. Let's assume I've performed steps one through three. I'll start with number four. In brackets I will put experiential narrative that is not a thought.

[peering into thought space]

[quietude, spontaneous movement of attention]

I wonder if I'll notice the thought when it comes.

Oh, that was the thought!

[starting again at number four]

[silence]

[some background ear-ringing]

I wonder if I'm doing this right.

Oh, that was the thought!

[starting again at number four]

[silence]

[Image of friend forms in my mind, along with a recent hike we went on together.]

[viewing thought image for a moment]

[starting again at number four]

[quietude]

[awake observing and flowing, no thoughts]

This is becoming peaceful.

Oh, that was the thought!

That's it. The exercise is as simple as that. If you find this enjoyable or informative, you can add other steps to the process. One step would be to write each thought down before letting it go. Another would be right before letting a thought go, check in with your body sensations. See if there is an associated sensation or feeling accompanying that thought. Another possibility would be to ask yourself the question, "Do I believe this thought?" See if some thoughts feel more true or more self-defining than others. Lastly, once it is clear that you are oriented toward thought instead of in an evaluative mode with thought, see if you can't begin to close the gap between what feels like you that is conscious, and the thought itself. This is best done gently and patiently. Here are a few pointers that will help make this process simple, enjoyable, and effective:

> It's best to do this in a relaxed way. See if you are able to approach this exercise from a relaxed sense inside your body, or even the space around your body. It is as if that relaxed space itself is what is doing the investigation. If this doesn't resonate with you right now, that is totally fine. Just recognize thoughts in whatever way seems natural to you. Over time, you might find a way to approach this in a more relaxed manner that feels simple and natural to you.

> There's no need to apply any force to this exercise or to thoughts themselves. If you feel like you are pushing against or fighting with thoughts, it's best to just relax and try this exercise at another time. Force is not required and can be counterproductive.

> The presence of any single thought, or thoughts in general, is never a problem, nor does it represent a failure. It doesn't mean you are unenlightened. It doesn't mean you are undisciplined. It says nothing about your progress when it comes to realization. So please don't judge yourself for recognizing there are thoughts, or that you were lost in thought. If anything, you should congratulate yourself for becoming aware of the thoughts as thoughts in that moment. Once we recognize that we were in a thought pattern, another thought will often come along and say something like, Oh, too bad you're still having all those thoughts. Here is your opportunity! You know what I'm going to say, right? That's right, this is just another thought. One single thought. It's no worse and no better than any other

thought. Recognize that and you are right back in your immediate experience—in presence.

➤ Don't expect immediate results. There are times when doing this will feel enjoyable and peaceful. It can feel like a huge release to let go of something you've been ruminating on. On the other hand, we aren't doing this to eliminate thoughts or to make anything go away. We are doing it to become clearer and more authentic about what is actually happening in a given moment. Sometimes this practice doesn't lead to immediate relaxation or the experience of vivid presence. That's perfectly okay; that's not its purpose. Its purpose is to see clearly that a thought is a thought, nothing more. It can take some time doing this to really start to feel like you are shifting into presence. So instead of constantly looking for results, I suggest learning to enjoy the process itself; the immediacy of it and the sincerity of it. Even if it feels dry at times, or sometimes brings uncomfortable feelings to the surface, this work is very potent. The effects occur deep in your identity structures, so trust and patience are prudent here.

➤ Consider establishing a regular practice. Even if you only do it for a few minutes daily, it's good to just to get into the habit of it. You could set a reminder to do this once or twice daily.

➤ You may find your own way of doing this investigation. I recommend trying to find inquiries and investigations that feel natural and relevant to you. As long as you maintain the spirit of this practice (to recognize a thought as a thought in the immediate), I think tailoring it to your own style and preferences is a great way to practice.

➤ Treat all thoughts equally. One of the effects of this exercise is you start to intuitively recognize thoughts as no problem, nothing to be alarmed about. Thus, you feel far less vigilant about paying attention to thoughts as if your life depended on it. One of the insights that make this possible is the recognition that no one thought has any more or less importance than any other thought. Feel into things as you continue this practice and see if you don't start to see the significance of this sameness, this equanimity. The content of thoughts will vary, of course, but the presence of thought (the "stuff" thoughts are made out of) will begin to have a certain familiarity and sameness to you. Recognizing this takes you out of the hot seat in a sense. You no longer have to remain constantly vigilant to thoughts and evaluate each one for its significance based on its content. It's more like a relaxed but alert interest when we are in immediate recognition of this.

➤ Don't create distance. This one is particularly important and tends to be counterintuitive. When we de-identify from a thought, which means recognize a thought as a thought, we sometimes tend to want to distance ourselves from it. Sometimes we imagine some vast empty space free of thoughts or thought objects, and without realizing it, we make this image a goal or an expectation of what de-identifying from thoughts should look like. This ends up forming a different kind of thought. Instead, when we de-identify we have the opportunity to turn our attention to the presence available in the immediate sense field.

Move Toward not Away From

One of the side effects of this practice, as described in the previous section, is that we often tend to distance ourselves from thoughts as we de-identify from them. This tendency manifests in different ways at different stages of realization. More precisely, when we are identified with thoughts, we are always holding a certain amount of distance between the seeming subject "me" and the thought object. The moment we de-identify, we have dissolved part of our relationship with the thought object (the belief), but the "distancing" often remains. So, the next step is to close that gap—to move toward not away from. This is an intimate and tactile sort of experience, not so much an intellectual or logical one.

There are many aspects of realization that are difficult to talk about, but this specifically I find to be one of the most challenging to convey. Ironically, this moving toward is not hard to do once you get the feel of it. The reason it's difficult to communicate isn't because it's complicated or because you have to have reached some special level of enlightenment to "get it." It's nothing like that. It's challenging to talk about because it's so close and so simple. We overlook it all the time, in fact. When I work one on one with someone on this, it usually takes a few minutes of back-and-forth exchanges, and they will often say something like, "Oh that! I know exactly what you mean now." It's as if they've remembered something they'd misplaced some time ago. The challenge in writing it in a book is I don't have the back and forth with you. I'll do my best to demonstrate this through an example. Let's say you and I are talking, and I tell you to simply become aware of your thoughts as they occur to you. You begin to examine your thoughts. Perhaps the first thought that comes is:

I'm not sure what he's asking me to do.

Oh, that's a thought!

[then quiet . . . sounds in room . . .]

I see how this can be peaceful.

Oh, that's a thought.

[quiet curiosity]

I wonder when the next thought will . . . ?

Oh, that's another thought.

[. . .]

As you go about this practice of observing of thoughts, there can be two "tones" to the feel of what you're doing. One tone is something like a hesitation tone. It's as if the moment you recognize a thought, some effort is introduced to make distance from that thought. Like you are trying to push your attention into some bare, thoughtless state. This is something like a suspicion about or mistrust of thoughts themselves. Would it surprise you to hear that this is often our default tone regarding thoughts?

The other tone is the opposite. It could be called a curiosity tone or even a fascination tone. It's as if the moment you recognize a thought as a thought, there is a familiarity with the thought form (remember the sameness), and you actually move toward it. Whereas the move away requires a bit of energy, this is an effortless movement. It might also feel like the thought merges into you, into the center of the aware part of you that just recognized the thought. This is like a coming home. It's intimate. It's an invitation and acceptance. Anything you wholeheartedly welcome will not harm you; indeed, it will liberate you. This tone is the one I recommend leaning toward. It can become quite enjoyable with practice. There are times when this can even become one of the most enjoyable things you've ever experienced.

Situational Advice

In this section we will discuss various situations involving thoughts that are often challenging. Then we will discuss specific strategies that may be helpful in those situations.

281

While Meditating

The most common comment I hear from people when they first learn to meditate is something along the lines of, "I feel like I'm bad at meditating. When I close my eyes for a couple of minutes, I'm bombarded with thoughts." My advice for this is simple: Accept it. Everyone experiences this. It's not a sign you are meditating incorrectly, nor is it a sign that you aren't making progress. In fact, it's exactly what's supposed to happen.

In the previous section we discussed a practice whose purpose is to actively de-identify from thought. During meditation we also de-identify from thought, but instead of doing it actively, we are passively de-identifying. Whenever we meditate there will be a spontaneous shift from being carried along by the thought stream to watching the thought stream as it flows by. This can happen gradually, or it can happen rapidly, but it will always occur during meditation to one degree or another. I'll use an analogy that might make this clearer. Imagine you are on a raft in the middle of a river. You are being carried along with the current. If you only observe the water and not the shore moving past, you will have no way of knowing whether the water is moving slowly or rapidly, nor would you be able to judge the volume of water being carried downstream. Now if your perspective were to shift, and you found yourself anchored to the shore, you would observe the water moving rapidly past you on a constant basis, and thus you could appreciate the rate of flow. You would be acutely aware of the massive volume of water moving past you. This shift in perspective is exactly what happens during meditation. When we begin to meditate, there aren't suddenly more thoughts. There is a shift in perception, and we become far more aware of the thoughts that were already there. Most importantly, we become aware of them as thoughts. This passive de-identification is quite valuable and requires no doing or technique to have a beneficial effect. It can be surprising how many thoughts are flowing through our mental stream as our perspective shifts during meditation. This understanding and acceptance of the phenomenon can have a

282

profound relaxing effect on the whole process once we realize nothing has gone wrong. Approach:

➤ Recognize that sometimes during meditation you will experience a lot of thoughts.

➤ If this happens, remind yourself this is perfectly normal and a natural part of the meditation process.

➤ Remember that there is no need to pay specific attention to any particular thought or thoughts as a whole. There is no need to evaluate or manage thoughts during meditation, just let them flow naturally and innocently.

When a Thought Feels Invasive

Sometimes a thought, memory, or image keeps asserting itself no matter how much we would prefer not to have it in our experience. In fact, when we try to avoid it or push it away, we often find that it comes back with vigor. The first thing to know about this is that resistance to the thought, image, or memory is exactly what keeps it coming back in a way that feels invasive. You've probably heard the saying, "What you resist persists." Well, when it comes to thought, this is exactly how it goes. So when a thought feels invasive or unwanted, the first thing to do is ask, "Am I adding resistance to this experience?" If you sense that you are adding resistance, then great, you've uncovered the key to the problem. The moment that we recognize we're resisting a thought, mental image, or memory, we have recognized that there is another thought lurking in the shadows. This hidden thought is what keeps "pushing against" the unwanted thought and keeping it prominent in our mind.

To illustrate, imagine you are standing face-to-face with another person with your arms are outstretched in such a way that your palms are firmly pressed against their palms. Now imagine that each of you has been incrementally moving your feet away from one another such that your upper bodies are leaning more and more toward each other. After a time, you will each be supporting the other and you will notice a large amount of pressure on the palms of your hands. Now if you suddenly forgot how you got into this position and did not clearly see and appreciate the physical arrangement keeping both bodies supported, you might wonder, Why in the heck is this person leaning so heavily on me? It's taking so much strength to resist them. I wish they weren't there. If you were to suddenly come to your senses and realize what was actually going on, you'd see that your limited perspective was the real problem. Because you weren't considering the nature of the two bodies pushing against (resisting) one another, it appeared as if you were being imposed upon. In actuality, you were as much responsible for the pressure and leaning as the other person was. Moreover, you were making it possible for them to be able to continue to apply this pressure and vice versa. When you stop leaning on them, they will have to stop leaning on you. This is exactly what happens when we find the hidden thought through investigating resistance. So, what is this hidden thought? The thought is:

That thought, image, or memory shouldn't be there.

Let's look at an example. Say I'm going about my workday at the office and suddenly an embarrassing memory comes into my mind. I might try to push it away, or I might even tell myself, "I don't want to think about that right now!" Of course, that doesn't work, and a moment later the image comes back stronger than before. It's an embarrassing image, so I don't really want to think about it, but it involves an "event" at the office Christmas party that occurred last Saturday. I went to the party dressed as a moose, and after a few glasses of eggnog I treated everyone to my impression of a moose running through the forest bugling mating calls. Now while that was funny to everyone at the time, and even seems to be providing some continued entertainment in the form suppressed snickers around the office when people are in the same room as me, I can't seem to find the humor in it when the memory invites itself back into my consciousness. What I actually feel is a combination of sheer embarrassment and dread.

So, what can I do instead of endlessly trying to push the memory away, replace it with another thought, or distract myself? Well, I might decide to stop and fully investigate the experience. I inquire, "Okay, what is it that's really bothering me?" I recognize immediately that this embarrassing thought keeps reliving itself in my mind. Then I ask, "Am I adding any resistance to this experience?" After a few moments of quiet contemplation, the answer comes intuitively—yes. I can feel it. Although it's a vague feeling at first, it's clear that I'm resisting this experience. Then I ask, "What hidden thought represents this experience of resistance?" When I sit with this question for a moment, it becomes clear that there is a thought here as well that says, "I should not have to relive this memory. That thought shouldn't be here." I sit there for a minute and move my attention from one thought to the next and then back. One is a thought image of my moose impression, and one is a thought that says, "That thought shouldn't be there." It strikes me as funny that two thoughts seem to be pushing against one another and that this feeling of resistance, of "this is not okay," seems to arise from the pushing dynamic and is not seeing the full perspective. As I allow both thoughts to be exactly as they are, suddenly the whole experience relaxes. The image of my moose impression is now in perspective. Sure, it was a silly thing to do, and I might not have done it sober, nor will I likely repeat it, but it gave people a laugh (including me) so what's the big deal? No harm done. That thought can be here; it has no charge anymore. And the resistance thought that says, "That other thought shouldn't be here" has now calmed down considerably. It doesn't feel compelling like it did a few minutes ago. It doesn't feel like I have an urgent need to do something about it. I can now see that thought in perspective as well. It's a simple misunderstanding. The thought states that

"that other thought shouldn't be there," but in reality, that other thought was already there so the resistance thought was more like a reaction to the first thought. Of course, it was okay for that first thought to be there because it already was there. It's okay for any thought to be here. Thoughts don't cause any trouble unless we don't examine them clearly and recognize them for what they are.

Approach:

➤ When an uncomfortable or invasive thought asserts itself, begin by asking, "Am I adding resistance to this experience?"

➤ Look for the hidden thought. You might try to formulate a statement about what the resistance in that moment might say if it had a voice. Another approach is asking, "What are my ideas or conclusions about the presence of those uncomfortable thoughts, images, or memories?" The answer is often something like, "This shouldn't be here," or "I hate this," or "I wish this had never happened," or "I would be in peace right now if it weren't for having to think about _____."

➤ Once you formulate that statement (hidden resistance thought), it is helpful to ask yourself, "Do I feel any resistance to this statement or viewpoint as well?" You might be surprised; often it is the case that we are feeling resistance both to the invasive thought and to the thoughts that say it shouldn't be there. This sense of resistance resisting resistance can really seem to cement these patterns if we don't take the time to look clearly at what's happening.

➤

If you follow the steps outlined above, you will be surprised how much of this can relax and dissolve. Be patient. These patterns weren't established overnight, and they don't resolve themselves overnight. If you work sincerely and with a willingness to simply see

286

things as they are, and then accept these previously unseen thoughts, impressions, and tendencies, things will soften more and more.

Another approach that can be helpful in the case of invasive thoughts is to speak directly to the thought itself. This approach is quite simple, but at first it can be counterintuitive. When a painful or recurring thought pattern occurs, try speaking directly to and assure it that it is perfectly welcome in your experience right now. This may feel awkward the first few times you do it because through habit we are usually inclined to do anything but accept an uncomfortable thought. You may even feel like you are being disingenuous for a time. With a little persistence and a willingness to speak from the heart as much as possible, you might be pleasantly surprised how quickly things can turn around. As I said earlier, everything in the universe just wants to be what it is. Well, difficult thought patterns are no different. They just want to be what they are. So, we can assure the thought or image, "You're welcome here. Please take the time and space you need to express yourself. Come and go as you feel is necessary. You can have my attention when you are here." Often when we do this, another thought will arrive soon after and it will say, "Wait! If I invite that one in, then what if it never leaves? What if I suffer forever?" You know what I'm going to say, right? That's right. Now that that thought has arrived, it needs your attention. These habituated thought patterns have life force. If you acknowledge their presence and give them permission to be what they are, they will stop being any kind of trouble for you. So, to this thought I might say, "Hello fear, hello alarm, I'm glad you've come to help. Thank you for being here. Please, make yourself at home. You have this space. You have my attention. Stay as long as you want." This can be called "self-parenting." If you make the decision to no longer abandon these little bits of life force that are searching for acceptance and a home, you might be pleasantly surprised how enjoyable and intimate this experience can become.

Thoughts Associated with Emotions

In the emotions chapter, we will delve deeply into the subject of feelings and emotions. For now, I want to give a few simple pointers for when we experience thoughts that are associated with or feel intertwined with emotions.

A simple and practical way to think about emotion is to look at it as a way station between the world of thought and the world of sensory experience. As such, we can say that emotions exist on a broad spectrum of experience. One end of that spectrum is represented by conceptual thought, internal dialogue, and personal narrative. The middle of the spectrum is characterized by various gradients of emotion. The other end of this spectrum is represented by pure sensory experience (body sensations). When we notice a thought or an internal dialogue associated with an emotion, our attention is somewhere on this spectrum. To be precise it is often moving between different points on the spectrum. As our attention moves from one area to another, feelings of ambivalence, confusion or disorientation can arise. We may feel as if we are being pulled in two directions at the same time. We may wonder which is more important to pay attention to, the sensation/feeling aspect or the storyline/thought aspect.

Well, first of all, when we recognize that the thought and the feeling are on a continuum or spectrum, we see that they aren't actually two things. This alone can give us some relief because we see that there is not some big decision to make about where to put our attention. We can trust the natural movement of attention even if it seems to move erratically at times. When our attention bounces back and forth between thought and emotion, it can feel a bit like a balance scale that has been disturbed and swings back and forth for some time before finding its natural equilibrium. This type of experience is common in emotionally charged situations. When it occurs, we have a great opportunity to learn a lot about our internal processes. If we observe with genuine curiosity and some patience, we find that at some moments our attention is more toward the feeling end of the spectrum, and at other moments it is more toward the thought end. We can remind ourselves that neither are wrong. Both have their place, and both are ultimately of the same essence.

When we recognize these movements, we can apply what we learned in the previous sections. We can ask ourselves, "Am I resisting either the thoughts or the feelings/sensations here?" Additionally, we can inquire, "Am I resisting the natural movement of attention from one end of the spectrum to the other?" If we find there is some resistance being introduced, we can apply the approaches described above to ease the resistance.

The self-parenting approach also works well in this situation. Let's run through a scenario. Perhaps you've had a recent disappointment or loss in your life. You are feeling some conflicted emotions and also feel like you are wrestling with your thoughts about these events. You might decide to try the self-parenting approach. You say out loud or quietly inside, "Sadness, you are welcome here. I can feel you in my body and I'm welcoming the sensation. You have a right to be here. I recognize you as a life form, and I see that all you want to do is be what you are. You can stay as long as you need to." You relax a bit and recognize that just directly feeling the sensation called sadness can be peaceful, even enjoyable. Then a thought might come, "But I can't just wallow in self-pity, I need to go live my life, not lay in bed feeling unhappy." Then you can welcome that shift from emotion to thought, remembering they are on the same spectrum, somewhat like the same life form showing you two different sides of itself. Staying true to your commitment to address your experience directly and with compassion, you continue: "You are welcome to shift as you feel is most natural to you. I trust your intuition and intelligence about where attention is most needed in this moment. Furthermore, I understand and recognize this thought and this narrative. It has a right to be here as well. It has its place. Welcome thought, I understand your concerns, stay as long as you need to. I will give you space to breathe."

Thought Storms

Thought patterns can be a lot like weather patterns. Sometimes things are calm and there are only a few thought clouds drifting effortlessly across the sky. Other times thoughts are coming so fast we can't make heads or tails of things. We can feel like we're truly caught up in a thought storm. We can't even get a foothold on a single thought to see what it's about and then another comes racing in, and then another, and then another. If you ever find yourself in this situation, here are a few suggestions to help you weather the storm.

➤ First of all, it is helpful to simply acknowledge what's going on. "Oh, this is a thought storm." Recognizing it as such and realizing that, like any weather event, this will come and go can help tremendously.

➤ Next, remind yourself, "Thoughts aren't going to hurt me even if they come faster than I'm comfortable with." Let them come. Let them come by the hundreds, thousands, millions— so what?

➤ Remind yourself, "I don't have to resist the thought storm, nor do I have to try to pay attention to any one thought. If they come so fast that I can't even tell what they are, then that's completely okay."

➤ Try to find a quiet and relaxing environment to settle into. Take a bath. Sit on your porch. Relax on the couch in a comfortable room with no distractions. Listen to soothing music. Take a walk in the woods. When you do move to a more relaxed environment, remind yourself that you didn't do this to make the thought storm go away. It doesn't have to go away. You are just putting yourself in a safe and relaxing environment for the thought storm to express itself.

➤ If it feels natural to move your body in intuitive ways, then do so while still giving some attention to the thoughts. Sometimes there is an unnoticed restlessness in the body during thought storms, and moving in intuitive ways can help harmonize that restless energy with the environment.

➤ Sometimes a bit of investigation into specific thoughts about the thought storm can be helpful. You might ask, "Okay, there are countless thoughts and they are coming fast, but what are my thoughts about this experience? What is making me uncomfortable about this?" You might notice thoughts such as: I can't handle this. If this goes on, I might go crazy. I can't think straight right now. I need to pay attention to these thoughts to orient myself. I understand that these can be uncomfortable thoughts, but when we recognize them as thoughts, we see they are just wisps of air in the larger weather pattern of the thought storm.

➤ If you approach the thought storm in these ways, you might be pleasantly surprised that like any storm, a thought storm can even become enjoyable. There will be times when you can even ride the waves of thought-consciousness, a truly sublime experience.

Disturbing or Obsessive Thoughts

Although it's not something most people talk about, everyone has disturbing thoughts at times. Sometimes they are associated with a strong emotion, such as a child having the thought, I wish she was dead about his mother when he is angry. Or when an adult has been insulted or embarrassed by another person and thoughts come of the offender being in a car accident or dying in their sleep. Other times disturbing thoughts come out of nowhere. You might be attending to the tasks of the day when suddenly a thought comes through your mind of hitting someone with a blunt object for no apparent reason. Years ago, Jim Carrey did a great stand-up bit about this. I'm paraphrasing, but he said it was a good thing that we don't actually do everything we think about. While shaving in the mirror we don't decide to cut our own throat, and we don't decide to turn into oncoming traffic while driving. Because Jim can make just about anything funny, he was able to make light of something that most of us never talk about, and if we do it's to a therapist. There is a lot of shame around some thoughts, as if they say something about our character. Luckily, they don't. A thought is a thought. They come spontaneously and are produced in mass quantities on a daily basis. As was mentioned in an earlier section, no one thought is any better or worse than any other.

It's important to point out that I'm making a clear distinction between thoughts and actions. To carry out a violent thought is, of course, not okay. If you have the desire or plan to carry out a violent thought against yourself or another, please seek help. There is a lot that can be done to assist you. What I'm talking about here are thoughts that simply come upon you and are recognized as thoughts. We might have a visceral reaction to them if they are of a disturbing nature. Here are a few pointers:

➤ Having a violent or disturbing thought doesn't say anything negative about your character. Everyone has them, and they cause no real harm. Like any other thought, they come and go like clouds forming and dissipating in the sky.

➤ If a disturbing or violent thought arises, then notice, "Oh, that's a thought." Let it be there. If you don't push against it or try to will it away, it will dissipate. If it returns, so be it. Over time, thoughts that we don't add charge to by trying to push them away will return less and less frequently. The point is to not make a big deal about it.

➤ Remind yourself that there is a big difference between observing a thought and acting out the content of that thought. If you find a thought disturbing and are afraid that simply having that thought might make you act it out, then that is a good sign that it is not in your character to do so. Here is an analogy to clarify this distinction. Imagine watching a violent scene in a movie. Perhaps someone murders another person in the scene. You might recoil internally and think, Wow, that's horrible. The very fact that you had a visceral reaction to that scene tells me that that kind of violence is against your nature. You experiencing a reaction of recoil to that violence makes it clear to me that you aren't going to go out and reproduce the violence in real life. The scene was simply something you observed, as was the violent thought. Recoiling in horror is quite a different reaction than watching a violent scene in a movie and deciding you want to go act out that violence in real life.

➤ If disturbing thoughts are recurrent and are negatively impacting your ability to function in day-to-day life and none of these suggestions help, then you might want to consider talking to a therapist. There are more targeted therapies for obsessive patterns that may be helpful to you.

Thoughts During Activity

Although thoughts are nearly constant companions to us, there are times when they quiet down or cease altogether. During activity, especially strenuous activity or activity requiring intense concentration, thoughts tend to calm down quite a bit. It's common that endurance athletes will experience a peaceful thoughtless state at times during intense exertion. Many describe this as meditative, having a peak experience, being "in the zone," or experiencing "flow." If you've had any of these experiences, you know how peaceful and enjoyable a thought-free or nearly thought-free state can be. These glimpses are but a mere taste of what occurs during an awakening. These are episodic and experiential, whereas awakening is a shift into that vastness, peace, flow, and equanimity at the identity level. If a peak experience is a 3/10, then awakening is a 10/10. Unfortunately, extreme physical exertion doesn't lead to awakening and liberation or all extreme athletes would be liberated.

Extreme athleticism aside, there are many other tasks and activities that quiet thoughts. Anything that requires focus or our attention to be in the senses tends to quiet the mind. This is why crafts such as knitting or modeling, or arts such as playing an instrument or painting can be so peaceful and enjoyable. However, if you look closely at your experience, you may find that even during these types of activities there are often thoughts churning in the background. You might notice that you are generally focused on the task at hand but in sort of a daydreamy way. You also might find you are thinking about things other than what is going on in the immediate. In this instance it can be helpful to thank your mind for doing its job of producing thoughts. It does its job very well. Then see if you can't "lean in" to the task a bit. Specifically, into the senses associated with the task.

Let's say you are building something. You've purchased a bookcase and are putting it together when you notice you are daydreaming about a discussion you want to have with your girlfriend the next time you see her. You realize that there's really no pressing need to think about this at this moment and decide to try leaning into the task at hand. As you pick up a screwdriver, you put your attention into the actual feeling of the cool plastic in your hand. You also notice the sensation of your feet on the floor. As you apply the tool to a screw, you notice the tension required to twist the screwdriver. You look closer at the screw and the surface through which it is moving. You notice the wood grain, the color patterns of the wood, and the metallic sheen of the hardware. Then you put the screwdriver down and reach for the instructions. As you transition between tasks, you notice some tension in your jaw, then feel a breath enter the body a little more clearly than you'd felt the previous one. You feel a sense of relaxation cascade down the body and into the legs as you exhale. When you pick up the instructions, you do so more slowly and with renewed interest, almost as if you can't wait for this next sensory experience. The shapes of the letters on the page, the sharp contrast between the ink on the page and the stark white of the paper look a little more vivid than before. You start to recognize a shimmering . . . but where? You can't even locate it because it's sort of inside and outside. It's in the wood, the paper, the hands. The sound of the music comes to you; it permeates and dances through the experience. Your attention moves into the sound as you watch your hands effortlessly reach for the next bracket and begin to attach it. The wood grain, the notes, the breath, the sensations in the hands and the face are all now becoming more vivid and alive. They are starting to commingle, it seems.

That is how you lean in. You can do this anywhere and anytime you have access to the senses, which is always.

Chapter 13:

Beliefs

Introduction

I mentioned in the second chapter that when it comes to waking up, being unwilling to examine and/or let go of beliefs will make the process quite challenging. This is because a refusal to question one's beliefs is tantamount to saying, "You know, I'm perfectly comfortable in the world of mind-identification. I like my illusions. I'm comfortable with them, and I'm not willing to risk change or discomfort to dispel any of them even if they cause me or others to suffer." If we aren't willing to examine the belief structures that bind our identity into the conceptual realm, and do so with some scrutiny, we won't get far. On the other hand, if we are willing to investigate all of our beliefs, especially the ones about ourselves and about reality, this process needn't take too long. The people that I see wake up the fastest are those who are willing to ruthlessly expose, examine, and let go of their obstructing beliefs, no matter how uncomfortable that process is.

What Is a Belief?

For purposes of this discussion, the usual meaning of belief will suffice. We don't need to adopt an esoteric definition to proceed. A common definition of belief is "an acceptance that a statement is true or that something exists." We can start there.

A Belief Is Essentially a Thought

Once we are able to clearly see and state the nature of one of our beliefs, it can be considered and treated as a thought, generally speaking. It could be said that all beliefs are thoughts, but not all thoughts are beliefs.

A Belief Is Partially or Fully Hidden

One distinction that differentiates a belief from a mere thought is that a belief has some hidden aspect to it. Depending on the specific belief, we may be partially aware or completely unaware that we hold the belief. There are two basic reasons a belief can be hidden from our awareness. One is that we never even considered that we held such a belief in the first place. A common circumstance where this occurs is when we have an overarching belief that is overt, and we "use" that belief to hide a deeper (often opposite) belief from ourselves. When this deeper belief is revealed, we are often dismayed because we'd had ourselves convinced that we actually believed the opposite. This occurs in many facets of our internal experience. One common area is in the realm of self-esteem and confidence. For example, someone might believe they have a high self-esteem and act outwardly confidant based on that superficial belief. However, if that person is willing to really dig in and get to the root of their belief structures around self-esteem and associated emotional blocks, they will often find some degree of self-doubt. The more primary underlying belief (the one driving self-defeating behaviors and cognitive dissonance) is that they aren't confident enough to handle the eventualities of life and aren't worthy in general.

The second situation in which beliefs remain hidden to us is when they are so fundamental to our views of reality that we wouldn't even consider questioning them. This tends to be true of our most deep-seated beliefs that are at the root of networks of more superficial beliefs. For example, consider the belief, "I am separate from that table over there." It's so taken for granted and frequently assumed in our communication, thinking, and experience that it would seem absurd to question that it could be anything other than true. On a side note, these "root" beliefs that seem absurd to question turn out to be the beliefs whose dissolution leads to incredible degrees of freedom and intimacy. This usually occurs in later stages of realization.

A Belief Makes Assumptions

A belief will always carry with it a certain amount of baggage. This baggage comes in the form of assumptions we may not realize we're making when we hold the belief. Let's look at an example. Consider the belief, "My sister ruined my day by speaking unkindly to me this morning." If we feel into a belief like this, it will probably make us feel uncomfortable. We might feel anxious, disappointed, or disempowered. I would suggest the majority of those reactions aren't so much due to the belief at face value, but to the assumptions we are unconsciously accepting when we believe it. First and foremost, we buy into the simple assumption that the belief is true, that the day is ruined and it's our sister's fault. Now let's look at a few other beliefs that are suggested and assumed by this belief:

A day can be ruined.

Is a day such a thing that can actually be ruined? Can you find the object called "day" to assess it's ruined-ness in the way you can pick up a piece of moldy fruit and assess that it's past its ripe period?

If one moment is unpleasant, it can cause every other moment to be unpleasant for a period of time.

We all know that interacting with certain people under certain circumstances can be unpleasant. However, it is possible to convince ourselves that an interaction lasting a few minutes can somehow "bleed" into other experiences, effectively lasting hours or even days. If we look at what is going on moment to moment, we will find that it doesn't really go down like this. It's more accurate to say that we have an unpleasant interaction, then when it is over, we recall it a few times throughout the day. Only in those moments of recall is our immediate experience "tainted" by the referent experience. So perhaps we have a ten-minute conversation that feels unpleasant. Then a few minutes after we recall how unpleasant it was, that recall might last a minute. Then we go on about tasks of the day. One hour later we recall the event again for a few minutes. After another couple of hours, we recall it a third time. At this point we conclude that the day has now been ruined. Yet looking back it was only unpleasant for a total of about fifteen minutes. Ten minutes of conversation and a few collective minutes of recall. The other several hours of the day were unaffected. Yet if we buy into this belief, we can convince ourselves otherwise.

The quality of my interactions with others dictates how I feel throughout the day.

Certainly, we can pick up various impressions and energies by interacting with people. However, it is quite possible to live in a state of presence where the momentary effect of any given interaction is dissolved once the interaction is concluded. In fact, the momentary effect can be so dissolved within simultaneity that nothing is noticed, judged, categorized, or held onto. Short of living in moment-to-moment dissolving presence, there is more freedom than we realize available in our reactions and responses if we are willing to question beliefs. For instance, we could easily walk away from such an interaction feeling put-upon, bitter, and resentful for how it affected us. However, we are also free to feel relieved, grateful for the fact that everything comes to an end, willing to let go with enjoyment and gratitude, and excited to see what the next moment brings now that we have been fully released into presence yet again.

Going . . .

Going . . .

Gone . . .

There are also subtler beliefs attached to the story about "my sister ruining my day." They may be less obvious until we get the hang of this process:

It's important to reflect on the conversation I had this morning (or any previous moment).

Is it? What would happen if you simply let go of that thought/ memory/conversation? What would happen if you let go of the past altogether?

I can't let go of that conversation this morning.

What is the cost if you belief this thought? If you buy into this thought, where does your attention go next?

It may seem like a lot of effort to disentangle webs of beliefs in this way, but it pays more dividends than might be obvious a priori. It can become enjoyable and freeing once you get the hang of it.

"A man should look for what is, and not for what he thinks should be."

—Albert Einstein

A Belief Feels Personal

Have you ever had a disagreement with someone about a principle or concept and it got heated? Does it surprise you when you or the other person gets angry because of the need to defend a concept or view? Does it seem strange that we can even feel aggression or ill will toward another person simply because they have a different belief than we do? We can all relate to these examples, but have you considered why certain beliefs trigger these intense emotional responses while others don't? For example, can you imagine getting incensed, angry, or feeling aggression toward someone because they think Chinese food tastes better than Italian food, whereas you believe the opposite? Most of us would have a hard time imagining getting triggered to the point of anger or aggression over such a conversation. On the other hand, it's not too hard to imagine becoming angry over a political disagreement.

Think back to a time you felt triggered due to a disagreement. Now ask yourself how that instance feels different than a debate over types of food you prefer. In the case of a topic causing a heated disagreement, it feels quite personal, doesn't it? It feels less like a difference of opinion than it does a personal attack. What causes a disagreement to lead to anger or aggression is that we take it to be personal—we take it to be about "me." This goes back to mind identification. To the degree that we have our identity intertwined with a belief or view, we will feel the need to defend that belief as if we're defending ourselves. The nice thing is that once we see a belief as a belief (a mere thought), we are relieved of some of this sense of needing to defend ourselves. We've already gone a long way toward disentangling it from our defense mechanisms and thus from our identity.

How Beliefs Are Formed

How Did We Get Here?

You may be coming to this chapter with a lot of experience examining beliefs, or you may have little practice in this area. If this is new to you, you might be wondering how we acquire all of these beliefs, and furthermore how they get so intertwined with our identity. The answer is simple and perhaps surprising. We never actually chose to believe most of what we believe. We have vast networks of interconnected beliefs constantly influencing our internal processes (thought and emotion). Yet we sort of just found ourselves here, didn't we? Do you remember that time during childhood when the BAB (Belief Acquisition Bureau) pulled you aside for a belief audit? They showed you a list of thousands and thousands of possible beliefs and let you select the beliefs you will adopt and operate from for the rest of your life. Yeah, I don't remember that either.

Mirroring

Although we never specifically chose to adopt most of the beliefs that define our experience, we have been actively adopting and incorporating beliefs into our views of ourselves and the world. We've been doing this our entire life. It happens automatically, and it occurs below our conscious awareness. I won't go into detail about how this occurs, but I will summarize by saying that we acquire beliefs largely through behavior and communication mirroring, which begins in childhood. We previously discussed theory of mind, which is the human capacity to perceive the internal world (thought process and belief structure) of other individuals. This faculty, combined with empathic mirroring, structures our own internal perceptions of self and life. This mirroring starts early in life and continues through every stage of development. The interactions we have with the outside world, and specifically with other members of our species (starting with our parents), shape and mold our consciousness, which is the raw material of thought, belief, and identity.

A House of Cards

Beliefs are like a house of cards. By the time we know what's happening, the house has already been built. It appears sturdy. It looks like a real and solid structure. We don't perceive it as a vast perceptual illusion of solidity built out of hundreds of flimsy cards. We simply take it at face value. We believe this "world" and "I" who navigate this world, constantly maneuvering, trying to protect, defend, and prove myself are solid and real. As we a start examining the most accessible beliefs (the top floor of the house of cards), we see how thin a single belief is. Then the wall connected to that belief-card falls.

Subsequently, we find ourselves in a more spacious environment. We might decide to settle into this increased sense of spaciousness for a time. If we decide to live there, not continuing to investigate deeper into the structure, we will miss something big. We may not notice that all the walls, barriers, and boundaries making up this house of cards are just as thin. If we are willing to continue on, we might find this whole house of beliefs is built out of nothing but assumptions and illusions. We might be surprised to find the solidity, the barriers, and the very rules that seem to govern our experience moment to moment aren't actually there.

Meta-Beliefs

The Sentinel Belief

There is one specific belief that has a tremendous influence on our experience of ourselves and of life. It dictates our ability to learn, grow, and adapt to life circumstances. It can be remarkably empowering or incredibly disempowering, depending on its polarity. It's an immensely powerful belief, yet we never learn about it in schools or universities. Most of us never consider where we stand on this belief, or that it's even operating inside us, constantly shaping our experience of reality. For reasons that will become clear, I'm going to call this the "sentinel belief." It's a funny thing, this sentinel belief. Those I've met who were on one side of it have enjoyed immense growth, accelerated awakening, and an extraordinary ability to adapt and respond fluidly to life circumstances. Those who fall on the other side of this belief seem to live with a lot of struggle and resistance to the circumstances of life. Yet it seems almost random which version of this belief we inherit from our past conditioning and experience.

It astounds me that such a simple thing (if we clearly see it and understand its implications) has such a dramatic effect on our ability to shift the courses of our lives. Like so many beliefs, this is a hidden belief to most of us. Yet it's power when examined and utilized to our benefit is extraordinary. This sentinel belief I'm referring to is our fundamental stance regarding beliefs themselves. That means it is a belief about the value of recognizing, examining, and questioning our own beliefs. You could call this a meta-belief, which simply means a belief about beliefs. The reason I call it the sentinel belief is that it is the gatekeeper that decides whether or not the incisive nature of truth is allowed passage into the inner framework that governs our preconceptions, perceptions, and experiences. Here it is stated in each of its polarities:

Empowering:

> *"I believe it is valuable, safe, and worthwhile to examine my beliefs. If a belief is found to be inaccurate, without evidence to support it, and/or causes perceptual distortion, I'm willing to discard it."*

Disempowering:

> *"I believe it is not a good idea to examine or question my beliefs. It could even be dangerous. To change a belief is to compromise myself in some way. Even a belief that appears to be inaccurate, without evidence to support it, or causing perceptual distortion, should not be discarded."*

"I am not going to question your opinion. I am not going to meddle with your beliefs. I am not going to dictate to you mine. All that I say is, examine; enquire. Look into the nature of things. Search out the ground of your opinions, the for and the against. Know why you believe, understand what you believe."

—*Francis Wright*

It can be of tremendous value to examine where you stand in regard to this sentinel belief. Do you generally fall on the empowering end or the disempowering end of the spectrum? Are there certain areas of your life where you are more likely to hold the disempowering polarity? How much freedom would there be if you were to release yourself from the apparent need to defend your beliefs, views, and positions?

Preliminary Exercise

In this section we will look into meta-beliefs (beliefs about beliefs). The importance of this is that certain meta-beliefs can make it unnecessarily challenging for us to examine and evaluate our own beliefs. Here are a few questions to consider as a primer to this discussion. If you take a moment to contemplate each one, this can be a powerful and revealing exercise.

➢ Do I believe there is something taboo about examining or discussing beliefs? Is it taboo to me personally? Are there taboos against it in society? With friends? With loved ones?

➢ Do I believe some beliefs are better than others?

➢ Do I believe certain beliefs are so obvious that they are unquestionable?

➢ Do I believe that beliefs define who I am?

Common Meta-Beliefs

Here is a list of common meta-beliefs. Each of these can have an influence on how we process new information, adjust to change, and perceive reality moment to moment.

➢ Having strong beliefs makes me a strong person.

➢ A person is defined by his or her beliefs.

➢ By purposely choosing to believe something, I will make it true.

➢ A person should never compromise their beliefs.

➢ Religion and spirituality are about what beliefs we have in common with others in a group.

➢ If I don't have strong beliefs, I'll be easily fooled or manipulated.

➢ Without beliefs, I'll get nothing accomplished.

Meta-beliefs are usually deeply imbedded, meaning they aren't always uprooted the first time we examine them. You may or may not hold any of the above beliefs to be true. If you do, that's fine. I'm not here to convince you of anything. All I will tell you is that if you are willing to consider the possibility that a meta-belief might be far more limiting and distorting than it looks on the surface, it can be profitable to inquire into your stance regarding that belief.

"When men are most sure and arrogant they are commonly most mistaken, giving views to passion without that proper deliberation which alone can secure them from the grossest absurdities."

—David Hume

Points of Inquiry

Here are a couple of questions that can be valuable in examining meta-beliefs:

"Can I think of an example in my life where this belief is demonstrated to be not true?"

As an example, you might question the belief, "You should never compromise your beliefs." Can you think of an example when you were sure you were right about something and that belief caused some confusion, discord, or harm to you or someone else, then later found out you were wrong the whole time? If you can then maybe this meta-belief is actually not true.

"Can I find support for this belief here in my immediate experience?"

For instance, consider the meta-belief, "If you don't have strong beliefs, you'll be easily fooled or manipulated." If you are in a conversation with someone and they are describing their belief or view, you might have an internal voice that is evaluating and rejecting their view as if it is contagious, somewhat like a virus. That is the meta belief operating. Once you are aware of this meta belief functioning in the background, you have the opportunity to catch it and see it as one single thought. That single thought is a discreet experience, right here and right now. That one thought experience is very much like a sensory experience, isn't it? It's somewhat like the experience of a sound or a body sensation. If you then put attention into your body sensations, the tones and pace of the voice of the person you are talking to, and the elements in the visual field, you might feel a certain relaxation intrinsic to that moment. You might find that your tendency to reject (opposing belief) and to internalize attention (meta-belief) have now dissolved into the sensory field. This can happen incrementally, so don't be discouraged if it doesn't happen the first time you try. Once the conversation is concluded, you will likely find that you weren't swayed to some distorted view, but rather you feel like you have a clearer understanding and feel for the person you were speaking with. You'll feel more presence and more equanimity. It's ironic, but when we are internally resistant to the beliefs of others, we get more set in our own unconscious beliefs and thus ignore and even deepen our own biases. On the other hand, when we can let it all in (the sense channels) and give the evaluator a rest, we find that we have neither resistance to nor feel compelled to believe the views of others out of a tendency to please. Thus, our natural discernment operates spontaneously and intelligently, releasing us to rest in presence.

A Case Against Beliefs

Belief Is Tied to Doubt

Whether we realize it or not, belief is always tied to doubt. The moment you feel certain about something, the opposite "side" of that certainty is already forming. This is due to the reflective nature of thought and consciousness. The thing about thought is that it puts an artificial construct called time over our experience. This construct can cause a perceptual delay in the cause-and-effect nature of certainty and doubt. Once this becomes clear and obvious, we stop holding so tightly to beliefs and views. Being aware of this can accelerate the process of clarifying this relationship. Anytime you feel certain about something, you can remind yourself that at some point you will feel doubt with a similar intensity.

Belief and Freedom

After many years of examining beliefs, how they operate, and their effects on experience, it has become clear that the quantity and intensity of beliefs one has about oneself and the world inversely correlate with the sense of freedom. The more deeply held and unconscious our beliefs are, the more natural freedom is enjoyed once they are dissolved. The most fundamental and seemingly unquestionable beliefs turn out to be the true gold mines when it comes to realization.

Beliefs Can Cause Us to Act in Unconscious Ways

One of the hardest things for us to see is that we can and do act out of unconsciousness. This simply means that we can do things that are maladaptive, self-defeating, or even violent due to the influence of unexamined views, distortions, and preconceptions. In the moments this is happening, we have gone at least partly unconscious. If our perspectives and views weren't skewed in those moments, we wouldn't perpetrate maladaptive behaviors. What makes this possible is a sort of hyperconscious experience of a belief that co-opts our attention, pulling us into a thought stream, or even a thoughtless stream, of disassociated consciousness. This overshadows and overrides our natural perspectives and tendencies that arise out of spontaneous action, empathy, and presence. There is another side to this process; we are simultaneously avoiding an emotional or physical experience. When we become aware that we are acting out of unconscious motivations, we can approach the inquiry from the belief side, from the emotion side, or both. Ultimately, we will have to explore both aspects thoroughly and repeatedly to calm this complex of tendencies to the point where integration and dissolution can come into natural equilibrium.

Realization and Belief

Ultimately, the process of awakening and deepening realization is about dissolving beliefs. There are no rules to how this occurs. Some people take up investigating beliefs as their central practice. Others primarily use meditation, contemplation, self-inquiry, or devotional practices, and the dissolution of beliefs occurs naturally. I don't have an opinion on the best way for a given individual to approach beliefs. I do, however, find that at specific times and with specific fixations, being willing to skillfully investigate beliefs directly can save you a lot of time and frustration. It can also get you out of a "sticky" phase of realization that you might not realize you are in. The most fundamental beliefs whose dissolution usually mark significant stages of realization include:

➢ I am separate from the senses.

➢ I am in here, and the world/my life is out there.

311

- A thought, belief, or identity has control over the apparent external world.

- Feeling "in control" is what I really want.

- Time exists.

- Distance exists.

- One thing can't be everything.

- Things are one way or the other.

- One side can't be both sides.

- There is substance, solidity, and continuity.

- Suffering is necessary.

It's hard to imagine experience without those beliefs, isn't it? Well, that's for good reason. It actually can't be imagined. This is because to imagine or form a view we have to induce the cognitive faculties that bring the effects of these illusory beliefs/experiences into consciousness. Luckily, though it's impossible to imagine, it's definitely possible to live without these distorting inflections. It's called liberation.

"An unquestioned mind is the world of suffering."

—Byron Katie

Relative Beliefs

When we talk about beliefs as limitations and points of fixation that will dissolve through the realization process, we're not concerned with relative beliefs. Relative beliefs are practical beliefs that don't necessarily get entangled with identity. Here are some examples:

➤ The year is 2021.

➤ Sushi is made out of fish and rice.

➤ You should have your oil changed when your car's computer indicates it is time to do so.

➤ The proper dose for aspirin is 81 milligrams.

➤ I own a pickup truck.

➤ Walking is better exercise than running.

➤ Jazz is the best type of music.

➤ I like pizza.

None of these are a problem, and none of them need to be examined or questioned in the ways we are exploring in this chapter. In contrast, the beliefs that concern the "big questions" are worthy of examination. We are concerned with beliefs about who or what you are, how you relate to life and the world, and what the nature of time, space, and reality is.

Beliefs Are Limitations

To the degree that we have identity intertwined with thought, belief, and consciousness, beliefs will come with a felt sense of limitation. Beliefs are dividing constructs in consciousness. These dividing constructs cause the experience of boundaries where none exist. If I believe that life is a certain way, then I automatically assume a lot of beliefs about how life is not. This might not sound like a big deal, but when something occurs that falls more along the lines of how we believe the world is not, we feel cognitive dissonance. In that situation we tend to go unconscious, to disconnect from our physical experience.

Let's say we hold the belief, "Life is fair." While that sounds like a belief that supports happiness and enjoyment of life, it can cause cognitive dissonance when something happens that is not fair. In that case there will be a tendency to "go internal." There will be a pull into that place where we feel like we have control—the thought world. In doing so we tend to disconnect from the senses, which leads to a deepening feeling of isolation and separateness. On the other hand, if we don't hold the belief that life is fair, we will effectively believe that life can be either fair or unfair. In that case we are not surprised and will be less likely to recoil inwardly in a situation where something unfair occurs.

Another example is the belief, "I'm a well-informed person." Again, this sounds like a harmless belief and one that might be empowering. The trouble starts when it is inevitably demonstrated that we are beyond the limits of our knowledge in one area or another. If we cannot accommodate this eventuality, then we will feel cognitive dissonance. This can lead to ignoring evidence (immediately available in the sense world) that would otherwise help us to gain or adjust knowledge according to the circumstances. This can lead to some awfully bad decision making and even harm to oneself or others. On the other hand, if we do not hold that belief and effectively believe, "I'm sometimes well informed and other times not," then we

314

can easily accommodate the circumstance where we lack knowledge. In this, we are far more likely to accommodate new information, adjust, and get along harmoniously with those around us.

"I am the wisest man alive, for I know one thing, and that is that I know nothing."

—Plato

Sacred Beliefs

You needn't hold onto or adopt any new beliefs as awakening unfolds. You can let them all go. You will be taken care of. Life has amazing ways of supporting you when you decide to let beliefs go. As discussed earlier, some of the beliefs we feel are the most empowering or helpful beliefs can be as much a trap as "negative" or disempowering beliefs. Holding the position that it's good to dissolve "bad" beliefs and replace them with "good beliefs" is unnecessary and will lead to confusion down the road. If you take the practice of directly investigating your beliefs, just know that there is no belief that is so sacred as to be immune from scrutiny. The more fundamental and preconceived or hidden the belief is, the more profitable it can be to examine it. It's okay to dig all the way down through the bottom of reality. There is a saying in Buddhism: "If you meet the Buddha on the road, slay the Buddha." This is not suggesting that we are to kill the historical figure on which Buddhism is based, but rather an important reminder that Buddha pointed beyond himself, beyond Buddhism, and beyond all doctrine. If you are a Buddhist, your own deeply held beliefs about and attachments to Buddhism itself may become your final obstructions.

Beliefs and Resistance

One of the mechanisms that keeps beliefs intact and operating is an avoidance tendency in consciousness. It's somewhat of a defense mechanism that keeps our attention directed away from beliefs. This happens largely through distraction. Like our network of beliefs, this tendency is also something we've learned subliminally through mirroring. When you really start to pay attention to beliefs and inquire to bring them to the surface, you might start to feel this avoidance mechanism. It can feel something like, "I know there's a belief hiding here, but for some reason it's eluding me." If you notice this, just remind yourself that it's normal. Sit with it a bit and the belief will likely surface naturally. Over time and with practice, this avoidance tendency will soften.

Recognizing Beliefs

We are almost always operating from distorting beliefs when we are conscious. This changes after awakening. From that point on, identity becomes far more fluid. There will be periods of operating from beliefs and views, interspersed with periods of experiencing pure presence or pure being. If the presence is clear enough, there will be moments when no distorting beliefs are operating.

After liberation, identity is essentially dissolved into presence. From this point on, beliefs are usually experienced as momentary fixations and dissolved spontaneously. Until that time it can be quite helpful to learn to detect when we are operating from a belief, especially one that is having immediate and distorting effects in consciousness. Here are some signs:

➢ A feeling of stuckness, especially in the mind. If you find yourself ruminating or stuck in a stereotyped, repetitive thinking circuit, there is almost certainly a belief (or multiple) operating to keep that circuit going.

➢ A feeling of rigidity or inflexibility to life circumstances. If it feels like you have difficulty adapting to certain situations, there are likely a few beliefs (probably competing with one another) hiding just beneath the surface.

➢ You have a strong sense of ambivalence about certain situations, or in general.

➢ You feel righteous indignation.

➢ Arguing.

➢ Refusal to see, or fear of seeing someone else's point of view.

➢ Fear of having your beliefs manipulated.

➢ Addictive behavior.

➢

"What is the most resilient parasite? Bacteria? A virus? An intestinal worm? An idea! Resilient . . . highly contagious. Once an idea has taken hold of the brain it's almost impossible to eradicate."

—*Cobb from the movie Inception*

Working with Beliefs

In this section we will discuss how to work with beliefs in a skillful way as we become aware of them during the realization process. This section in concert with the inquiry chapter will give you many possible approaches, techniques, and points of inquiry that can help to elucidate and dissolve beliefs and the experiential fixations they are associated with.

Develop an Interest

If the prospect of investigating and dissolving your distorting beliefs excites you, then great, you're in a good place. It's something you can work on any time you think to do so. If you find the subject boring, uncomfortable, or uninteresting, I will suggest giving it a chance. Take some time to see if it doesn't become more enjoyable and lead to experiential insights. I think one of the biggest barriers preventing us from taking on this type of work is simply that there isn't much support for it in our human value systems and social code. It's the kind of thing you have to give yourself permission to do because no one else will give you that permission. Give it an honest try to see where it leads.

Indirect Methods

Meditation: Simple meditation does have some effect on belief structures, but it can take a long time to dissolve beliefs through meditation alone. This is especially true early in practice. Deeply rooted beliefs, and the resulting distortions they cause, can easily go unnoticed for decades even if one has a consistent meditation practice. Once there has been an initial awakening, however, this process of passive belief dissolution is accelerated. Belief structures dissolve much more readily when we have access to unbound consciousness and experience of pure being, which clarify after awakening. Even still, complimenting meditation practice with inquiry and belief investigation will greatly accelerate the process.

Asking for help: A great way to break through belief barriers is to ask for help. Who do you ask? The Universe? Life? God? Take your pick. Having the intention to give your will over to a power or intelligence that is beyond you is an exceedingly powerful gesture. What would that look like? Well, it depends on you, but it could be something like, "All I ask is that false beliefs and distortions in perception are seen. I am willing to make the effort to uncover them. I know I don't always have the capacity to see through them, so I give this over to (fill in your favorite higher power). I am willing to let go of what's false even if is uncomfortable to do so."

Direct Methods

Examining beliefs: This is a simple and straightforward process. Choose any belief that comes to your attention. Sticky beliefs, charged beliefs, and beliefs that seem related to recurring mental or emotional patterns are always a good place to start. State the belief as clearly as possible in words. Then feel into it. How does it make you feel to believe that? Can you get closer to that thought/belief in your mind? Can you close the gap, even come into contact with it? You can ask questions such as:

➢ Where is this belief rooted?

➢ Can I remember a time when I started to believe this? If so, was it relevant or adaptive at that time in my life?

➢ Is it still relevant?

> What does this (meaning current experience) feel like without that belief?

> Is this belief (or letting go of it) associated with any specific emotion?

> If so, can I move closer to the physical experience of that emotion in my body?

> Can I fully accept that this belief is here and that it is a single thought?

> What does that acceptance feel like?

> What does it feel like if I let go of the need to make this belief either true or false?

> In what ways can this belief limit me?

> What has believing this cost me?

> Are there times when I believe the opposite?

When you feel stuck: Sometimes in practice or in life we just feel stuck. It can feel like no matter what we do or how we think about things, the stuckness remains—unmoving. In this case, one specific line of questioning can be helpful to dispel the stuckness:

> What belief am I holding onto?

> What belief is operating in the background?

> What am I assuming to be true right now?

> What belief am I not seeing?

> What am I resisting?

> What am I avoiding?

Sometimes the answer comes immediately, such as, "I'm holding onto the belief that I can handle anything. My current circumstances are beyond my control and capacity to manage." Sometimes the answer doesn't come immediately or in clear form. Be patient when asking these questions. It can take a while for things to loosen up.

Disentangling the web: Take any belief and examine which beliefs are fundamental to it. This is a good way to get to root beliefs.

Looking for evidence in direct experience: If you are willing to really push a belief to its limits, you might arrive at some particularly interesting insights. To do this, take any belief and ask yourself, "Can I find any evidence of this belief being true in my immediate (direct) experience?" For instance, we might notice the belief, "The experience of presence and clarity that was here yesterday seems to be gone today." Then we put our attention fully into the sounds in our environment. Is there evidence here for or against this belief? No, there's just a buzz, click, click, hiss. How about in the body sensations? There is a sensation in the face and some sensations in the chest and hands. Those are just what they are; they carry no "information" outside of their pure experiential nature. Then we can examine the visual field. Looking around, I see some hues, some lines, and shapes—nothing that is outside of this immediate vivid experience. There is also the movement of thought and consciousness. When I look right there, then move into contact with that thought, there is nothing solid anymore, just clarity and expansiveness. "So what belief was I investigating anyways?" That's how it goes.

The key to this type of work is consistency and a willingness to revisit a belief and continue to inquire until the belief is dissolved. This usually comes with a release of the sense of fixation around that belief, situation, or circumstance.

Chapter 14:

Emotions

Introduction

If I had to name one aspect of the awakening process that I see causing the most confusion, it would probably be emotion. There is a wide range of advice you can find on emotion, both in spiritual and in nonspiritual literature. I always found it interesting that in spiritual literature some teachers seem to talk almost exclusively about emotion, while others essentially ignore the topic. I don't think there is a right or wrong approach in this regard, as different teachers bring different talents to the table. However, it can be confusing for someone going through this process to see so much divergence in teaching methods when it comes to emotion. One has to wonder what part, if any, emotion plays in awakening.

What I can tell you from my experience is that emotion is not necessarily the most important or the salient aspect of the realization process. However, if it's not addressed properly, it can be the biggest sticking point, especially in later stages of realization. In this chapter we will explore various aspects of emotion and how they play into the process of awakening. Please understand that there are many ways to talk about and break down the topic of emotion. This chapter will approach it in a way that I've found best facilitates the awakening process without neglecting the full spectrum of the human experience.

"To suppress the grief, the pain, is to condemn oneself to a living death. Living fully means feeling fully; it means becoming completely one with what you are experiencing and not holding it at arm's length."

—Roshi Philip Kapleau

An Emotion Is Never Wrong

When working with emotions, it is good to keep in mind that there is no emotion that is fundamentally wrong. It could be said that an emotion doesn't have a truth value (having to be either true or false) in the way that a belief or an assertion does. If an emotion is felt or experienced, then it's okay just as it is. It doesn't need to be evaluated. Its very presence is sufficient evidence that it has a right to be. You may not know why a specific emotion has arisen. You may not know where it has come from, or how long it will last. You may not know if there is some lesson attached to the emotion. What you do know is that the emotion is valid and has a right to be a part of your experience. It has a right to live. This knowing, when applied sincerely and consistently, leads to a certain kind of peace. At first this peace might be subtle, or even go unnoticed. If you continue to honor this truth and attune to the peace that results, the peace will deepen gradually until it permeates all of your experience.

There is no wrong emotion.

So, what to do with an emotion once we recognize its presence? Is it enough to simply notice, acknowledge, and experience the emotion to the best of your ability? Yes, it is. It always is. This is great news. Imagine what life will be like when:

> You don't have to analyze emotion.

> You don't have to fight emotion.

> You don't have to suppress emotion.

> You don't have to deny emotion.

> You don't have change emotion.

> You don't have to explain or justify emotion to anyone, including yourself.

> You don't have to run from emotion.

> You don't have to hide your emotion.

> You don't have to blame emotions on others.

> You don't have to meditate emotions away.

> You don't have transcend emotions or wake up from emotions altogether.

What will happen is a tremendous amount of energy will be freed up as the struggle with emotion subsides. You will start to relax internally in a way that you never had before. This is the value of taking the time to acknowledge and allow emotion into your experience. Instead of spending most of our waking hours masking our true emotional states and playing the game of convincing everyone how together we are and thus abandoning the truth of our internal worlds, we can begin to live a life of sincerity, authenticity, and congruence. This means that our external world, including relationships, interests, and creative impulses, harmonizes with our internal world on an ongoing basis.

"Feeling is deep and still; and the word that floats on the surface is as the tossing buoy, that betrays where the anchor is hidden."

—Henry Wadsworth Longfellow

Mistrust of Emotion

What I see in human culture is a pervasive mistrust of emotion. Mistrust and misunderstanding of emotion have reached epidemic proportions. It's evident in the media. It's evident in entertainment. It's evident in world affairs. It's evident when interacting with people on a day-to-day basis. We don't trust our emotions. We don't trust our bodies. We don't trust our instincts. We don't trust our own intuition. We live in a world of personas constantly trying to project the image that we are stable, unafraid, and "have it together." We share this currency of persona among one another, constantly reconvincing ourselves that it is what is real about us. Yet we know the truth, don't we? We feel the underlying truth—that this currency of persona is a house of cards. It only exists so we can agree to remain in complicity with one another about what's real and what's a projection.

The projection is that we feel okay; what's real is that we are suffering. Deeply suffering.

There is a common turning point I see among people who are in the process of waking up. Sometimes it occurs before initial awakening, sometimes after. It is not a stage or insight of realization, per se. It is more a mark of spiritual maturity. To put it bluntly, it is when they stop faking it. The turning point is when they drop the pretense and persona and shift into authenticity with me and with themself. When this happens, they see clearly that this mistrust of emotion affects all aspects of experience, not just for them, but for the vast majority of society. By letting go of our own mask of "I'm okay," we suddenly become clear that nearly every human we encounter is wearing the same mask in one form or another. Dropping this mask doesn't necessarily mean that we suddenly realize we are fundamentally not okay either. It is simply an acknowledgment that the business of hiding, of projecting okayness, is a waste of time and a distraction from attending to what we are really experiencing. Of course, sometimes we feel okay and sometimes we don't feel okay. This is natural. We are far more a dynamic process than we are a fixed persona dictated by social agreement. This turning point typically marks the beginning of one's sincere interest in emotion and shadow work.

In this section we will investigate this mistrust of emotions. We will look at its mechanism and how to begin to reverse the habituated patterns that keep us in the dark about our own emotional truths. Before we move on, I want to point out that these patterns of mistrust that operate in us are not something we consciously chose to adopt. We are not the guilty party here. These patterns of avoidance and repression gain access to our psyches through the mechanisms of mind-identification. They are learned behaviorally and unconsciously. So while this material can be challenging at times, it is helpful to remind yourself that you never chose to mistrust emotion; it is something that came upon you without your notice or permission.

Negative Emotions

Mistrust and avoidance of emotion is so common in our culture, communication patterns, and internal experience that it actually feels quite normal. I find that it's usually only after awakening (and upon further refinement of insight) that people will see this clearly. Many people have said to me, "You know, I never really understood why you stressed the importance of investigating emotional repression until now. It's so common that it feels normal. It feels like what it means to be a normal person." I have to say if I would have heard about all of this before awakening, I'm fairly sure I would have thought:

That's not about me.

That doesn't sound important.

Why would I waste my time learning about this instead of just going out and trying to get what I want out of life?

Here is a simple example that demonstrates a common way of thinking and speaking that, when examined closely, betrays our mistrust of emotion. Have you ever heard someone use the term "negative emotions?" Have you used the term yourself? Have you ever considered the implications of believing some emotions can be negative and others can be positive? If we recognize that an emotion is our immediate physical experience, representing how we feel in the moment, then to label it as negative (implying not okay/wrong) suggests that perhaps something about us is not okay. It's to take a superficial layer of identity (conceptual identity) and try to use that to override and invalidate a more fundamental layer of identity (emotions, feelings, and physiology). We can't, of course, override a deeper level of identity with a more superficial layer. What we can do is use the avoidant mechanism of mind-identification to further

327

intertwine our identity with concepts, thus further distancing ourselves from our emotions, our heart, and our connection with all of life.

One reason that we consider there to be positive and negative emotions is that we mistake behaviors with emotions. For example, someone might lose their temper and cause emotional or physical harm to another. We could interpret that person as having "acted out of anger" and conclude that anger causes harm and is thus a negative emotion. While this might make sense logically, it is a complete misunderstanding of how emotions and emotional repression work. In this example, the person causing harm to another was actually acting out of repressed anger. Anger is an emotion that arises when our boundaries have been threatened or violated. If we are comfortable with and can embody the emotion of anger, then we have no need (or very rare need) to act violently. We will sense when our boundaries are being threatened far earlier and trust ourselves to communicate that and/or adjust our situation to mitigate that threat. When we trust the emotion of anger, we know intuitively how to structure our boundaries so that we don't put ourselves into situations where they are violated to such a degree that we have to resort to violence to defend ourselves. On the other hand, if we ignore, avoid, and repress anger, then we are much more likely to allow our boundaries to be violated to the point where we lash out with overt anger or even violence. When we understand this, we can see that there is nothing negative about the emotion of anger at all. If anything could be called negative, it would be our misunderstanding of the emotion and the disallowance and denial of its intelligence.

Emotional Repression

In my earlier life I had no idea what emotions I was feeling. In fact, I wasn't even aware that I was feeling most of the time. If you'd have asked me then, I probably would have told you that I was feeling "fine." This is not because living in a world of emotional repression feels good; it's because a big part of emotional repression is hiding the fact that you actually feel terrible. We hide it both from ourselves and from others. My internal experience was one of confusing thoughts, anxiety, isolation, and dysphoria. I didn't know there was another way of experiencing reality. To someone who is emotionally healthy and articulate, it might sound strange to hear that I had no idea what I was feeling. They might ask, "Well, isn't feeling terrible internally a feeling?" The thing with emotional repression is there is such a pervasive fear of feeling emotion that we don't even stop to acknowledge a single emotion. It's as if acknowledging how bad I actually felt would have been so devastating, that it was easier to remain in a sort of denial and to continue to distance myself from myself by putting ongoing energy into thought and distracting behaviors. One distracting behavior, ironically, was continually putting on a front of looking like I felt okay, even though I felt like I was dying inside. This was exhausting, but I had no idea I was doing it. There was a momentum to it that I didn't know how to stop.

Now I'm pretty confident that I understand emotion better than almost anyone I know. This isn't because I'm special or because I'm smart. It's because I was lucky enough to be unlucky enough to have lived with severe emotional repression and thus had to learn how repression functions and how emotion functions. Since I had to learn it intentionally and from the ground up, I made a point to learn it in exquisite detail.

"One does not become enlightened by imagining figures of light but by making the darkness conscious."

—Carl Jung

When I look out into the world now, I see a landscape of varying degrees of emotional repression. There are some unfortunate ones who have it worse than I did. There are many who have a much milder case than I did. There are a few I've met who, because of favorable conditions, have healthy internal emotional lives. Even so, emotional repression is situational and varies depending on the emotion in question. There are certain emotions that almost every human represses to some degree. The beautiful thing about the realization process is that at some point we will move through and integrate emotions at every level, including and especially those most deeply rooted and hidden within our identities.

Pure Emotion vs. Repression

So, how can we become aware that we are repressing emotions? Luckily, there are usually clues. Two specific qualities of an emotional experience that can provide evidence of repression are the duration and clarity of the experience. The experience of a pure (embodied, unrepressed) emotion is short, perhaps a few minutes. The duration of an "emotion tone" of repression may be days, weeks, months, or even years. A pure emotion is clear, obvious, intimate, fully felt in the body, and physiologic reactions to it are freely expressed. It passes through the physiology rapidly and without resistance. The emotion tone of repression is unclear, hidden, or partially hidden from our notice. It is distant, isolating, and there is resistance in our physiology. It may feel like we're "bracing" ourselves but don't even know what for. It may feel like we are driving with the brakes on. There are often a lot of thoughts with emotional repression. It has a certain cognitive dysphoria. On occasion, this cognitive dysphoria can take the opposite polarity when it comes to thoughts. It can result in few or no thoughts. This is when repression becomes so severe that we repress thoughts as well as emotions.

I remember a moment that beautifully illustrated the experience of a pure emotion. I was with a friend at Disney World right after she had a profound awakening. She was in pure presence and childlike amazement throughout most of the day. It was quite beautiful to watch. At one point we were walking, and she asked if we could stop for a minute. We sat down somewhere, and I watched her entire physiology change like a shifting weather pattern. I could feel sadness overcome her. I could feel it in her, in my own body, and in the environment. Tears started streaming down her face. After about a minute she asked in total amazement, "Is this what sadness actually is?" She was like a child who had discovered a gem buried in her backyard. She couldn't believe it. She said, "I always thought it was a story about something, about me, but now I see it's just this, this purity. Water comes from the eyes. It's so light! There's nothing here, and it's perfectly expressing itself as sadness." Then as quickly as it came, the sadness dissipated. She let go of it completely and moved on to whatever was next. It was as if an afternoon rainstorm had moved through and in its wake left everything fresh and glistening in the sunshine. That is the freedom of fully experiencing a pure emotion—without distance, without hesitation, without a narrative. It is pristine, sublime, innocent. It is interconnection with nature.

Why Do We Repress Emotions?

There is no why. This is a wholly unconscious mechanism. If we knew what we were doing and knew the cost, we wouldn't do it.

How Does Repression Occur?

We learn it both empathically and overtly. Young children are incredibly empathic. They physiologically mirror those around them. This physiologic mirroring ingrains in them behavior, emotion, and thought patterns that are avoidant in nature. In addition to this empathic learning, children often learn to repress emotions overtly from parents. Parents have the difficult job of teaching children which ways are appropriate and which ways are inappropriate to act on their emotions. Unfortunately, parents often throw the baby out with the bath water when we teach children not to act out callously, selfishly, or violently when they are experiencing emotion. Children have to learn to be functional and adaptive adults, of course, but the message they often receive is that it's not okay to acknowledge, articulate, or feel emotions, along with the message that it's not appropriate to act out in unhealthy ways when they are experiencing emotions.

Self-Talk

As we've already touched on, when there is emotional repression, it can be quite difficult to identify what we are feeling. Moreover, there are often defense mechanisms in play that prevent us from even wanting to investigate what we are feeling. Luckily, it is still quite possible to investigate what's happening in our emotion-body even if there is repression. A simple willingness to investigate this part of yourself, even if it's uncomfortable or confusing, is key. If you do suspect there is emotional repression in play, then I just want to urge you to be patient with yourself. This work can be incredibly valuable and rewarding, but initially it may go slowly. It can feel like a lake surface that has been frozen over. Little by little as it melts away, you will be able to begin to wade in and feel what's going on under the surface.

One approach that is helpful when there is ongoing repression is to listen to our internal self-talk. This is especially true when there are emotional themes. For instance, I've had many people tell me they frequently have thoughts such as, I don't fit in. Nobody understands me. I've never felt like I belong. Or, I hate myself. While we might not be in direct contact with the feeling of the pure emotions associated with those thoughts, the thoughts themselves certainly point to a certain emotion tone, don't they? You can almost sense underneath that barrier there are emotions that are trying to express themselves but don't have a voice. Simply noticing this is valuable. If you are willing to watch your internal dialogue and notice any emotional themes, you might find a lot of entry points into your emotion-body. You can ask the question:

Which emotion is represented by this thought or belief?

Once you ask this question, be patient. The answer might not come right away. It might not come for some time. Yet it is still a valuable question. You are orienting your interest and attention to your emotion-body. That, in and of itself, can work wonders over time. Let's look at a few practical examples of how this might work. I'll use real examples of common situations I've encountered.

Example 1:

I might be talking with someone and they tell me something along the lines of, "I don't feel anything (referring to emotion)." Shortly after, they will say something like ". . . and it's horrible." Then I'll usually ask, "Can you think of an emotion that

333

represents what you just related to me in those two statements?" Depending on the person and situation, it may or may not be immediately clear, but I'll usually work with them until it dawns on them: "Oh! That's frustration!"

Example 2:

When someone is feeling frustrated, I might ask, "Can you tell me what it's like to look from frustration? What story does frustration have to tell?" They might think about it and say something like, "I'm not making any progress. I think I'm fundamentally flawed because of my childhood." I'll address that directly by seeing if I can get them to recognize what that new dimension they brought into frustration represents. "Well, now the frustration has a target. It's like I'm blaming something for my frustration." Then I jump up and down in excitement at this recognition because I love to see this kind of clarity in people. It leads to such a good place. I'll reflect back, "Yes, that's blame!"

Example 3:

I might notice a thought or impression that says, "Something feels uncomfortable." As I notice this thought, another follows it, saying, "It's probably because of what so and so said five minutes ago." Then I'll recognize, "Oh, blame . . . welcome to the party!" As attention moves into the experience of blame, blame dissolves into the boundless clarity of consciousness. Attention moves naturally into the pure body sense. With this, the story of that comment five minutes ago disappears. Then the narrative of feeling uncomfortable disappears, and underneath all of it a bit of sadness is released and moves through the physiology. Within a few moments it is completely gone and has been replaced by some other experience.

The takeaway from these three examples is that if we ask the questions with a spirit of curiosity and acceptance, we can move through the emotional cascade and often will find a pure emotion at the root of our experience. Regardless of which emotion we encounter, we will now have the opportunity to fully integrate that experience with clarity and interconnectedness.

Descriptions and Modifiers

It's also possible to repress emotions not by avoiding the acknowledgment of their existence, but by altering, modifying, and overemphasizing them in quality or intensity. In short, we turn the emotion into a dramatic narrative and thus avoid the pure experience of the emotion. A good way to investigate whether we might be doing this is to look at our descriptions of emotions. How do we talk about our emotions or feelings to others and ourselves? We can look for clues by examining our narratives. We tend to use modifiers that amplify or accentuate our experience when talking about certain emotions or experiences such as:

Intense

Intolerable

More than I can handle

Debilitating

Horrible

Sometimes we go further than adding simple modifiers to our narratives. Sometimes the central theme and main communication of our narrated experience is overtly dramatic. I've heard all of these descriptions and many more:

My body's burning.

I feel like I'm dying.

The pain is constant.

I'm in hell.

I'm on fire.

This is excruciating.

There's no relief.

This is torture.

I'm destroyed.

I'm devastated.

While this way of experiencing and expressing emotion is generally healthier than complete repression, we are still avoiding full and honest acknowledgement, acceptance, and embodiment of emotion.

On the surface it would seem that someone using these types of descriptions is clearly feeling the emotion. In fact, their communication is emphasizing just how much they are feeling it. Upon closer investigation, however, this type of communication (even with oneself) is actually a way of distracting from the full experience of the emotion. How is this happening? It has to do with self-soothing through a plea for sympathy. As children we learn that our ability to articulate our discomfort can lead to us being soothed. This is hard-wired into our mammalian brains. If we can convince our mom or dad how uncomfortable, troubled, or upset we are, then they will offer words of assurance, comfort, and affection. This is adaptive and a necessary part of our development. However, when we develop an internal self-reflective identity, we learn to use this mechanism to self-soothe. Because of the distortions described in the chapter on mind-identification, the echoes of this child-parent interaction go on and on, outliving their usefulness and ultimately leading to the opposite effect of which they were intended. We recognize that the usual descriptions of discomfort don't bring about the same soothing that we enjoyed as a child, so we up the ante. We begin to overdramatize our suffering in our self-talk.

The more clearly you understand yourself and your emotions, the more you become a lover of what is.

—Baruch Spinoza

I've found that this can be one of the most challenging things to see and accept about ourselves. We tend to be resistant to hearing this message because our belief that this type of communication can definitively soothe us (contrary to all evidence) is so deeply rooted in our psyche. I can tell you that when we see this about ourselves and start paying close attention to the descriptions we use (especially the dramatic and inflammatory ones), we begin to recognize that there was a very high cost to doing so. When we are able to stop overemphasizing emotions, we are able to start feeling the emotions and are invariably surprised how enjoyable, peaceful, and equanimous an emotion can be.

Unexamined Beliefs About Emotions

Certain beliefs we have about emotions can pretty quickly turn emotional intensity from a 3 to a 10. Often we don't even recognize that it's a belief and not the emotion we are so uncomfortable with. So here are a few questions that can be helpful in uncovering hidden beliefs about emotions (especially when the emotions are uncomfortable):

➤ What are my beliefs about this emotion?

➤ What scares me about this emotion?

➤ If I were to fully feel this emotion, what could happen?

➤ What have people told me about this emotion?

➤ Have I seen anyone act on this emotion in a way that caused themselves or others harm?

If any of these questions reveal beliefs about a specific emotion, then you've done quite a lot. Merely bringing those beliefs to the surface will relax things and begin to rectify distortions. It might take some time and repetition, but when it comes to hidden beliefs, revealing and acknowledging is what counts. If you want to further investigate, then the following questions can be helpful:

➤ What is it like to feel this emotion without the accompanying belief?

➤ Where do I feel this in my body right now?

➤ Am I able to remain in contact with this area or sensation for a few minutes without trying to heal or fix anything?

Asking these questions may not always bring about immediate change, but you might be surprised that it often releases tension and resistance surrounding an emotion. Thus, you are free to experience the emotion in an undistorted (direct) way.

Resistance

Emotions are never a problem. Even when they feel like they are a problem, they are not a problem. Even when it feels like anger is raging on inside of you and you feel like it might burn you up; even when it feels like you are going to drown in an ocean of sadness; even when it feels like the shame and guilt are endless, the emotions are not a problem. It's the resistance to the emotions that is the problem. Well, even the resistance isn't a problem in the grand scheme of things, but it is the resistance that causes the emotional experience to seem like such a struggle at times. Resistance is what causes us to mistrust emotions. It is what causes us to act out in unconscious ways and perpetuate violence. For a while you may have to take this on faith because the way we are conditioned makes it challenging to see the effect resistance has on our experience of emotion. It is hard to see resistance as such.

> Resistance leads to mistrust of emotions, not vice versa. There is nothing intrinsic to an emotion that compels us to resist it.

Here are some signs that there is resistance to emotion:

➤ You are afraid to feel or express certain emotions, even if you are comfortable feeling or expressing other emotions. For instance, you may have no problem with sadness but are afraid to feel and communicate anger. Or maybe you can easily express anger but compensate for a fear of feeling shame by using a persona of false confidence.

➤ You believe or communicate to others that you don't feel emotion.

➤ You notice frequent distracting behaviors, especially surrounding certain people or situations.

➤ Someone you are close to and that you trust tells you that you are emotionally blocked.

➤ Someone you trust tells you that you are an angry person, and you don't understand why. You don't feel angry.

➤ You feel uncomfortable talking about emotions or feel uncomfortable when others express emotions.

➤ You often experience a general feeling of numbness.

➤ You believe that the awakening process itself has something to do with overcoming or living without emotions.

If any of these are the case for you and/or you aren't sure but want to investigate whether there may be resistance to emotion going on, questions such as these can shed some light:

➤ Am I resisting an emotion here?

➤ Which emotion am I resisting?

➤ What does this feel like without resistance?

The Empath

With few exceptions, humans grow up being naturally empathic. Some more so and some less so. Young children respond to and absorb the emotion states of those around them. This happens so spontaneously, so instantaneously, that the child is completely unaware of it happening. Our nervous systems are wired for vibing with, bonding with, and mirroring the emotional states of others. This is especially true of those we are emotionally connected to and those we are dependent upon for survival. This empathic capacity and resulting affinity for emotional bonding is essential for our species to survive and to propagate.

As we grow and develop, we maintain the emotional patterns we were imbibed with as we developed a sense of self. You could say that physiologic empathy was the interface through which our emotional software was downloaded as children. As we mature into adulthood, we learn to put filters over our empathic interface. We develop a set of beliefs, behaviors, and skills designed to modulate what we feel. These filters are in place to prevent us from feeling certain emotions in certain situations, and around certain people. It also goes the other way. We use filters to prevent our own emotions from rubbing off on or burdening others. The only problem is this doesn't work. We can't actually filter our empathic interface. All we can do is tie our identity into spaces that are more and more distanced from the direct experience of that empathic interface. All we can do is become more mind-identified. No matter how many layers of identity, repression, and avoidance we construct, some part of us is still reacting to the emotional states of others. Isn't that wonderful?

"How much we give to thoughts and things our tone-painting, And judge of others' feelings by our own!"

—Letitia Elizabeth Landon

People who are inclined to wake up are often (but not always) more on the end of the spectrum where their empathic interface is wide open. This means that as children we were more apt to feel what others felt. We would absorb and even metabolize others' emotional pain. What's more, as the awakening process unfolds, we become less able to use the false filters of belief and identity to avoid our capacity to immediately and spontaneously respond to our environments in an empathic manner. At some point it becomes clear that we have to be intelligent about how we live with this inborn empathic mechanism. Here are some pointers:

> It's important to recognize that the discomfort and intense feelings you feel around others aren't always your feelings. I don't mean to suggest that you blame emotional states on others, but to take on others' pain without realizing it can and does lead to dysfunctional relationships and ineffective boundary setting.

> As an empath it's imperative that you learn to set and communicate boundaries effectively. There are many people who do not have good boundaries, and you can easily form an unbalanced relationship with them. Make it your business to understand physical, emotional, and energetic boundaries.

> Develop your emotional intelligence. An empath who is not clear on and accepting of their own emotions will find themselves in confusing and compromising emotional landscapes frequently.

> Learn to trust and embrace empathy (once good boundary habits are established). Empathy is a powerful and wonderful attribute of being human. To deny or resist this part of ourselves will lead to unending internal struggle.

Emotional Intelligence

As we practice traversing our inner (emotional) landscape, we will naturally develop and hone our emotional intelligence. We will become better at recognizing what we are feeling, whether we might be avoiding an emotion, and how to experience emotions more directly. This leads to the ability to accept and integrate emotions into the totality of our experience on a moment-to-moment basis. This section will describe various aspects of emotional intelligence and offer actionable guidance that can be helpful to facilitate this process.

Pure Emotions

Previously, I characterized pure emotions based on their experiential qualities, but I didn't specifically identify which emotions I was referring to. Before I do, I want to say that I'm not suggesting that some emotions are impure and some are pure from a moralistic standpoint. Nor do I mean that pure emotions are preferable, more important, or more real than other emotions. By pure I mean physiologically pure, undistorted by thought and interpretation. I could also call these "simple" emotions or "basic" emotions. They are:

➤ Happiness/Joy

➤ Fear

➤ Sadness

➤ Anger

➤ Surprise

➤ Disgust

All of these emotions have physiologic functions. They are adaptive and important for our survival. These physiologic responses can be observed in various forms in nonhuman animals. What I've found is that complex or composite emotions will have one or more of these emotions at their root. When we are able to soften the distortions that are often components of composite emotions, we begin to feel the pure emotions underneath. Over time, the purity of natural emotion moves unhindered through our experience and becomes quite natural and enjoyable.

Compound Emotions

I consider emotions that are distorted by beliefs, interpretations, concepts, and identities to be compound in nature. While a pure emotion can be experienced directly, a compound emotion is more clearly experienced when we are aware of its individual components. This allows us to experience closely, fully, and with integrity. There are far more compound emotions than pure emotions, but many of them you can appreciate because they are rooted in a pure emotion. Here are some examples:

- ➤ Anticipation

- ➤ Guilt

- ➤ Shame

- ➤ Pride

- ➤ Frustration

- ➤ Envy

- ➤ Grief

- ➤ Resentment

- ➤ Boredom

- Anxiety

- Impatience

- Disdain

The Axes of Distortion

The distortions that inflect emotion and result in compound emotions can generally be delineated as existing on two different axes. The first axis is the distortion of self-other. The second axis is the distortion of past-future.

The self-other distortion incorporates the cognitive perception of separation such that "I am here, and others/things/situations are out there somewhere, and clearly separate from me." This leads to inflections on pure emotions, resulting in compound emotional experiences, such as inadequacy, shame, and guilt, which lie toward the "self" pole of this axis of distortion. It also leads to inflections that lead to emotions such as annoyance, disdain, and contempt, which lie more toward the "other" pole of this axis.

The past-future distortion incorporates the cognitive perception of time such that "I have a definite past and a definite future that exists in the way the thoughts about it make it appear to exist. I live on a timeline and 'my life' stretches out behind and in front of me on this timeline." This leads to inflections on pure emotions, resulting in compound emotional experiences such as regret, which lies toward the "past" pole of this axis of distortion. It also leads to inflections, resulting in emotions such as worry, which lies more toward the "future" pole of this axis. You can refer to the chart to see where different compound emotions fall on the grid defined by these two axes of distortion.

To investigate a compound emotion distorted by time perception, you can ask yourself, "What does this feel like when I experience it without the time thought?" For example, you might be feeling worry. If you ask yourself what you are feeling without the thought of future, you might be surprised what you actually feel in that moment. It might not be what you thought it was. It might feel closer, less distorted. This can take some practice, so be willing to work with it as emotions arise.

REJECTION OF SELF

Shame

Inadequacy

Guilt

Regret

Humiiliation

Worry

PAST

Anxiety

FUTURE

Suspicion

Annoyance

Resentment

Disdain

Bitterness

Contempt

REJECTION OF OTHER

To investigate a compound emotion distorted by self-other perception, you can ask, "What does this feel like when I don't imagine distance or separation?" For example, if you are feeling annoyance, you can ask, "What does this feel like if there's nothing apart to be annoyed with?" Again, it may take some practice, but you might be surprised with the results if you keep at it.

Emotional Awareness

As a simple approach to improving our emotional intelligence, it can be valuable to cultivate some curiosity about your emotional states throughout the day. This will naturally result in an improvement of awareness of how different emotional states affect your responses to various experiences. It also teaches through experience that no specific emotion is a problem, and that no specific emotion lasts forever. The emotional landscape is an ever-fluctuating field of experience.

At any moment you can ask, "What am I feeling?" Once you ask this question, give yourself a moment to tune in to the emotion-body. If it is immediately clear what emotion you are feeling, then great. The work is done. Just feel. If it feels unclear, it can be helpful to reference a list of various shades of emotion to help articulate the experience. The labels themselves aren't the point, but they can help hone our skills of emotional observation and articulation. Here is a list you can use for reference:

Adoring	Friendly	Peaceful
Amazed	Frustrated	Proud
Angry	Furious	Rebellious
Annoyed	Gratified	Rejected
Anxious	Grieving	Relaxed
Ashamed	Happy	Relieved
Belligerent	Helpless	Resentful
Bitter	Hopeful	Sad
Bored	Hurt	Satisfied
Callous	Impatient	Scared
Comfortable	Inadequate	Serene
Confused	Insecure	Self-conscious
Content	Inspired	Shocked
Depressed	Invalidated	Silly
Determined	Irritated	Sublime
Disgusted	Jealous	Suspicious
Distracted	Joyful	Sympathetic
Eager	Lively	Tense
Elated	Lonely	Terrified
Embarrassed	Lost	Trapped
Energetic	Loving	Uncomfortable
Enthusiastic	Melancholy	Validated
Envious	Miserable	Worried
Equanimous	Motivated	Worthless
Excited	Nervous	
Flawed	Overwhelmed	
Foolish	Passionate	

Evolution of Emotion

Whenever I do emotion work with someone, I first try to discern what their experience of emotion is. People can mean vastly different things when referring to their emotions.

➢ For some people, emotions are clearly divided into "negative" and "positive" categories. Generally speaking, the goal is to cultivate positive emotions and avoid, heal, or transform negative emotions.

➢ For some, emotions are a waste of time, a distraction, and something we should avoid making decisions based on.

➢ For some, emotions are inspiration for their creative impulses.

➢ For some, emotions are an important part of the texture of life. They are the "juice" that makes life enjoyable and meaningful.

➢ For some, emotions are messengers. They are a mode of transit for information between the instinctual or subconscious parts of ourselves and our conscious self.

➢ Some people say they don't experience emotions at all, or they experience very few.

➢ For some people, emotions are the energies of life force experienced directly as the energy movement itself.

What I've found is there is a consistent evolution in one's experience of emotion as their realization matures. Toward the beginning, the subject of feelings and emotions can be quite heady. The interpretation and narratives about emotions are taken to be the emotions themselves. We fool ourselves at every turn because we convince ourselves that the more we analyze, talk about, and relate our emotional experience, the more emotionally authentic we are, when in actuality all of that mental activity is being used to avoid actually feeling the emotion.

As realization deepens, we begin to see the absurdity of putting so much energy into the activity of using narratives about emotion to avoid emotion because it feels increasingly uncomfortable to do so. With this, we begin to feel emotion more directly. I should point out that as this occurs not everyone refers to these "closer" experiences as emotion. Yet there is clearly a more "experience-close" aspect to our internal world. As this tendency to avoid emotion through mental activity and/or communication begins to subside, we also become more aware of the patterns of resistance that had been underlying those mental activities. Feeling these resistance patterns in the raw, along with the emotions we had been avoiding, often leads to the conclusion that feeling emotion is an unpleasant, afflictive, or overwhelming experience. With maturity, it becomes clearer and clearer that what causes this dysphoria is not the emotional energies themselves, but the resistance to them.

Over time, the resistance patterns begin to dissolve, and we experience more directly, more "from the side of the emotion." We become aware of the resistance as such, instead of fooling ourselves with narrative and analysis. It becomes clearer that the direct experience of emotion is perfectly okay and does not exist in any contexts of "positive" or "negative," nor does it have anything to do with a narrative. It becomes thoroughly enjoyable at times when we are able to feel directly, without resistance.

Dolphins read each other's emotions by sonar and it's the inside of the body, the configuration of the viscera, that lets dolphins know whether the dolphin they are meeting is tense or happy. Their emotions are much more connected with the insides of each other's bodies. We don't have that. It's like denying 90% of what we are physically, not knowing it.

—David Cronenberg

At some point, the energy of emotion is experienced with zero-distance (nondualistic) clarity. With this, it's understood and becomes instinctually obvious that we'd been running from and resisting that which we most desire—wholeness. The bliss of intrinsic intimacy radiates from vivid sensory (body sense) experience. There's no receiver of this other than the experience itself, which also self-releases only to be replaced by other nondualistic phenomena. This replacement doesn't happen in time, and nothing is lost or gained. Nothing begins or ends here.

Wherever you are on this spectrum, it can be valuable to ask yourself:

➤ What is my experience of emotion?

➤ What are my ideas about emotion?

➤ How is this (current emotion) experienced when I drop all narratives and labels?

> What is the experience of the current emotion in its most natural form?

> If I drop even the category of experience called "emotion," what is left right here/now?

Working with Emotion

In this section we will cover general hands-on approaches to working with emotions and emotional states.

Healing

There are two ways we can approach healing. One is from the point of view of the conceptual or cognitive identity. From this point of view, healing is a challenge. It takes time, work, and sacrifice. It is not a something-for-nothing transaction, so we will negotiate. "When am I really ready get to work on healing at the cost of comfort so I can start to face the difficult emotions that have been avoided for so long?" These concerns have merit. To the degree that some of our identity rests in the conceptual mind, we can't deny that some of this negotiating will go on. The side effect of this approach is that it is somewhat divisive in nature, so that as much as we work at healing, and even succeed to various degrees, we are subtly reinforcing a certain view, an identity. The identity we are reinforcing is the identity of "the one that needs to be healed." It's extremely easy to rebuild the hurt one by endlessly trying to repair it. That doesn't mean this approach is useless, but it does takes time and effort. It can be confusing, and it has the potential for self-sabotage and replacing one identity with another.

The other approach is a bit harder to describe. This is not because it's abstract or mystical, but because it's so close. This approach is to simply occupy the wholeness that already fully exists and is none other than this exact instant. It is the position of the body in this moment. It is the sounds in the room. It is the colors and shapes and movements dancing before your eyes. It is every sensation in the body. It is the somatic sensations such as the feet touching the ground, the sensations in the hands and fingers, and the sensation of the tongue and lips. It is also the more vaguely located visceral sensations in the gut, chest, neck, and head that may or may not correspond to certain emotion, belief, and identity patterns. When we rest in this directness, then any emotion state that occurs is automatically given a home. The healing is automatic. We can feel that these emotion states were never in need of repair. We were never in need of repair. The truest healing is the experience that feeling is healing. When we feel from the most intimate position, then there is nowhere to go. There is nothing to fix. There is no need for repair. The thoughts can make a distinction between unhealed and healed, but the immediate experience of no-distance reality can easily accommodate both states simultaneously. Rest here.

Just One

We only need concern ourselves with the emotional state that is in our immediate experience. There is rarely a need to go digging into our pasts or our subconscious minds to reveal or expose repressed or unaddressed emotional states. Life is brilliant; it will present exactly what is needed in any given moment. If we are able to stay with this momentary flow, realization will unfold with the synchronicity and intelligence of the cosmos. Whatever is hidden will be revealed. Whatever is buried will be uncovered. Whatever is repressed will ultimately be expressed in consciousness. This happens naturally and effortlessly.

*"For there is nothing hidden that will not be
disclosed, and nothing concealed that will not be
known or brought out into the open."*

—*Luke 8:17* NIV

As you learn to relax into this process of unfoldment, you will feel more and more that what needs to be seen and felt will come in its own time. It will be right on time. There is a traditional Japanese scroll hanging in the meditation hall of my home that says in Japanese calligraphy:

Enter Here

This is a way of saying that the entry point to your deepest truth is always exactly where you are. You do not have to search for the entry point; all you have to supply is sincerity and a commitment to see clearly. Clear seeing means recognizing a thought as a thought, an emotion as an emotion, and a sensation as a sensation. This work is simple. The challenge is to not over-complicate things; to develop a deep trust in the intelligence of life to bring forth exactly what is needed moment to moment.

The Emotion Sequence

In this section we will look at the sequence through which an emotion evolves in consciousness. If we look closely at a singular emotional cascade, we will find a pattern by which that emotion evolves from a physical experience based on momentary conditions to a narrative in our minds.

The first step or inflection in the sequence is that there is a physiologic response in the body to momentary conditions (both internal and external). This consists of a pattern of sensations associated with body responses. The responses may be very subtle, such as mild, often unnoticed muscle tension, or a slight increase in heart rate. Or they may be much more obvious, like sweating, shaking, or a physical startle response. As this physical experience occurs, there is an immediate inflection in consciousness that could be called the most fundamental distortion of perception. It happens so quickly that most of the time we completely overlook it. That is that we decide (based on predispositions and experience): What general category does this emotion or experience fall into? The two basic categories are "I like this," and "I don't like this." The experiential fork could also be described as desirable/undesirable. This defines our most fundamental reaction to an emotional experience as desire or aversion. We could also say that this step defines our most basic position in relation to an experience.

Example: "This is uncomfortable, I don't prefer it."

The second step/inflection in the sequence is to provide emotion or experience with a label. This also occurs so quickly that we usually overlook this step of processing. We could say that this labeling both defines the emotion and categorizes it.

Example: "I'm feeling envy."

The third inflection in the sequence is that a narrative is developed in response to the first two inflections. This narrative will have the overarching feel or "mood" of the first inflection (desirable/undesirable). It will also be a narrative that fits the label and category of experience defined by the second inflection.

Example: "I am envious of John's relationship with his girlfriend."

The fourth inflection in the sequence is that we identify with the narrative. The important point about this step is that we've stopped perceiving the experience as an emotion or reaction that we are experiencing and have now attributed our perception to the outside world. We have removed responsibility for this experience from ourselves (usually unconsciously) and placed it on objects of our perception. In doing this, we begin to deflect, project, and blame. We begin to see our own distortions, prejudices, and hidden beliefs and assumptions as the outside world.

Example: "John always gets what he wants. Why don't I have what he has? Life isn't fair."

Clearly, every emotional experience we have doesn't run the entire gamut of this sequence. However, we can all relate to this happening from time to time. Some of us live more toward one end of this spectrum than the other. Certain emotions or situations may be more likely to trigger us to complete this sequence into full identification and thus effectively avoid the direct physical experience.

Generally speaking, it is more profitable to orient our attention toward the direct feeling end of the sequence than toward the thought or narrative end. If we practice becoming aware of where our attention is along this spectrum, especially when we're feeling triggered, blocked, or uncomfortable from an emotional standpoint, we will begin to intuitively orient in this way.

Blame

When blame is operating and we are not aware of it, it causes us a lot of unnecessary pain. Once we become aware of it, we have the opportunity to stop giving it so much energy. Over time, situations in our lives that had felt completely unmanageable begin to feel far more manageable. We often find that what had previously felt like an insurmountable problem in our life has completely ceased to be a problem at all.

One sign that blame is operating is when we feel powerless, frustrated, and/or angry, and the more we think about the situation, person, or circumstance that is causing us to feel this way, the more powerless, frustrated, and/or angry we get. If you find yourself in this situation, it can be revealing to ask:

"Am I blaming my unhappiness, frustration, powerlessness, or anger on someone or something?"

If that question feels triggering or heavy, you can start by asking:

"Who or what is causing my unhappiness, anger, frustration, and/or feeling of powerlessness?"

If the answer to the first question is yes, then you have already done most of the work. You have acknowledged blame. You now have the opportunity to welcome it into this moment. This will always bring experience closer to some degree. Good follow-up questions are:

"Where do I feel blame in my body right now?"

"How does it feel if I release _____ from all blame in this moment?"

You might be surprised at how much relief this process can bring, especially if practiced consistently.

Psychological Fears

When it comes to the topic of fear, I sometimes find it valuable to make a distinction between situational fear and psychological fear. Situational fear is the type of fear that causes a fight or flight response when facing an immediate physical threat. This type of fear is necessary and adaptive. Psychological fear, on the other hand, is what we will be addressing in this section. This designation represents a gamut of fears that are related to mind-identification and can have physiological effects similar to situational fear. A key difference is that psychological fear has an additional set of effects that are long-lasting and become incorporated into our identity. These fears are rooted in important developmental stages of our lives, and at the times they come online they are a normal part of human development and maturing. Through mind-identification, they accumulate and solidify our internal experience, having effects on our perception and experience of reality far beyond the moments in our lives when they were immediately relevant. This accumulation contributes to our doubt-mass, lack of spontaneity, preoccupation with thoughts, and tendency to distance ourselves from life.

We will discuss four psychological fears that I find to be the core of our tendency to self-avoid, self-abandon, and construct an internal mental world to use as an experiential buffer between our false-self and the flow of life. They are:

➤ Fear of humiliation

➤ Fear of intimacy

➤ Fear of abandonment

➤ Fear of helplessness

I listed these in roughly the reverse order of which they develop. Before we discuss them in detail, I want to offer a few suggestions to help frame this discussion in way that won't lead us to mishandle these potent and deeply rooted emotions:

➤ Never make these emotions wrong. They are part of all of our psyches. We're not here to throw anything out or to judge. We are here to see and experience what is actually going on inside us.

➤ You'll almost certainly find patterns of resistance associated with these emotions. Resistance may come in the form of denial, distraction, justification, anger, or despair. Resistance can even come in the form of trying to use spirituality or awakening to resist or avoid things we don't want to experience. This is normal. It's not a problem. You can always start by accepting resistance itself.

➢ Be patient with these emotions. They rarely disappear or integrate fully by our coming into contact with them one time. We often incorporate them over time and through successive interactions with them. Take your time.

➢ Have an adventurer's spirit. This is uncharted territory for most of us. What a wonder and a privilege that we find the event horizon of experience right inside us.

➢ Don't push too hard here. Inquiry is fine, but be gentle.

➢ You have the right and the capacity to explore these spaces. Every human does.

➢ To the degree that you can, try to keep some attention in the body sense (even fingers or toes) as you navigate this territory.

➢ There is no need to dig. These fears will come to the surface at various times during the process of realization. After initial awakening, they tend to come with much more clarity and regularity.

➢ Treat this space like sacred ground. If things get difficult, remind yourself that you are fortunate to be able to come into contact with these parts of yourself. Many people never have this opportunity.

Fear of Humiliation

Fear of humiliation manifests in various forms. It could also be called:

➢ Fear of losing approval

➢ Fear of being an outcast

➢ Fear of being judged

➢ Fear of losing validation

- Fear of embarrassment

- Fear of looking like a fool

Associated behaviors include:

- Preoccupation with status

- Being judgmental of others

- Preoccupation with trends

- Trying to impress people

- Acting like you know things you don't know for fear of looking unintelligent

- Avoidance of social situations

- Avoidance of public speaking or performance

The fear of humiliation begins to operate in us when we become socially aware. This typically happens as we approach puberty. While the roots of this fear touch into earlier developmental stages, such as the fear of losing approval from parents, the fear of humiliation doesn't blossom and hijack a large part of our identity until we become socially aware. Anyone who has watched a child grow into young adulthood knows exactly what this looks like. The transition from having the parents and family as the center of a child's concern and their source of validation, to having their social group be their main concern and the source of their validation is stark. It can happen rather quickly. It is a normal stage of healthy development to learn to navigate social contexts and develop an identity within social structures. Along with this dawning of social awareness, we develop fears around what could happen if we were to suddenly lose validation or were to be cast out of our social group.

As with all psychological fears, fear of humiliation remains with us to various degrees, even after we have learned to successfully navigate social contexts and situations. It influences our behaviors and perception of self throughout the remainder of our adult lives.

"Humiliation is Liberation."

—Tony Parsons

Because of the "sticky" nature of psychological fears, this fear intertwines itself into various aspects of our identity and personality that it doesn't necessarily apply to. For instance, we might imagine ourselves being humiliated, not knowing what to say, or looking foolish, and then those mental images result in us avoiding an activity that we otherwise would be interested in. An extremely common (probably ubiquitous) manifestation of this is social anxiety. Instead of walking into a social situation as a "clean slate," we imagine how we might look in that situation before it occurs. If we imagine embarrassment, we might become fearful, resulting in us deciding to avoid the situation altogether.

When you come into contact with fear of humiliation, here are some suggestions:

➤ Welcome it! Seeing this fear as a fear is the only way to disentangle our identity and behaviors from it.

➤ Recognize that the fear and associated thoughts (imagined humiliation) is usually far worse than actually being in situations that could result in humiliation. Avoidance is always more stressful than trusting spontaneous action.

➤ Be willing to recognize areas of your life where this fear might be hiding, compelling you to avoid activities you would otherwise be inclined to involve yourself in.

➤ Don't underestimate this fear. I've seen many instances in both others and myself where this fear causes us to make choices that are very much in opposition to our natural tendencies. I've even seen this fear lead people to do things that are harmful to their emotional and even physical well-being.

Fear of Intimacy

It may seem ironic, but the fear of intimacy is closely tied to the fear of abandonment. When we truly allow ourselves to feel into the fear of being abandoned or losing someone we are emotionally connected to, we will have an automatic "distancing" response. This isn't necessary or adaptive, but it seems to occur almost without exception among humans. It could be stated as such: "When I see how important that person is to me emotionally, it becomes clear that to lose them could be emotionally devastating. So, I'll hold a little distance between myself and them so I'm not so devastated if and when they depart." Understand that this is neither an obvious conclusion nor is it a conscious decision. I've met a few people who are emotionally articulate enough to describe it exactly this way, but most of us have no idea we're actually doing this. It manifests in various forms and intensities among humans. The "distance" we hold is often in direct proportion to how much emotional pain we were exposed to with emotional connections earlier in our lives. Here are some of the associated tendencies and behaviors:

- Avoidance of emotional connections

- Inability or unwillingness to trust those closest to you

- Feeling more "in your head" than "in your body" around those you are close to

- Stonewalling or "pushing away" our loved ones

- Discomfort with physical contact with other humans, or even with animals

- Sexual dysfunction or avoidance

- Volatile relationships

Here are some pointers that can be helpful around fear of intimacy:

- Acknowledge it, at least to yourself. So much of the resistance charge around this emotion can be relieved by mere acknowledgement.

- Communicate it to your partner or loved one if it feels safe and relevant to do so. You might be surprised that they also experience fear of intimacy.

- Avoid blaming it on your partner or loved ones.

- Make contact with those you are close to. Sometimes physical touch, whether it's a hug or hand on the shoulder, can diffuse so much tension and "headiness."

- Practice direct and honest communication. Make eye contact and speak simply and directly from your own experience. Don't "filter."

Fear of Abandonment

This fear has its roots very early in our development as humans. It begins to form as soon as our rudimentary sense of self begins to form. This is between one and two years of age. The moment we begin to perceive our self as a distinct entity, we also begin to perceive our primary caregiver and our emotional bond with them as necessary to our survival. This is a critical stage in our development, and if there is a disruption in the formation of this primary bond with our caregiver, it can result in pervasive and longstanding psychological and emotional impediment.

Fear of abandonment is so deeply buried in our psyches that most of us are totally unaware of how much influence it has on our choices, our beliefs, and our sense of self. As was mentioned, it is tied into our fear of intimacy. It is also tied into other perceptions and behaviors, such as:

- Fear of loneliness
- Remaining in dysfunctional relationships when it's clear it would be healthier to leave
- Needy or "clingy" behaviors
- Lack of interest in independence and autonomy
- Being unnecessarily dependent in relationships or only feeling loved when the other person displays dependent traits
- Feeling uncomfortable being by yourself
- Displaying manipulative behaviors toward loved ones to cause them to remain close to you, depend on you, or fear losing your validation
- Extreme jealousy
- Any form of violence in relationships

When you come into contact with the fear of abandonment, slow way down. Give this experiencing some space. You are on sacred ground. You are in the vicinity of some of the most primal energies in human consciousness. These instincts are intrinsic to mammalian bonding and survival. Here are some pointers:

➤ First and foremost, stop and feel. Refamiliarize yourself with this tactile aspect of this territory. There's nothing to think about or analyze here. In actuality, there is nothing to do here at all except to feel.

➤ Ask yourself, "Can I hold this experience without having to act on it? Can I simply feel the fear of abandonment, or abandonment itself, without having to blame anyone for it, talk about it, analyze it, or heal it?"

➤ At first you may only be able to come into contact with this experience briefly. That's okay. You will get more comfortable with it over time.

➤ As you become more comfortable in this space, you can ask yourself questions like, "Where do I feel this in my body? How does it move? How can I act more consciously with regard to this part of myself?"

Fear of Helplessness

This fear has a special place in my heart. It is the most surprising emotion of all when you truly get to know it. It's more fundamental than the psychological fears we have already discussed. The reason this one is so surprising is that it is the final barrier. This is something I might call the impulse of existence. This impulse is common to all life forms. I might even go so far as to say that this impulse is intrinsic to the most primal urge for there to be anything at all in existence. All of physicality as we know it and don't know it— the entire universe and its contents—are a result of this most subtle and marvelous urge to exist.

Helplessness, it turns out, is a direct conduit to what's "on the other side" of that urge. The transition point between the most viscerally personal and the most radically impersonal yet vastly intimate is right at the very core of the entire cascade of human emotions. In that core is a singularity. It has no name. It is a paradox. It is a placeless place that will deliver you from existence as an endlessly suffering, discrete being to an indescribably free and peaceful reality, which is not bound by the distinction between existence and nonexistence.

We humans do everything we do, and construct every identity we have, specifically to avoid passing through this gate. We have no idea we're doing it either. All of our defense mechanisms equate to various levels of protection to assure we never come face to face with this primordial truth. Even the spiritual paths that lead us into the vicinity of this barrier will usually turn away once this ultimate transit point is sensed. And yet . . . there's a possibility here. A few will carry on and be awarded with the most surprising and indescribable of gifts. To put it in Zen terminology, "Everything will be changed, you will think that heaven and Earth have been overturned."

I don't want to say too much about the fear of helplessness. I don't want to spoil the surprise for you. Let me just say that you will face it at some point. If you penetrate it, you will come into direct contact with that which it says it's protecting you from—helplessness. In reality, it is not protecting you from helplessness; it is protecting helplessness. It's keeping this most sacred of truths hidden just enough that only the most unguarded can pass. Only those who are willing to approach with full vulnerability will gain admission.

Helplessness is our direct physical connection with all of nature. It is sublime. It is without compare. Here, the most fragile is the most powerful. Here, the deepest wisdom is innocence itself.

"Blessed are the meek for they will inherit the Earth."

—Jesus, Matthew 5:5 NIV

Shame

Like helplessness, shame reveals something surprising when we get to its core. It's not at all what it appears to be. Yet it's the kind of thing that most of us avoid for years, or even for our entire lifetimes. This avoidance isn't something we choose. It's a habituated tendency we learned at a young age through communication and behavior modeling. This type of learning happens instantaneously and situationally and usually goes unnoticed. Most of us never consider the possibility that there is any possible orientation toward shame other than avoidance. This avoidance pattern becomes so ingrained in our cognitive and emotional processes that we often overlook the very fact that shame exists at all. The most effective form of avoidance is to forget that the object of avoidance ever existed. It could be said that this forgetting is the mark of identifying with avoidance.

If I could give shame a voice, it might say something like, "Don't look here! This is a bad place, and it has to do with you. If this part of you is exposed, you will be ruined! Hide this from everyone, even from yourself. Never mention to anyone that this place is here inside you. The core of what you are is corrupted."

Clearly that's pretty intense stuff; but really, it's just a lot of talk. That inner voice is just doing its job. It's using scary language to make sure you never get close, much less journey right to the center of that core of shame. So what happens when we finally decide to venture into that space? Does it mean our destruction? Does it reveal something about ourselves so accursed that we have no ability to handle it? No and no. What happens is that we experience relief. We experience rest. We experience peace. This relief, rest, and peace aren't situational or fleeting emotions. They are clearly felt, in that moment of contact, to be the substance of emotional experience itself. This means that to come into contact with emotion is to come into contact with true peace and true rest. This is the ultimate relief.

This takes some time. It rarely happens overnight. However, there is good news waiting for you once you've traversed sufficiently beyond those resistance barriers. What is at the core of you is not a curse. It's not a problem. It's not something you need to expend energy hiding anymore.

Emotional Themes Common to Awakening

In this section we will touch on a handful of emotional themes and situations that are common during the process of awakening and realization. Almost everyone who goes through this process will experience some form of these at one time or another.

Falling Away

The experience that there is something being let go of or falling away is so common during the process of awakening and realization that it's effectively ubiquitous. It can occur early on, before any obvious shifts in identity. It's even more common after an awakening. Either way, you will almost certainly encounter it at some point.

This phenomenon sometimes feels like a gentle letting go. Other times it feels as if something quite substantial is being removed from us. We often can't articulate what that something is. It may be subtle, or it may be prominent. It may be in the background, or it may be in the forefront of our experience. It may feel familiar, or it may feel foreign to us.

For many people, this falling away experience is distinctly emotional in nature. I've heard it variously described as a sense sadness, loss, or grief. It may even feel something like the experience of losing a close friend or loved one. You may feel like crying a river at times.

Others do not experience it as emotion, per se, but will instead have a profound visceral instinct that something is disappearing or has already been lost. If it doesn't feel particularly emotional to you, it's not an indication that there is something wrong with you. Everyone processes things in different ways.

It's also common to have this falling-away experience without a precipitating external event. This feeling often occurs when life seems to be moving along as usual. There may have been no recent changes in your close relationships, no loss of a job or health related challenges, and yet you experience a profound sense of loss. We tend to believe that if we feel a certain way there must be a reason, and so we look for that reason. Well, when realization starts to flower, all the usual rules get turned on their head. When you experience this falling-away sense, there is no need to identify what circumstances are causing you to feel it. The mere experience can be a good teacher if we are open to the lesson. We have an opportunity to begin to trust and take reference from our direct (sensory-emotional) experience regardless of what our thoughts are saying about it. When we do this, we stop being so concerned with how we should be feeling and become more interested in how we actually feel. You can trust that it's happening to you exactly as it should happen. This trust naturally leads to a returning to our innate ability to feel without the need to explain or describe what we're feeling.

With all of that said, there is some value in understanding the underlying mechanism of this experience of loss. You're actually letting go of quite a lot, from one perspective at least. From another perspective, you are letting go of essentially nothing.

In one way of perceiving, you're letting go of worlds of beliefs, imagined futures, and cherished pasts. You're letting go of security and assurance that you have things figured out and that you know how things are going to go in life. Something deep inside knows that these all exist only in the dream world of thought. As our identity disentangles itself from this dream world, we feel as if something very real is dissolving. From the perspective of that thought world, that's exactly what is happening. This is because anything our identity has itself intertwined with will feel quite real, even if there is sufficient evidence to the contrary. We know that daydreaming about the future can't really allow us to physically escape present circumstances, yet we indulge anyway. We know that trying to remember something happening in a way other than it actually happened does not change our current circumstances, yet we sometimes convince ourselves that it can. Well, once we start investigating our true nature, these kinds of attempts to pull one over on ourselves get more and more difficult. A result of this is that we feel the loss of this internal pacifier of imagination we often use to make ourselves feel better.

As we let go of these escape movements of mind, we begin to enter the world of unfiltered experience. The side effect of this is we experience the loss of the comfort of those inner worlds we have been using to maintain the illusion of escape and control. In this sense we are grieving the loss of quite a lot.

In another way of looking at things, we are losing essentially nothing. As we traverse this territory, the more fundamental movement is a transition of identity from the illusory world of thought and escape to the actual world of sense phenomena, presence, and intimacy. The loss of an illusion from the standpoint of the world we have been using that illusion to ignore is no loss at all. It is a rebirth indeed! The thing to know is there is usually a gap here. The illusion has to subside for the primary, authentic experience to reveal itself naturally. So that in between time is where we tend to experience a lot of this sense of falling away, grief, and loss.

When you find yourself in this territory, it can be helpful to remember a few things:

> This experience is perfectly normal. It is a necessary part of the transition you are going through.

> You can honor the experience primarily, knowing there doesn't have to be a reason or explanation for it. The experience itself is reason enough for it to be there.

> This experience of falling away will come and go at various times, and your experience of it will evolve. It may feel quite uncomfortable at first, but over time you will likely find that it becomes natural and even enjoyable.

> It has no specific pattern. It can come in short bursts. It can stay for a while. It can come in early stages of realization and/or later stages. It knows how and when to manifest, so you can trust it.

> As always, look to see if any resistance patterns are also present. If so, then acknowledge those as well.

> However your body reacts is perfectly okay. If you feel the need to lay in bed and stare at the wall or cry for a day, there's nothing wrong with that.

> You don't need external validation for this experience. If you feel like sharing it with others, that's fine. Just be honest with yourself about why you are sharing it. Are you sharing it to use sympathy as a distraction from the experience itself? Are you looking for validation as if it's only okay to feel this way if others agree or approve? These times of falling away are an

intimate and personal experience. You have every right to make space for yourself to give them your attention.

"Pleasant feeling is impermanent, conditioned, dependently-arisen, bound to decay, to vanish, to fade away, to cease—and so too are painful feeling and neutral feeling. So anyone who, on experiencing a pleasant feeling, thinks: 'This is my self', must, at the cessation of that pleasant feeling, think: 'My self has gone!'"

—Buddha

Bliss States

It is common throughout the awakening process to encounter exceedingly enjoyable states from time to time. We might call these euphoria, bliss states, mystical states, or experiences of sacredness. These can happen during meditation. Sometimes they last for a few minutes and sometimes they last throughout the entire meditation. They can also happen at random times when you are going about your daily activities. Occasionally there will even be a bliss state that lasts for a few days.

The most important thing to know about these is that as good as they feel, there is no point in attaching to them. If we let them come and go as they please, we will not suffer. If we attach to them, identify with them, or make them the goal of our practice, we will suffer. Key points:

- Bliss states are essentially uncaused. You don't need to figure out the recipe to bring them about. Doing so will just be a distraction. It's far better to attend to whatever shows up in the moment and let go of whatever occurred in the previous moment.

- Bliss states are not the goal of realization.

- A bliss state is not an awakening (even a prolonged bliss state).

- When a bliss state comes, give yourself permission to fully immerse into it. Paradoxically, this will make it easier to let go once it passes.

Existential Fear

Existential fear is another phenomenon that seems to be nearly ubiquitous among those of us who have traversed this path. You might get tastes of it before awakening, but after awakening you are more susceptible to it in its unfiltered form. While it's typically short lived, it can be surprising in that it arrives out of nowhere and can be quite disturbing. It feels like the fear of death or the fear of not being, in its most raw form.

It was a high counsel that I once heard given to a young person—always do what you are afraid to do.

—Ralph Waldo Emerson

The good news is that in the end this fear of extinction turns out to be a misinterpretation. We are fearing the death of an illusion. The death of an illusion can be quite alarming, however, when we take ourselves to be that illusion. As we disentangle our identity from thoughts and beliefs, these moments of existential fear soften considerably. They also become our teachers. A few pointers for when existential fear shows up:

> It's okay. Everyone goes through this.

> It rarely lasts long.

> To the best of your ability, try to embody the experience. Let yourself feel it. Notice the difference between the narrative in the mind and the physical sensations in the body.

> Give this experience some space. Although it might be a disorienting and difficult experience at first, it has a lot to teach you. Try not to avoid it or distract yourself when it comes. Don't resist it.

Acceptance

In the end, emotion work is all about acceptance.

❖ *Can we accept instead of analyzing?*

❖ *Can we accept instead of judging?*

❖ *Can we accept instead of trying to heal?*

❖ *Can we accept instead of trying to transcend?*

How do we accept? We feel. It's quite simple. Let the thoughts do their dance. Let the narrative carry on. Let the labels label. None of that is a problem. As all of those experiences are happening, we can also give some of our attention to the bare sensation. If you're feeling frustration or restlessness, you can ask, "Where is this felt right now in my body?" Then go there. Or better yet, let that body space come to you. Let it fill up your experience. Swim in it. Feel it wash over your flesh, your bones, your limbs, and torso. Let it demonstrate it's magic. Let it show you its shapelessness. Let it show you its lack of edges. Just plummet right into its depths. It's inviting you . . .

Chapter 15:

Inquiry

Introduction

"The important thing is not to stop questioning. Curiosity has its own reason for existence. One cannot help but be in awe when he contemplates the mysteries of eternity, of life, of the marvelous structure of reality. It is enough if one tries merely to comprehend a little of this mystery each day."

—*Albert Einstein*

What if I told you there was one particular approach to investigating your true nature that is so potent, so incisive, that it makes all other spiritual practices pale in comparison? Well, it's true. The approach I'm referring to is inquiry. What I'm talking about is a particular method of inquiry, of course. Here are a few things to know at the outset:

➢ Inquiry can bring about profound transformations, including awakening, that often elude spiritual practitioners for decades. I'm talking about sincere practitioners who consistently use meditation or other common spiritual practices. What's more, it can do it in a very short time. A few months or less is not uncommon if inquiry is done correctly.

➢ Many people "stumble upon" inquiry almost as if by accident, yet it still works as well as if they had learned and applied it in a deliberate and structured manner.

➢ Inquiry works for anyone who is willing to apply it sincerely. This is largely because it is customizable and, if properly applied, will be adapted specifically to you with all your unique characteristics and qualities.

➢ As far as I can discern, every person I've encountered who has had awakening and refinement of insight beyond awakening has utilized some form of inquiry.

➢ You don't have to understand inquiry for it to work, but you do have to be willing to acknowledge your own deepest yearnings and make sincere effort based on them.

As we have explored in previous chapters, there are many facets and approaches to the process of awakening. These areas of investigation, techniques, and practices all have their place. With proper timing and application, all can be powerful entry points. Inquiry is the entry point that ties all of the other aspects and approaches together. In fact, it is at the core of all other techniques and practices. You could say that other approaches are preliminary or preparatory movements until you are ready for true inquiry. Inquiry is something magical. It's something of a glitch in the Universe. It's a loose thread that if, for whatever reason, you become curious about and start tugging at following wherever it leads, begins to unravel all false identities. This unraveling reveals something marvelous and surprising.

In this chapter we will discuss the nature of inquiry, when and how to use it, and how it changes throughout the process of realization. We will also discuss specific approaches to inquiry and how to customize them to best suit you.

Before we begin, I want to make a general statement about inquiry that relates to how I'm presenting it to you here in this written format. I'm going to break this process down into a great amount of detail. I'm also going to break it into phases. Please understand this is an artificial deconstruction for teaching purposes. I want to assure that you will learn everything you need to know about the nuances of inquiry, as well as the potential misunderstandings that can arise, so that you have a good overall sense of how the process works and confidence that it can work for you. The difference between using inquiry effectively and using it ineffectively is night and day as far as results are concerned, so I don't want to leave anything out. However, it's important for me to convey to you that inquiry itself is not complicated, abstract, esoteric, or conceptual. It's actually a simple and intimate process. My goal is to get you to the point where you can do effective inquiry on your own in a meaningful way without having to think about the details.

It's sort of like learning to ride a bike. When you begin to learn to ride a bike, it can be frustrating, and at times you feel like you might never get it. Trying to coordinate several new tasks simultaneously can feel quite daunting at first. You have to pedal, you have to steer, you have to brake, you have to keep your balance, and you have to watch for obstacles. At times you will make mistakes. You will forget one task, such as peddling or steering, while focusing on other tasks, like finding the brakes or watching the path in front of you. You will sometimes overcorrect, and even fall. If you learn the various tasks but leave one out, you won't get very far. For instance, if you learn to balance and brake but you don't pedal, you won't go anywhere. If you learn to pedal and watch the road but don't know how to balance, you'll fall. If you can balance and pedal but look down at your hands and feet and don't pay attention to where you are going, you'll hit an obstacle. In the same way, inquiry doesn't get very far if you miss one of the important aspects.

The salient difference between riding a bike and inquiry is that with riding a bike, the necessary tasks to learn are obvious and someone is almost always there to point them out. With inquiry, the necessary aspects are all internal. What's more, the process of inquiry is subtle so if you're overlooking something, you may feel frustrated but won't know where to look or who to ask. This is why I go into great detail in this chapter; so that nothing is overlooked. With both riding a bike and with inquiry, if you learn all of the necessary aspects as well as how to coordinate them, and you keep at it, in a relatively short time you'll be doing all those things simultaneously without thinking much about them. Then you can just relax and enjoy the ride, the scenery, and the adventure of it all.

Lastly, I would like to point out that none of the aspects (tasks) involved in inquiry are completely new to you. They are inherent capabilities you already possess. They have just been overlooked. Many years ago, when we learned to go about the business of being a good person and living a good life, we put them on the shelf and now have forgotten about them. If this process is about anything, it's about learning to regain trust in your intuition. It would be nice if I could just tell you to follow your intuition. The challenge with that is that we've been thoroughly conditioned to mistrust our own intuition, especially when it comes to our innermost truth. What I find is that once a person has been reminded of their innate ability to inquire, they do so naturally and with a certain serene confidence. The process can become quite enjoyable. This leads me to the final point I want to emphasize in this introduction:

> I am not the expert on the best way
> for you to do inquiry.
> You are!

What Is Inquiry?

A basic definition of inquiry is the act of asking a question. In the context of awakening, it is a specific type of question being asked in a specific way. With that said, there is a lot of leeway as far as which questions you ask and how you ask them. Once you really get a feel for how inquiry works, you can even drop the question and the inquiry becomes an instinctual movement of curiosity and fascination.

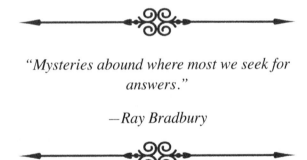

"Mysteries abound where most we seek for answers."

—Ray Bradbury

Inquiry manifests differently for different people and will also change as realization evolves. Sometimes inquiry is a distinct and specific practice; other times it is more like the overarching flavor and tone of the process of awakening. I know people who have woken up who would say they rarely if ever asked specific questions, but their yearning for truth, realization, or to end their own suffering clearly aligned with inquiry as it will be presented in this chapter. Quite simply, inquiry is a method of investigating your fundamental nature and the fundamental nature of reality in a direct, nonconceptual way.

Mechanism

As we discussed in the chapter on mind-identification, one of the most fundamental movements of the ego or the sense of separate-self is seeking. The egoic movement endlessly seeks the illusory "missing piece." It is by definition never satisfied, as the constant seeking continually reinforces the sense of lack. Because our identity is so intertwined with the seeking mechanism, it's impossible for us as the seeking mechanism to undermine the seeking process and reveal the fundamental error (the presupposition of separation). If we try to use the seeking mechanism to discover the truth that there is indeed no actual separation anywhere, we will be thwarted at every turn because it will be the false identity that's running the show. Another way of saying this is that the sense of lack itself will continue to seek a solution and thus reinforce its own existence. We all do this to some degree because it's impossible not to. Simply becoming aware of this hide-and-seek we play with ourselves is important and helpful, but that awareness alone usually doesn't break the spell of the seeking process. It has too much momentum.

Inquiry is a clever way of hacking this system. It takes the seeking mechanism that simultaneously reinforces the sense of lack as it seeks, convincing itself that it can somehow find the answer to its dilemma, then directs it right back into its own source. Inquiry, when properly applied, short-circuits this the machinery of a false sense of separation, causing seeking, which in turn reinforces the sense of separation. Over time it slows this seeking machinery down and ultimately it will come to a stop. With this, the illusion of separation in your experience will come to an end. You will experience reality as undivided, profoundly intimate, without boundary, and center-everywhere. A famous Indian sage named Ramana Maharishi (in his book Who Am I?) compares this with the process of stirring a fire with a wooden stick. As you stir, the stick gets burned up more and more until it's completely gone.

These descriptions point to subtle experiential truths that may not be clear initially. Don't be intimidated if you can't find these subtleties in your experience right now. I want to reiterate that you needn't understand the mechanism of inquiry for it to be effective. It is just as effective whether or not you know why and how it is working. At some point this will all become far more obvious.

Deceptive Simplicity

Through proper use of inquiry, you can accomplish in a short time what it might take decades to achieve through other means. I've seen awakening occur within two to six months in numerous people who applied inquiry properly and with wholehearted (sometimes half-hearted) dedication. When I had my first awakening, I had been meditating for four years but had taken up inquiry only about a month before. No one taught it to me outright. I sort of stumbled upon it and was able to surmise how it worked through trial and error. Even in that month's time I was mostly fumbling through it until it finally became clear. Something clicked, and I instinctually knew exactly what inquiry was and how to do it. It felt quite familiar and intimate. Once that click occurred, it was only a few days until the awakening.

I'll concede that the majority of people who get involved in spiritual work do not see this rapidity of transformation. One of the main reasons for this is they overlook and/or underestimate the value of inquiry. This can happen for several reasons. I will summarize the important ones here:

➤ It seems way too simple to work. "Something as important and transformative as awakening or enlightenment must require extraordinary means to achieve. Asking a simple question couldn't be a legitimate way to go about this."

➤ We don't know what question(s) to ask.

➤ It's not something we've encountered outside the subject of awakening, so we are learning something new and unfamiliar. Sometimes we are adverse to learning something unfamiliar or outside of common experience.

➤ We feel loyal to a certain technique (like a certain type of meditation), tradition, or teacher that doesn't involve inquiry. We are afraid we are somehow "cheating on" something or on someone we've committed to in the past.

➤ We have some interest in inquiry, but it has never been explained to us in an actionable way, so we don't know how to proceed.

➤ We've tried inquiry and found it frustrating, confusing, or it seemed like nothing was happening. We thus concluded either that we were doing it wrong or that it doesn't work.

➤ We read or listen to someone's description or instruction on inquiry and think we "get it" but never actually attempt inquiry ourselves in real time.

➤ For whatever reason, inquiry just doesn't sound interesting or useful to us; therefore we don't investigate it or attempt it with any sincerity.

Less Common

> We engage in inquiry and subsequently have an intense emotional experience, such as fear, disorientation, or sadness. This can occur immediately, or it can be delayed. We conclude that inquiry caused that experience, so we are afraid to "open the door" again.

If you can relate to any of the above, it's helpful to know that almost everyone has come to similar conclusions at one time or another. This doesn't mean that inquiry can't or won't work for you. You have as much potential as anyone, past or present, to undergo great transformation through proper application of inquiry. Here are some simple suggestions that may help orient you to this process in a realistic and empowering way:

> Don't overlook inquiry due to its simplicity. Indeed, its power is largely due to its simplicity.

> Give it an actual try. Don't think about it or think about what you think about it. Do it and see what happens.

> Don't expect immediate results. Sometimes you will notice something shift immediately upon inquiring. Other times you won't. Both are fine.

> Don't let an uncomfortable, frustrating, or confusing experience lead you to conclude that you are doing it wrong or that it doesn't work. Those experiences will happen on occasion, and like everything else, they will pass.

> There is no need to constantly assess whether it's working. It is. Sooner or later the evidence that you're experientially touching into something more real, natural, and free will present itself.

➤ Give it some time. When you take up inquiry, commit to doing it for a few months before reassessing.

➤ If for whatever reason you try inquiry and it doesn't seem to work, or you have an uncomfortable experience with it, don't completely give up on it. Put it aside for a while and readdress it with fresh eyes and an open heart in a few weeks or a few months. Sometimes it's a matter of timing.

If you follow these suggestions and apply what you learn in this chapter, I have no doubt you will be pleasantly surprised with how things start unfolding for you.

The Vehicle

Asking a good question is important in inquiry, but the question is only the vehicle. What is carried by the vehicle (the yearning for truth and the intuition that it is your birthright to embody that truth), and the fuel propelling that vehicle (the willingness to enter the unknown and the paradoxical doubt-mass or suffering that led us here in the first place), are far more important than the vehicle itself. A simple way of saying this is that what you put behind the inquiry is more important than choosing the perfect question.

"Whether you succeed or not is irrelevant, there is no such thing. Making your unknown known is the important thing—and keeping the unknown always beyond you."

—Georgia O'Keeffe

So let's talk about yearning, intuition, and willingness. Above I mentioned the yearning for truth. This isn't the kind of truth that can be written out in a set of rules or principles. You aren't going to find it in a book. This kind of truth doesn't refer to anything that you have to learn or acquire. This is because it's a living truth and it's intrinsic to what you already are; that's the beauty of it. This living truth is that which you hold most sacred regardless of anything you have learned or anything anyone else has taught you is important. I'm talking about a living reality that is so real, so self-obvious and intuitive, that no belief or opinion could blemish it. So, what is your deepest yearning? What is driving your desire to awaken?

> ➤ *Is it to end suffering?*

> ➤ *Is it to experience reality as it actually is, unfiltered by thought, perception, distortion?*

> ➤ *Is it to see through the illusions of separation and isolation once and for all?*

> ➤ *Is it to regain your innate innocence and spontaneity?*

> ➤ *Is it to live in peace?*

> ➤ *Is it to live free of the fear of life?*

➢ *Is it to know and embody your deepest truth?*

➢ *Is it to live in a natural state of intimacy and effortlessness?*

➢ *Is it to know eternity in this moment?*

If the answer is not immediately clear to you, that's okay as well. Give it some time. Ask yourself the questions, "What is the most important thing to me?" and "What is my deepest yearning?" These questions can clarify your natural point of inquiry. Ask, and then let them settle to spaces deep inside you. Give it a few days or even a few weeks. Readdress them periodically along your journey. The answers may evolve as realization evolves.

It's important to be honest with yourself when the answers come. Don't disregard answers, such as "to find the perfect partner," or "financial security," or "safety," or "to find a community that welcomes me as I am." These are all relevant yearnings. It can be helpful to further ask, "What do I think that will give me?" and see where that question leads you. When you get into the territory where you sense that no set of external conditions is going to ultimately satisfy your deepest yearning, you're coming into harmony with the impulse to awaken to your true nature.

When you start to really feel this deep yearning for living truth, finding an end to your suffering, or whatever feels most authentic to you, then put that urge or impulse behind the inquiry. It will be as if the yearning itself is inquiring. It may feel far more intense than yearning; it may even feel like desperation. That was the case for me. If so, it's perfectly okay. Allow yourself that and you will be in the company of many who came before you who realized great transformation through great desperation.

Willingness means that we are giving ourselves over to this process. We are trusting the unknown. We see and admit that the old ways of thinking about ourselves and our lives haven't led to true, lasting peace and equanimity. We are willing to let go of old beliefs if they are revealed to be causing us to suffer. We are willing to open to experiences we have been avoiding, repressing, and overlooking as well as experiences that we have sought yet somehow they have evaded us. In short, we are willing to enter a great big mystery. When you take up inquiry in earnest, you will invariably begin to notice there are powers greater than you at work. You begin to feel processes in motion that are beyond your control and understanding. There can be a paradoxical sense of randomness as well as a certain mysterious synchronicity at play. If you take it as an adventure, then there is space for amazing things to happen. You won't believe what comes to your aid. Intuition is the instinct that there is an unseen possibility, that it is possible to realize our true nature—that we were not born to suffer.

These three qualities come together to form a potent catalyst for transformation. The raw fuel is the suffering itself. The doubt, angst, and frustration with life as usual, mixed with a profound yearning for living truth, an intuition that it doesn't have to be this way, and some willingness to give yourself over to the transformation process are the perfect mixture to propel your inquiry to the very depths of your identity and beyond.

Formulating the Question

Deciding which question to ask needn't be a monumental decision. The function of the question is to direct all of that yearning, willingness, and intuition down into a one-pointed, simple investigation. The simpler the better, in fact. Inquiry questions can generally be categorized into two basic types:

1. Momentary or practical questions

2. Fundamental or core questions

Momentary questions usually arise out of simple curiosity when we are investigating or contemplating our thoughts, emotions, or senses. For instance, you might be spending some quiet sitting time observing thoughts. You might wonder, What is a thought actually made out of? Can I experience it directly? Can I touch that 'thought-stuff'? That is a perfectly valid point of inquiry. Or maybe you're watching the flow of thoughts and suddenly become curious about what is it that is noticing the thoughts and yet also remains as the "noticer" between the thoughts. Another great area of inquiry: Perhaps you are working with putting attention into the emotions. You feel some sadness and recognize that the label, "sadness," is in thought, and there is also a sensation in the body that seems to correspond to that experience of sadness as well. You might wonder, Are the thought and the sensation linked? or Can I get closer to that sensation? or What is that sensation made out of? These are also great questions arising out of practice and natural curiosity. They are perfectly legitimate points of inquiry. These types of questions have come up thousands of times for me personally as well as when I'm working with others on the inquiry process. Occasionally one of them will "catch fire" and suddenly plunge the inquirer down into the depths of their being.

"Who in the world am I? Ah, that's the great puzzle."

—Alice, Alice's Adventured in Wonderland

As far as core-type inquiry questions, they generally come in two varieties. One we can call a "natural" question or point of inquiry. It may seem as if that one question has been with you your entire life. In fact, it may be what has led you to read this book. The other type of core inquiry question I will call a "derived" point of inquiry. This is just as real and fundamental as a natural question. The difference is you might have to dig a little to find it. The third possibility is that there is no specific core question that is a driving force in your inclination to wake up. This is okay as well. It doesn't mean inquiry won't work for you. You may still find that certain inquiry questions feel relevant at certain times, and others at other times. Still another possibility is that you are inclined to do inquiry without a specific question, I'll call this pure inquiry. That may sound absurd, but it is a very real thing, and by the end of this chapter you'll know exactly what it is and its significance.

Finding Your Core Question

A good approach to finding your fundamental inquiry is to simply ask yourself, "What is my core question?" or "What is my most essential inquiry in life?" or "Which question really stirs something in the deepest part of myself?" When you ask yourself these questions, give it some time, or bounce them off a trusted friend or teacher.

You may find it helpful to brainstorm and write out possible questions. Sometimes just allowing the free-flow of ideas will help to hone in on your fundamental inquiry. Here are some common inquiry questions:

➤ *Who am I?*

➤ *What am I?*

➤ *How do I live a life free of suffering?*

➤ *What is eternity?*

➤ *What is this that is aware before, during, and after a thought?*

➤ *What is consciousness?*

➤ *Is it possible to be conscious without thought?*

- *Where Am I?*

- *What is reality?*

- *What is true peace?*

- *What is the deepest truth of this moment?*

- *Who is observing thoughts?*

- *Who is aware of this experience?*

- *What is sound?*

- *Who is hearing the sounds?*

- *Who is feeling the sensation?*

As you can see, these are all simple questions, and they are all easy to understand even if the answer is not obvious. There are some traditions, such as Zen Buddhism, which use similarly simple questions, but questions that make no logical sense. The point of asking these types of questions is that they immediately disarm the intellect. Strangely these types of questions, when applied properly, lead to the exact same experiential insights.

- *What is Mu?*

- *What is the sound of one hand?*

- *What was my original face before my parents were born?*

Clearly there is a great variety of inquiry questions. You can use any one of these that you resonate with. Work with it for a while. If it seems to be opening something for you, keep at it. If it feels distasteful or unhelpful, try a different question. You may come up with your own as well. There is no wrong question as long as it comes from authenticity and leads to experiential insight instead of conceptual answers. Here are some guidelines that can be helpful to formulate a question. Don't take these characterizations to be gospel, but they are a good starting place:

Who and What Questions: These are powerful questions if aimed at your deepest truths and/or your immediate experience (what you don't have to think about). I recommend using who or what questions most or all of the time.

Why and How Questions: I generally recommend against using these questions for inquiry, especially early on. To put it simply, they almost always lead to conceptual answers, more thoughts, and more confusion. For example, if you ask yourself, "Why do I suffer so much?" your brain will get busy coming up with all kinds of reasons, and they will be entirely conceptual and almost always disempowering and unhelpful. You'll usually receive answers like, "Because I'm fundamentally flawed," or "I'm a hopeless case," or "Because all of life is suffering." Don't you feel worse just reading those answers? So don't give your already overworked mind fuel to make you feel worse with no benefit.

When and Where Questions: These questions can be extremely potent, but they can be a bit tricky to use early on. They become quite powerful in later stages of realization. However, if a when or where question captivates you early on, by all means go for it. I know someone whose fundamental question was, "Where Am I?" and it worked very well for him.

"This is your last chance. After this there is no turning back. You take the blue pill, the story ends; you wake up in your bed and believe whatever you want to believe. You take the red pill; you stay in Wonderland and I show you how deep the rabbit hole goes."

—Morpheus, *The Matrix*

Asking the Question

Once you've settled on a question that represents your innate yearning for truth, or a practical question has arisen through momentary practice, it's time to inquire. In this section we will discuss when, where, and how to ask the question.

Setting: There really is no wrong time for inquiry. During silent sitting or meditation is a great time to inquire as it minimizes distractions, and you can give the investigation all your attention. Being in nature, especially when free of distractions, is also a great time to inquire. While lying in bed and drifting off to sleep is an excellent time to do it. This allows you to carry an inquiry off into the subconscious realm. You can even inquire while engaged in tasks such as doing housework or yardwork. At first you might find it easiest to do inquiry in quiet environments where there are few to no distractions. Over time, you'll probably find that inquiry can be done in many different settings. You can dedicate a certain amount of time to inquiry, or you can simply engage it at any moment the inclination hits you, even if for only a few moments.

How To Ask the Question: Just simply ask the question with all of the curiosity you can muster in the moment. Ask it as if it is the most intriguing question in the world . . . because it is. It's okay to say it out loud, but it is not necessary. You can simply ask the question internally and then look (but not for a thought answer). If you are able to keep looking and keep that curiosity after answering the question, then great—just keep on. If you find yourself distracted, lost in thought, or off task, then just ask the question again with curiosity and look where it leads experientially. At first it may feel like nothing is happening. With a bit of practice, you will start to notice a small gap between asking the question and when the thoughts return. This is exactly what is supposed to happen. Inquiry isn't something you are supposed to think about; its purpose is to lead you into direct experience. There is no need to repeat the question over and over robotically. If you find yourself doing that, then take a break. When you return, remind yourself to ask with curiosity and willingness to direct your attention into the immediate experience that reveals itself after the question is asked, whether or not there are thoughts there.

Beyond the Question

The real magic of inquiry begins after the question has been asked. This is because that yearning for truth and questioning heart fueled by the doubt-mass and desire to find an end to suffering has been loaded into the inquiry vehicle and launched into the unknown. In a sense, you've done your part, and now you release the inquiry to the life impulse that flows through everything. In short, you surrender to the inquiry process.

The most beautiful thing we can experience is the mysterious. It is the source of all true art and science.

—Albert Einstein

Although it's largely out of your hands at this point, it's important to acknowledge that this phase after the question has been asked and released is where the true work is done. This acknowledgement comes in the form of your attention and your regard for the process itself. It's the most important part of inquiry. Your job now is to not get in the way of the process. A very smart friend of mine put it this way: "It's like when you're going in for surgery. You have two jobs: don't move, and don't try to be the surgeon." So from this point on in the process, your job is to surrender to the inquiry. Here are the qualities of surrendered inquiry:

Nonconceptual

We are never looking for a conceptual answer. As per the description in the chapter on thoughts, anything you could write down or speak in words is considered a concept. There is no need to think about what inquiry is teaching us. The whole point of inquiry is to lead you into nonconceptual immediate experience. Any conclusions or judgements are conceptual here. One way we can bind ourselves unknowingly into conceptualization during inquiry is by taking thoughts about the process or technique itself to be your thoughts. This means that during inquiry we might find that after we ask the question, there is a lot of internal debate about whether we are doing this right. Maybe I should put my attention here instead of there, or Now my experience seems to be shifting. Should I ask the question again or just go with the shift experientially? The presence of these thoughts during inquiry is not a sign you've made a mistake; they are simply normal thoughts. They do not pose a problem. Just don't convince yourself that you are the confused one or the doubting one by believing those thoughts to be produced by you. If thoughts are noticed, so be it. Just keep looking. If thoughts or conceptual answers seem particularly insistent, then you can further inquire, Oh, this is a thought. So what else is here that is not a thought? After some practice, you'll know the "feel" of allowing your attention to flow into nonconceptual, experiential inquiry.

Suspend Judgement

Once we start to recognize the feel of nonconceptual experience, we might still feel like we are "wrestling" with our experience to some degree. This is caused by our habit of constantly evaluating and separating "good" experiences from "bad" experiences. With inquiry you can give that discriminating mind a rest. If it seems insistent upon wrestling with experiences as if trying to find the "right" one and avoid the "wrong" one, you can affirm, "In inquiry, there aren't better or worse experiences, there are only experiences."

Find the Sweet Spot

There is a magical middle ground between intention (wanting to know truth, wanting to wake up) and surrender or yielding (letting yourself be overtaken by the experience). When you don't overemphasize either of these aspects, you'll find inquiry to be nearly effortless and enjoyable.

If Attention Moves into the Senses, That's Perfectly Okay

If you find your attention going to the sounds in the room (without labeling or contemplating them), that's not a bad thing. If you find your attention moving into in the sensations in the body, then by all means let it rest there.

Let Go of the Need for an Answer of Any Kind

This is an extension of the caution against looking for conceptual answers. It may seem counterintuitive that we ask a question with a burning desire to know truth and then let go of even the expectation for an answer in any form. It's okay if this isn't intuitive at the outset. Over time it will become clearer. What happens is the openness and the nonjudgmental investigation of our immediate experience becomes deeply enjoyable. When this enjoyment comes, you will start to sense the natural curious innocence that inquiry is touching into. This curious innocence as we surrender to this sacred rite is the exact set of conditions that can open a portal—a portal to infinity. As Christ said in the gospel of Matthew, "Truly I tell you, unless you change and become like little children, you will never enter the kingdom of heaven." That is the kind of innocence I'm talking about.

Don't Strain or Struggle

If at any point during inquiry it feels as if you are pushing or struggling, or things feel forceful, this is probably a sign of some expectation of a specific outcome. This expectation might be unconscious. It's quite possible to unknowingly push for some sort of resolution even if we aren't clear on what we think that resolution is. If you are feeling this sense of pushing for an outcome, you can ask, "Is there something I am expecting out of this right now?" or "Am I demanding something of this moment or experience?" If you sense that you are, then that's often enough to relax the whole situation. Sometimes it helps to dig a bit deeper: "What am I trying to get out of this right now?" The following stanza may help to clarify this:

> Just be willing to look. And keep looking.
>
> Don't judge. Don't pick and choose. Don't throw anything out. Don't try to add anything.
>
> Keep looking until the looking is all that's left, and that looking is nondualistic, meaning intimate beyond compare and thoroughly satisfying. This is not a complicated process.

Natural Inquiry

You will never hit a point in inquiry where you suddenly realize the job is done. There isn't a stage of maturity after which inquiry is no longer necessary in any form. However, there are refinements of this process that naturally occur, and so it can be said that the process itself matures with experience. So, what is it like when the inquiry process matures? Well, it will be different for everyone, but the following description may be helpful:

When we begin inquiry, we can't help but look for and expect certain types of experiences. We all come with our preconceived notions about what it might be like when we are more awake, more clear, more . . . whatever. After some practice, we begin to realize that all of that is simply the busy mind doing what it does best, making thoughts. Early on, this can distract us from recognizing the simple and natural process of engaging our immediate experience spontaneously and directly. After some practice, we will learn to effortlessly discriminate conceptuality from immediate experience. With this, we learn to trust that immediate experience more and we start to "get" the whole point of inquiry on an experiential level. This is a mark of maturity in inquiry. By this point, we've really started to trust the process and to intuit its power. Even at this stage, we will harbor unconscious expectations about what we will get out of inquiry and out of the whole awakening process. As those hidden beliefs surface, the somatic structures they have become tethered to through habituation will start to relax. It is often seen in retrospect, once belief and identity structures have dissipated, leaving more vastness, clarity, and effortless flow.

With this, we begin to dissolve the expectation tone (not only with inquiry but in various areas of our lives) and begin to realize what a blessing it is to remain in that wonder and fascination with the mystery of life. We dissolve into the innocence and mystery of natural inquiry. At some point we realize inquiry isn't something we do, and it never has been. It's much more something we are. Or rather, it's a radical immersion into something sacred, wondrous, humbling, and rather intimate. We begin to genuinely enjoy occupying this mysterious space, which isn't just available during silence and meditation but is now recognizing itself in the moment-to-moment flow of life, regardless of the activity or circumstance. What a blessing to need nothing and have immediate access to this intimacy with everything. Life takes on a radiance, richness, and depth we had never known. And the inquiry continues, now of its own accord. And the mystery deepens.

We will conclude this chapter with a quote by renowned Zen Master Dogen:

"To study the Buddha Way is to study the self. To study the self is to forget the self. To forget the self is to be actualized by myriad things. When actualized by myriad things, your body and mind as well as the bodies and minds of others drop away. No trace of enlightenment remains, and this no-trace continues endlessly."

—Dogen

Chapter 16:

Awakening

Introduction

Well, we're finally here. We've come so far and covered so much ground. I really want to congratulate you for sticking with this. This kind of work isn't easy, and nobody is making you do it. It's been your own love of truth that has been guiding you all along. Truth can be a challenging ideal. It is often neither interested in your priorities nor in your expectations. Yet if you continue to attune to it, it pays huge dividends. In this chapter, we will discuss the awakening event. The purpose is fivefold:

1. To prepare you, as much as possible, for the shift. Much of this preparation will be in the form of encouragement. Things can get rocky and disorienting as awakening approaches. It often feels like things have totally gone off the rails. So a few words of encouragement can be what's most needed at these times. Yes, I know this is not what you expected. I also know that all the work you've done up to this point seems somehow unrelated to where you find yourself currently. I know you

have often been frustrated and sometimes wanted to give up. I know that you can't even remember why the heck you were exerting all this effort. I understand the "spiritual stuff" that sounded so romantic in the past now seems like it was in your imagination. Here's the thing. You're in good company. Many people have walked this path before you and come to this exact impasse. We've all felt as lost as you do. We've all questioned ourselves endlessly. We've all come to the end of our capacity to carry on. We've all exhausted those seemingly endless mind roads and collapsed in utter exhaustion. You're in the right place, even though it feels like your foundations are crumbling.

2. To describe practice approaches that can help you breach the veils of false identity and the illusion of separation.

3. To address the obstructions that come into play during that final push. Some of them were discussed earlier in the book. There are also a few common sticking points specific to the period immediately before awakening.

4. To transmit the "flavor" of awakening through descriptions of what it's like going through it.

5. To discuss how to proceed as awakening begins to unfold.

I'm sure you've gathered by now that talking about awakening as an event is slippery business. Neither I nor anyone who has gone through it can tell you exactly what it is or how to go through it. The only way to really know is to go through yourself. So how in the world am I going to prepare you for this? Well, in one sense I can't. You'll never be truly prepared for this, and that's just how it goes.

However, my plan is to point at the event and precipitating circumstances from a few different angles. Partly, I'm relating experiences that others and I have had prior to and during awakening. I'm also summating the countless discussions I have had with people as they've moved through this territory. That's the best I can do in the form of writing. I'd love to personally walk with you to that threshold as we stare into the abyss together. In a sense, I will be there with you. I've shared this sacred rite of passage with many people, and their experience and my experience will be distilled down for your benefit. I promise you that you have the support of every single being who has crossed this threshold. Their collective voices echoing up through the millennia are saying to you, "This is what you've come for. Don't hesitate another minute. Step through the gate-less gate. Step off into the Great Unknown."

The following sections will vary in approach and pointing style, but all are designed to get you to that threshold. Once you're there, it's up to you to take that step into the mysterious pass. No one can do that for you. Good luck.

"Long seeking it through others,
I was far from reaching it.
Now I go by myself;
I meet it everywhere.
It is just I myself,
And I am not itself.
Understanding this way,
I can be as I am."

—Tung-Shan (806–869)

How It Went Down

As I sit to write the story of my awakening, it dawns on me that I've never written about or even discussed this in depth before. I've never described it to anyone in the detail with which I'm prepared to share it with you. I have certainly shared various aspects and insights related to these pivotal events many times, but I've never reconstructed the story in this way.

Before I tell the story, I want to make a couple of points about the act of describing one's awakening experience to others. First of all, it's impossible to truly relate what happened. It's the kind of thing that you only "get" by going through it. There are very good teachers out there who are averse to talking about the details of their awakening process. In fact, I know teachers whom I respect and to whom I refer people that avoid even using the term awakening. There are good reasons for this. To put it plainly, no matter how much I caution someone about trying to mentally recreate the "story" of my awakening, I know that to some degree this will happen if I talk about it. This is the normal functioning of the human mind. It collects data, then tries to use that data to recreate desirable results. With rare exception, I didn't even mention this event for about fifteen years after it occurred. I didn't feel a need to hide it. I simply knew there wasn't anything I could say about it. Furthermore, I could see that it is extremely easy to mislead people.

I no longer hold the view that it's always detrimental to discuss one's awakening. However, I feel strongly that it has to be done with discernment and in the proper context. One of the reasons I feel it's valuable to share the story in this chapter specifically is a personal one. One of the catalysts that triggered the awakening for me was reading a collection of stories written by people who had gone through awakening themselves. Hearing stories related in the words of regular people somehow made it clear to me that this can and does happen. I also feel comfortable sharing it now because I've made several cautionary statements in this book regarding the futility of thinking

406

one's way into an awakening. I trust that you get the point that what is to be gained from these stories isn't a conceptual or literal reproduction of my story, but rather a deep, intuitive sense that a transformation at the most fundamental level of your being is possible for you. That can only happen in a way that is unique to you and the conditions of your life. As opposed to being a result of following a scripted narrative that you gleaned from others' experience, awakening will be a radical deviation from all scripts and narratives, culminating in a dissolution of the limitations of your identity.

This shift occurred almost twenty-five years ago now. Yet the energetic essence of what happened is still here. It's never gone anywhere. In fact, it is far clearer and more integrated into all aspects of experience than it was at the time. That integration didn't happen overnight. It took a lot of inquiry, acceptance, and letting go. The work continues, although in a very different way now.

A few weeks before the event, I could sense something shifting. The perfume of change was in the air, but I didn't have any idea of the magnitude of what was coming. This was not a happy time. I was in deep despair. Years of anxiety, self-doubt, and constantly questioning my own thoughts had culminated in a pervasive sense of hopelessness. I had been meditating for several years by this time. I did find some solace in those moments during the day when I could relax my mind while sitting. However, the relaxation was inconsistent during meditation, and outside of seated meditation there was no solace to be found. I honestly felt like I was in a mental pressure cooker on a day-to-day basis.

I had heard of awakening and enlightenment before, but it was still mostly conceptual for me. As I mentioned in chapter one, all it took was one person who somehow managed to plant a seed a few years before. I think that seed needed time to germinate. One night, by seemingly random chance, I picked up a book about Zen Buddhism that I had gotten for Christmas a few years before. I had never actually opened it. If I remember right, I hadn't read it because my impression was it was probably full of some old boring stories about monks sitting around in monasteries. For whatever reason, I opened the book that night. Reading the table of contents, I noticed the chapter "Eight Contemporary Enlightenment Experiences by Japanese and Westerners." The book was The Three Pillars of Zen by Roshi Phillip Kapleau. This stirred my curiosity, so I started reading. I was immediately struck by how relatable these people's experiences were. Each was autobiographical and clearly written in their own style. They were mostly lay practitioners of Zen, meaning they lived regular lives—were married, had jobs, etc. The stories described their experience before, during, and after awakening. I was awestruck by these descriptions. It was too good to be true. I knew this was it. I knew this is what I was after, and I knew I wouldn't settle for anything short of awakening (kensho, as described in the book). Please understand I wasn't confident I could do it and still had a lot of doubt. But I knew I had to give myself over to this. In fact, it was the only thing I'd ever come into contact with in my life that I knew I could fully give myself to. I remember thinking, Even if I die trying, I'm not giving up on this because otherwise it's just unending suffering. There had been no real rest or satisfaction for the first twenty-four years of life, so I was pretty certain it wouldn't get better without some fundamental shift that I had never sensed anywhere except in this possibility of kensho.

Reading these stories lit something deep inside me. Something was stirring, something big, something beyond the dimensions of how I'd learned to understand myself. Strangely, I barely noticed this stirring at first because my mind was still making so much noise. Thoughts, thoughts, thoughts. I had nothing to go on except these inspiring stories that clearly communicated a possibility that I was pretty sure most people didn't know existed. If they had, wouldn't everyone be talking about it? I didn't have the faintest clue how to go about this. I had no teacher. I didn't know of any Zen temple nearby. I didn't know any Buddhists. I had never met anyone "that" had happened to. Yet I was determined. The only other clues I could find were in another chapter of the same book. It was a chapter called "Private Encounters with Ten Westerners." This was (and still is) an extremely rare glimpse into the inner workings of an aspect of Zen that is almost always kept completely secret. The Japanese term is dokusan, which means a private interview with a Zen teacher. This is not an ordinary conversation; it is a student's opportunity to present their direct understanding or insight into awakening and realization. It's an instinctual exchange and it follows no specific script. It usually consists of only the teacher and student in a closed room so they can work in private and the student can demonstrate understanding in a focused way. If they are working on a koan, they can do so without spoiling the process for others who have not broken through with the same koan. In this rare case, the Zen master (Roshi) gave permission to have the exchange recorded by a scribe, omitting specifics about koans so as not to give anything essential away.

The Zen master would give very direct practice instructions, words of encouragement, and direct sorts of pointing, all with the intent of helping the student awaken. A lot of what I read I didn't understand because I wasn't really familiar with Zen. However, two things stuck out to me, and I put them into practice as best I could. The Zen teacher had told the students to not separate from their practice at all. "Not even a hair's breadth." This sort of mystified me. It was such a simple instruction, and yet I couldn't quite get what he meant experientially. He also said something to the effect of, "Imagine you're on a train track that goes on forever. Stay right on that track as regards your practice and don't deviate." This also mystified me and hit me at a deep level.

Although these were obscure pointers and I had no context or Zen experience, there was a clear recognition of the "flavor" of what he was pointing to. It was almost like an ancient memory locked away in my DNA. There was something in me that wanted to purify my focus, my mind, and my reality into a singular experience. My attention started to become more focused on practice, even though I didn't really know what "my practice" was. Things were starting to feel paradoxical both when meditating and when going about the activities of the day. In one sense I could feel something focusing like a laser beam. I could feel resolve building in my gut. Yet this wasn't the kind of resolve that results from planning and becoming determined to make something happen in the usual ways we talk or think about. It was a resolve that wasn't completely me. I felt both in control in a way I never had, and yet radically out of control. There were things moving inside me and around me that I didn't understand, and yet I trusted and was in awe of. It felt like I was participating in an ancient ritual, a primordial rite of passage. Yet I had no idea what the heck was going on or where I was headed. I stopped caring about where I was headed, yet I carried on down that railroad track. I wasn't going to deviate now, even though I truly had no idea what that even meant.

In practical terms, I was taking my practice off the (mediation) mat. I would stay with it as I went on about my daily activities. When I walked, this practice walked. When I cooked, practice cooked. When I would drift off to sleep, I carried this with me to the last glimmer of consciousness. Then I'd pick it right back up the moment I realized I was awake again. I stayed on that track. You might be wondering what I mean here by "practice." Well, the strange thing is I can't tell you exactly because I didn't even know myself, and yet I intuited some direction that was not of conventional dimension. The more I refused to separate myself, the more momentum this gained. It was scary at times. It was confusing most of the time. It was exciting. There was still a ton of doubt, there was still suffering, but my body, mind, and soul had turned into a leviathan of blind faith directed through a laser-like precision of concentration. Directed toward . . . well, I didn't know what. Does this sound crazy? Yes, it was crazy. It made no sense, and yet it was the first thing in my life that really made sense instinctually. I wasn't deviating—I refused to. And since I didn't know what I was refusing to deviate from, I was opening a portal into the unknown. I didn't know how I knew how to do this, but through sheer desperation and a willingness to push through the veil of the unknown, the lock dial was turning, and the tumblers were falling . . .

Click. . .

Click. . .

Click. . .

The following passage written by St John of the Cross describes this experience well:

*"To come to enjoy what you have not
you must go by a way in which you enjoy not.*

*To come to the knowledge you have not
you must go by a way in which you know not.*

*To come to the possession you have not
you must go by a way in which you possess not.*

*To come to be what you are not
you must go by a way in which you are not."*

I was off the map. I had abandoned the script. I didn't care what happened to that old life. I could feel it starting to slough off like the skin of a snake. I was still functional. I could dress myself and I could go to work. However, when I returned home, I'd go right back at it. Right back into that unknown.

If you're asking yourself how I was orienting myself to the unknown, you're asking the wrong question. This is because any answer I could give you would be orienting you to the known. Instead, you might ask the opposite question. Ask, "What is the unknown?" Then look there. I'll give you a hint: It's not a thought. Any thought is the known, so then what in the world is the unknown?

❖ *What is there when there are no thoughts?*

❖ *What is between thoughts?*

❖ *What is aware of thoughts?*

❖ *Look there. Again, and again, and again, just like a train on a track to infinity.*

That's exactly what I did. One night I was meditating, and it became very clear. If I didn't deviate from that mystery, from the unknown, then any thought would only be a distraction. A thought could say nothing about this. With this recognition, I became extremely interested in thoughts. I wanted the next thought to come just so I could call it out as "not truth." A thought would arise. Wow things are so clear now, and I'd immediate recognize, Oh that's another thought, and let it go. Another thought would come, Well, without thoughts I won't be able to do anything. I'd immediately dismiss this with, Oh! Another thought. What else is here?

"I could become insane doing this."

Thought!

"Oh my gosh, there are no thoughts!"

Thought!

"This must be enlightenment."

Thought!

"Okay, I must not know what enlightenment is."

Thought!

"I'm exhausted."

Thought!

"Well, that was fun and interesting, but I should really go to sleep now."

Thought!

"Oh my God, even I'm tired is just a thought. I've believed thoughts about 'me' for so long, I never stopped to look outside of thoughts. What is this space outside of thoughts? Can I stay in it without thoughts?"

Thought!

Then . . .

"......"

I kept at this, becoming more and more fascinated with what was there between thoughts, and also there when there wasn't a thought at all. Then I noticed something simple and peculiar. I noticed that I could clearly notice there were no thoughts in this mystery-practice without having to think about it. I can't tell you how strangely surprising and yet relaxing that was. The gap between thoughts grew longer and longer. Understand, I wasn't pushing thoughts away. If anything, I was welcoming them because it was such a joy to release each thought, each belief, and each judgment, and then just return to this mysterious awakeness that didn't have to think about anything. It was almost as if the thought-producing machine had just given up once it realized it couldn't trap my attention anymore. It was quite enjoyable, but there was no internal comment about it. It was sort of joyously neutral . . . and quiet. I can't tell you how much of a relief it was to have that kind of quietude after years and years of being bombarded with thoughts, doubts, and mental experiences.

So, I just stayed with this. This is where things get tricky to talk about. Let me just say that if you find yourself in this place of pure awakeness with few to no thoughts, then you are in a good place. Just stay with it. What I found is that by staying with it (I don't know how long it was because it was hard to judge time and there was no interest in doing so), the quality of it started to change, to deepen perhaps. Then there was a simple but very fundamental shift. Suddenly it was clear that I was in a far more vast space of existence than I had known previously. It still had that thoughtless pure-awakeness aspect, but the instinctual depths of being became suddenly fathomless. Everything became exquisitely light and fluid. It was clear that I, and everything I had previously encountered and perceived as my life (other people, and the world out there) were all exactly the same "stuff." The sense of being a struggling me always at odds with my thoughts and emotions had completely dissolved into an intimate pool of pure, unconditioned existence. The relief was beyond description. There was no internal comment about this, just a pure enjoyment of aliveness without boundary. It was clear that this wasn't an experience because the mental faculty that had been (seemingly) carving up reality into discreet experiences had stopped altogether. Now there was just pure being without parts. The access to this infinite pool of pure, undivided consciousness-being has continued to this day.

At that moment I could never have imagined I was only on the precipice of what was to come. It didn't matter, that undeniable, self-validating, all-encompassing consciousness was all that mattered. I drifted off to sleep that night with a peace a hadn't known was possible for the first twenty-four years of my life.

A Few Reminders

> ➤ As the first line in this book states, you can wake up from the dream of separation. You have what is required, even if you don't know what that is. Without fail, everyone I've known who was sincere about wanting to wake up, and has been willing to work toward it, not backing off when things start to shift, has woken up. You can do this!

➢ No amount of intellectual understanding, reading, imagining, mapping, or planning can cross you over. You have to go beyond concept and thought to penetrate this barrier. You have to go directly into the unknown.

➢ At some point you will be moving on pure instinct. I can't tell you what that feels like, but you'll know it as it starts to happen. If a thought is saying, "Is this it, or isn't it?" That's not instinct. When you get tired of entertaining that thought and proceed on without the crutch of thinking, that is instinct. You won't know exactly where you are going, but you'll recognize that the doubt that has weighed you down for so long is only thought. There is a way to go beyond even doubt. Don't think about this, do it.

➢ There are forces ready to come to your aid when you have exhausted all of your mental avenues and yet are still determined to move forward into the unknown. What you're involved in is beyond the scope and limitations of your identity and life as you know it.

➢ If you penetrate this identity barrier, you won't be disappointed, but you will be astounded. It won't be any way you've imagined it; it's too real to be imagined.

➢ When the bonds start to release, you might feel intense sensations, particularly at first. Many people describe pressure, disorientation, fear, or panic. Some people even feel like they might die. I know these are intense descriptions, but I want to prepare you for the possibility. It's not uncommon that when I point someone past conceptuality, they say something to the effect of, "Every time I let go of thoughts, I feel this intense sensation like pressure or dread. I think it's because I'm overexerting myself. I worry that's not a good way to practice." In some contexts that might be a valid conclusion. However, when we come to this seeming impasse, it's important to be very clear about what is a thought and what is real. Do you see

416

how the thought seems to be throwing you a life preserver to save you from that "dangerous place" out there beyond the conceptual realm? Don't be fooled! Thoughts have a lot of experience at reeling you back in. They know just what to say. A little stubbornness here can even be helpful when you realize it's time to shed these mental shackles and find out what's really real.

The Puzzle Pieces Come Together

Here are the factors that often come into play when someone is close to awakening. With each description/pointer I will provide questions you can use as points of inquiry to help clarify and penetrate that aspect of experience. Of course, the timing of much of this is out of your control, but sooner or later you'll start to recognize these fires being lit in your life. When you do, I encourage you to stoke those fires. They are the catalytic flames of transformation.

Any of these questions can take you all the way in if you're ready to throw yourself 100 percent into the questioning and accept no answer short of authentic awakening. Ask the question and then follow its trajectory fully into the unknown like an arrow fired in slow-motion directly into infinity.

"In each moment the fire rages, it will burn away a hundred veils. And carry you a thousand steps toward your goal."

—Rumi

Going Beyond Conceptual Self

You've read it many times now, "Awakening isn't about concept or understanding," and yet it's not until you become genuinely curious about this truth that the cracks start forming. At some point you become truly dumbfounded that although you sense something beyond the boundaries of your life as you can possibly think about it (the conceptual you), it's a complete mystery what that something could be. If you really consider this, it can lead you into a subversive sort of curiosity. Once that curiosity starts to permeate your mind and your heart, you will become willing to let the conceptual self go to find out what is truly beyond. It's the only way.

> ➤ "What am I right now when I don't 'remember' myself through memories of a past, imaginings of a future, or referencing any facts I think I know about myself?" Look there right now and don't look away. Don't grab onto that life raft of knowing.

> ➤ "What is here that is not a thought or image?" Go there and don't turn back.

> ➤ "Can I become curious without wanting any thought or conceptual answer to satisfy that curiosity?" What . . . Is . . . This?

Abandoning Spiritual Knowledge

Even your accumulated spiritual knowledge will do you no good here. By the time we've come this far, it's likely we've picked up many beliefs and expectations about awakening and spirituality. In fact, we've often developed a sort of spiritual identity. Well, when it's time to move into the unknown, we have to be willing to let that mass of acquired knowledge and all spiritual identities go. This moment is a raging fire burning up everything that tries to enter or leave it.

> ➤ "What is true right now if I forget all the knowledge I've accumulated about awakening and/or spirituality?"

> ➤ "What is this experience like if I have nothing to compare it to, meaning I can't reference any previous experience, be it spiritual or otherwise?"

> ➤ "What is this like when I don't reference the past, or the future, or even the present? Where can I look now?"

> ➤ "What is this like when I dissolve all expectations of what it should be like?"

Being Fed Up

You have to be willing to see that all the ways you've tried to make yourself feel better, make your life work, and find rest and salvation have failed to deliver what you'd really hoped for. This is a hard pill to swallow, and a hard thing to admit. However, suffering is the match that lights the fire of awakening, so it's necessary to be brutally honest with yourself about this and stoke that fire of dissatisfaction. Sure, in the short term it feels good to accomplish things, deepen our relationships, and set and achieve goals. These activities have their place in our lives and deserve our effort and attention. Yet something is still missing, isn't it? Something you won't find by following any external path. None of those things brought you deep peace and lasting relief, did they? If they did you wouldn't be here. So we have to be willing to see that all our efforts to make ourselves feel better, find peace, and live fulfilling lives have resulted in only brief periods of satisfaction. Furthermore, they were often followed by the opposite experiences of feeling unsatisfied, isolated, and confused.

This is exactly how I felt right before awakening. I knew I could accomplish things in life. I knew I could connect with people. I knew I could set goals and achieve them. Yet that wordless question still burned inside me. It was something I couldn't talk to anyone about. It was too personal. I knew I had to go beyond myself somehow. When I gave myself fully to that impulse, everything changed. We have to get to the point where we are ready to try something radically different. We have to be willing to throw away the map.

> If you're really honest with yourself, have you ever had lasting peace and equanimity with the things you sought and then acquired/accomplished?

> Even if there were short periods of enjoyment following an accomplishment, did dissatisfaction follow closely behind?

> If so, did you let go into that emotional experience and dive all the way down through it, or did you start seeking something else to take your mind off the disappointment?

Letting Go

This isn't going to sound good, but I find this movement to be consistent among those who experience awakening, so I have to mention it. At some point, you will have to be willing to let go of your life as you know it. I know that seems radical, but when you really start to move into the unknown, there are well-hidden defense mechanisms that come into play. Whether we realize it or not, the only thing that actually prevents awakening is that when we start sniffing in the right direction, these defense mechanisms get activated. More times than not, before we even realize we are operating in defense mode, the thought stream had already grabbed us by the nose ring and led us down some avenue of distraction. Outwardly this will usually just feel like an impulse to contemplate something else, or a change of mind. However, if we refuse to be deterred by yet another

420

thought, distraction, doubt, or fear, we will find that a shedding of the conceptual structures that seem to hold our life together is underway. Once we've been through this process enough times, we realize, "I have no choice but to go beyond myself if I want to realize living truth." All thought roads lead to the same hamster wheel of seeking and craving—promising everything and delivering nothing.

The mental alarms that go off know how to get your attention. If you ignore the distracting thoughts, the musings, and the philosophical chatter, your mind will kick it up a notch to get your attention. It will say things like, "Your life will be over if you go any further!" "You'll die if you keep on like this!" "You'll go insane!" Of course. These are just thoughts, but to disentangle yourself from them, sometimes you have to get to the point where you say, "Well so be it, if I die then that's how it goes, but I'm going to keep moving in this direction because somehow I instinctually trust it." I've never heard of anyone dying because of awakening, but I have talked to many people who felt like they might die right before it happened. For me, there was one incident where I felt a massive fear of plunging into the unknown, so I backed off. Later I had the instinct that if I ever came that close to the edge again, I'd just go ahead and let go. When the opportunity presented itself again, I did let go, and that time there was no fear at all.

> What would it feel like to let go right now? I mean let go of everything. Does that bring up any emotion? Do you notice the thoughts that flood in, saying, "Well, you can't just let go of everything. You have to hold onto something!" What if you continue to let go despite the emotions and/or thoughts? Where does this lead? Try it and find out.

> What if you give over your will to living truth right now, even if it has nothing to do with what you think truth is? How would you go about that?

Moving on Instinct

I remember approximately a week before awakening something clicked for me. I was still suffering. I still had endless thoughts, doubt, and anxiousness/tension in my body. Yet I was suddenly aware of something "new." I can't say exactly what that was, but it was like a little smile coming out of the fabric of reality. It was not anything specific, yet it was always there when I remembered to put my attention on it. No matter what circumstance I was in, it was there. It didn't immediately end my suffering or change anything outwardly in the environment, but it was a sort of beacon. I trusted it in a way I had never trusted anything before. I also knew that it wasn't exactly new. It had a familiarity to it. When I would put my attention on it, something interesting would happen. It would be like I was suffering and also was not suffering. The thoughts were there but in that "place" I could attune to, they were also not there. Can you sense what I'm talking about? If so, turn your attention there and don't worry about what any doubts say because the doubts can be there, and with this they are also not there. Do you see?

This wasn't yet awakening, but it was like I was tugging on a string that had somehow come loose from the fabric of reality, I just kept following that string . . .

Where is your string?

Find it right here and keep your attention there, even if thoughts, doubts, or activities occur. It's not apart from any of those, but it's also not bound by any of them.

Being Willing to Stop

More precisely, be willing to be stopped in your tracks, because even trying to stop is still doing something. When you're completely stopped, you're in a great position for a force that is beyond your understanding and dimension to come to your aid. Here's what it looks like:

- ❖ Stop trying to gain anything.

- ❖ Stop trying to lose something.

- ❖ Stop trying to fix something about your life.

- ❖ Stop convincing yourself that more seeking will get you what you want.

- ❖ Stop imagining awakening or enlightenment.

- ❖ Stop running into the future (thoughts).

- ❖ Stop running into the past (thoughts).

- ❖ Stop believing you know anything about reality.

- ❖ Stop trying to find something.

- ❖ Stop faking it.

- ❖ Stop pretending you're happy when you aren't.

- ❖ Stop filtering your experience right now.

- ❖ Stop interpreting.

- ❖ Stop managing.

It may seem contradictory that I'm telling you to stop, yet throughout this book I've described various approaches and techniques that sounded very much like something to do. Well, what if they aren't two different things? It sounds contradictory, but all contradiction resides in thought. One we've crossed over, reality isn't contradictory, and we see that thoughts stumble all over themselves in contradictory ways, trying to keep up with raw aliveness, but they never can. What if doing and stopping are not apart from one another? What would that look like? What if stopping is the inevitable effect of not getting on the thought train anymore? This is exactly how it is. All doing and effort exists solely inside thoughts. When we no longer look through the lens of thought, there is only spontaneous action.

An Artist Awakens

A good friend was generous enough to record her awakening story to include in this chapter for your benefit. She told me that she really wanted to support anyone going through this and encourage them. However, she also wanted to be clear that it's not always bliss and roses. She said for her it was often a painful process, but she wouldn't trade it for anything. Here is her story:

"As a child I had always had a sense that there was something I needed to turn toward. This continued into adulthood. I didn't know what it was, but it terrified me. So I continued to search for home elsewhere. It felt energetically like something was always following me. It was as if there was a ghost following me around, just waiting for me to give it my attention. Yet I was always on the run. I really thought I'd find that one thing that could complete me. Rather, I thought I'd find something that would allow me to ignore this pain and the sense that something was not quite right.

Even with all this running, I still felt like I was between worlds. I felt alien to this life. I didn't feel attached to the stories of the trauma of my past, but I did feel personal attachment to making a better future and to stop suffering. I felt like it was my responsibility, having come from such a chaotic upbringing. I was both running and seeking, and nowhere felt like home. For years I experienced shifts in reality, but intellectually I had no clue what was happening. I intuited something immensely powerful in me that seemed to keep on, leading me right where I needed to be. I didn't feel this path was spiritual at all, I just wanted to stop suffering. I wanted to know life more deeply. I felt this energy in my chest that wanted to burst open, but I got the message somehow that it wasn't okay to let it. I sensed that it was more painful to contain this energy, but I didn't know how to let it open. So I chose things that kept it closed.

I changed jobs multiple times. I traveled the world. I got married and I got divorced. No matter where I looked, I wasn't able to find this home I had always been searching for. I was at a loss. I was at my end. I felt defeated and I lay in bed for eight months in the worst depression of my life. This depression continued until one day something got me out of bed. Something else seemed to be carrying me. Perhaps it is what had been carrying me all along.

I had no context for awakening whatsoever. I met Angelo one night in an improv acting class, and he was the first person to tell me to trust what I was going through. Trusting a stranger's words at that moment felt oddly perfect. He was a stranger, but it also felt like he wasn't a stranger at all. He knew this 'ghost's' energy that I have been running from. He knew about what I had thought I could never share with anyone. After that night, I began to turn inward, taking his advice about trying meditation and self-inquiry. I trusted this guidance. I knew it was time. Everything else had failed me. It felt right in a way that nothing had before. This is where it becomes extremely hard to talk about because the memory doesn't exist on any sort of timeline.

Since I wasn't working at the time, I sat on my patio all day and all night. I kept asking, 'What am I?' I felt I was at the edge of knowing who I was anyway, so I thought, 'Why not ask?' It was challenging at first. My mind would wander, and I would cry. I would go into memories of childhood. I would relive the experiences that I always guarded myself from. I sat on that balcony for three months, and that balcony became my best friend. Watching the movement of the trees in the wind calmed me. One day I was messaging with Angelo about identity, and I realized that identity isn't this one thing I had been looking for. It's a web of thoughts, movements, and identities. I was shocked that there were more than one.

I have a vague memory of getting up from the balcony in the middle of the night and staring at myself in the mirror for a long time. The reflection looked strange to me. I eventually went to bed. The next morning, I wrote a powerful poem. This was the first poem I'd written since I was in elementary school. I don't even read poetry, but somehow I started writing it. Later in the day I was mediating on the couch. When I came out of mediation, something felt very different. Even now I can't describe it. I ended up in the car not knowing why or where I was going. Then I walked into a Chipotle, ordered my food, and sat to eat. As I sat there eating, I looked out the window and saw people walking by. However, things didn't look like they usually did. It looked something like the movie The Matrix. I could see the people and also see through the people and scenery. I could see the code of existence. I got kind of spooked and went back to my car. I messaged Angelo and we talked a bit. I went to drive home but I couldn't remember where my home was. I drove in circles for a while until I finally ended up back at my house. Angelo suggested I stay with this at home for a few days. I had no clue who I was, or even where I was for that matter. I went back to my balcony. I felt like I kept opening. I kept expanding. My memory would fade. My pain was gone. The magnitude of stillness and connectedness

426

was beyond anything I'd known before. I felt so alive, an aliveness beyond description.

From this moment on I laughed a lot. Life became so funny that my stomach would cramp. I used to cry at the drop of a hat, but now I laugh at the drop of a hat. I spent six months laughing. I fell on the floor laughing constantly. It felt so good to laugh. My body would release so much stored-up energy when I would laugh. This was grace; grace giving this sweet child of trauma a chance to laugh freely without care. Giving her the space to express her heart and enjoy. Giving her space to open.

During this time, I found a love for food when I was normally very picky. I noticed that my picky eating had been a way to feel solid in identity. Now that the need to construct an identity was gone, the flavors and textures and visual experience of food became so fascinating. Whereas before I had rejected many of my experiences of life, now I couldn't imagine saying no to my experience anymore. I found myself in love with life and finally felt like "I am home." Finally, home. Since I wasn't working, and I didn't have a plan for what was to come next, I began painting. This led to me starting a career as an artist. Being an artist is my truest existence because I can express my array of emotions and tap into my intuition. Most importantly, I can share it. I can share a part of myself that I had kept hidden for so long. My heart bursts open every chance it gets.

After six months of blissful laughter, amazing sensations (including food), and a newfound love for painting and writing poetry, life put me right back into the pain. There was more to see, more to feel. The next eight months were challenging. I didn't lose my laughter, but I had to face a very dark shadow side. My practice became about paying close attention to delusion and unconscious behavior. There was a lot of time spent alone and with the sensations of physical and emotional pain. I discovered ways of welcoming the lost children inside me who had never had a voice. I learned how to express the sides of myself I still wanted to stuff away. I was afraid, but there was nowhere to go but in. Consciousness kept pulling me toward truth. It wasn't easy, but I knew it had to be done. As far as shadow work, I found that you can't skip over the shadow; you must become the shadow to really see where it illuminates.

This journey of awakening isn't an easy path. However, it is far more rewarding than any dream. It's been over a year now since my dive into the shadow work and back, and I truly don't have the words to describe what's here. After these few years all I can say is, "What a shift." All the seeking for home and all the bliss of being welcomed home, I now have nowhere to rest my head, nor a need to do so. Life doesn't look how I imagined it would. Awakening didn't happen how I wanted it to or how I pictured it would. It is not bliss or pain, it is where everything is welcomed. I know this is absolutely possible for anyone willing to turn inward. We are not alone. What we experience as humans is the same, but we each have different story lines.

As I sit here now and write, I'm aware it's a beautiful opportunity to feel the sensation of this story again. To listen to the birds in the yard, to feel the couch beneath my bum. I love life, and the experience of it is far beyond what I could have imagined. It's a dynamic dance, and I am beyond grateful for it. I could have never guessed it was possible to love life this much, even through all the fluctuations, through all the coming and going. What great stillness. Somehow, out of this going nowhere-ness of it all, it no longer matters if there is suffering or bliss. When I look directly into your eyes, I see an aliveness dancing. In the eyes of a stranger, I see my greatest lover. I see colors dancing. I see life loving so deeply. Even in a shallow pond I see this radiant, unspoken life. I no longer see suffering, though my heart could never ignore your pain. What a paradox to search lifetimes for an end to suffering, only to come to this place where I don't have a care whether it comes or goes. What brilliance.

All of it leads to right now. The act of going anywhere in time is lost—vanished as quickly as the sun sets in the sky. It's seen to have ceased to be—to have never been. It had always felt like I was going somewhere. The inevitable truth is that we are going toward death if toward anything at all. That is what we know for certain. So, with this certainty and this seeing that nothing is certain, then any ultimate way of being, any ultimate truth, is an inevitable trap leading back to the now. When I look for the memory of what was, it only appears in this now. I find it in the arrival and passing of each breath, the heart beating in my chest, and the clinch in my throat. This ambient light that is radiating now, this alive nature of all things, it's momentary. It's infinite. Language has a beautiful way of describing this or that, in or out of time, but this is neither in time nor is it out of time. It is both in time and out of time. It makes no sense. It is neither logical nor illogical. It is neither toward nor away from. It seems perhaps time and no time aren't existent unless arising together. Like two particles, one and the same, yet going different directions.

One paradox is coherent to one ripple of a pond. All of what I remember as my story doesn't feel personal anymore. It's a blip on the radar. It's a drop in a bucket. It never was, yet always is. Awakening is such a precious, personal dance, until it isn't. So, then, who is there to awaken? This is a valuable question. In my opinion, it is the most valuable thing one can address in any lifetime."

—*Violet*

Two Approaches

We have explored many practices, techniques, and points of inquiry in the preceding chapters. None of them is intrinsically better or more potent than any other. Which will work best for you is matter of your temperament and what most effectively potentiates your drive to awaken. It is also a matter of timing. Trust your instincts. It only takes one act of complete relinquishment, at the right moment, to breech the veil of the illusion of separation. Once that happens, you will naturally realign with what is beyond.

As you approach that moment of dissolution, it can be helpful to concentrate your intention to break through into a singular focus. A point of inquiry or a question that you find particularly engaging is a perfect way to accomplish this. You may have already found one. If so, wonderful. If you haven't, I want to offer two approaches that are specifically geared toward this final push. They are particularly potent in that period when we sense awakening approaching. The two approaches are:

➢ Self-Inquiry Approach

➢ One-Pointed Approach

The self-inquiry technique is a particularly direct approach to awakening. It can efficiently dissolve the mental barriers that keep you locked in the thought-prison. The key is to give yourself fully to it. This approach can also be a valuable practice after awakening. It can help to both clarify the initial insight and continue to dissolve false identity structures.

The one-pointed approach differs in that it's an exquisitely potent catalyst for first awakening but is less valuable afterward. How you choose between these approaches is largely intuitive. Try them out, and if one feels more aligned with your instincts and temperament, then use that one.

Self-Inquiry

We've touched on the question, "Who am I?" a couple of times. Now we're going to take that point of inquiry and give it a boost. We'll use this self-inquiry vehicle as a sort of depth charge. Its purpose is to plunge you down through all those layers of belief and personal narrative, right to the core of identity. If we do this the right way, it will detonate when it reaches that core. This detonation will blow a hole right through the bottom. "The bottom of what?" you might ask. The bottom of everything. We are going to blow a hole right through the bottom of reality. You didn't come all this way for nothing, right?

Blowing a hole through the bottom is obviously a metaphor. The transformation that we're talking about here is so radical that even dimension (bottom, top, near, far) will be seen to be an illusion. Still, it's a reasonably apt description. After my own awakening, these were the exact words that occurred to me. A couple of days into reality as I knew it dismantling itself, I was talking to a friend about what had happened. I knew I couldn't adequately put into words what had taken place. I also knew it was impossible to describe what had replaced the struggle and isolation I had previously considered to be "normal life." Yet my friend could sense that something had dramatically changed in me and asked what had happened. The words came: "I was meditating, and the bottom fell out." It was exactly like this. Oddly enough, when the bottom fell out, there was nothing for everything to fall into. The framework of reality as I had known it had completely deconstructed itself. What was left was something like a deep and pervasive peace, and that's how it remains. It's obvious that whatever I thought was real before was only a very small "model" of reality, something like a shadow on a wall. I had stumbled upon a possibility, a way of investigating the nature of perceiving, that completely altered the way I experience reality.

Self-inquiry has the power to bring this about for anyone who is willing to take the plunge. By imbibing it with the will to awaken to your true nature, you give the self-inquiry vehicle power beyond the limits of what you are capable of on your own. In this way, the inquiry becomes something of a portal or a conduit through which we can come into contact with forces altogether beyond the limits of the human dimension. Once this happens, you can no longer know yourself in the limited and definite way you had previously learned to perceive yourself. Your identity will find a new equilibrium with unbound consciousness, which is essentially limitless. The limitless experience of consciousness-Being, while astounding, is but the staging area for the more radical unfolding ahead. Yet it is an important milestone in the process of realization.

Like any catalyst, this method of self-inquiry functions best when the environmental conditions are favorable. Let's spend some time discussing the optimal conditions to support this process before we will delve into the mechanics of the inquiry itself. Here are the conditions:

Alert: This inquiry works best if you are alert, without straining. You don't want to be slack with your attention, daydreaming, or mind-wandering. On the other hand, it's unnecessary to be hypervigilant or to strain your attention into a hyperfocused state. You want to be alert enough to assure that nothing escapes your attention, including any thought. A relaxed and dilated (open) attention, engaged in the process of inquiry is ideal. It is something like driving an automobile in a city you are unfamiliar with. Unlike taking a long drive down the highway where you might zone out or daydream a bit, driving in an unfamiliar city requires you to keep your attention on the immediate environment. You won't be daydreaming or imagining events and places that aren't in your current experience. It can take a bit of practice to strike the right balance between alertness and relaxation. Keep practicing, and you will find that sweet spot where you are neither daydreaming nor straining.

Curious: Genuine curiosity is necessary for this approach to work. It's my responsibility to relate the mechanics of this inquiry in a way that compels genuine curiosity. It's up to you to be willing to acknowledge that innocent curiosity and let it carry you deeper into inquiry. We often circumvent natural curiosity by moving our attention to a familiar but artificial mental construct when we find ourselves in the unknown. We do this to feel some sense of certainty. This means that when faced with the unknown, we often cling to old, habituated patterns of thinking to help us avoid admitting to ourselves that we really don't know. When this technique is applied correctly, you will find yourself in the unknown rather quickly. The paradox here is that using thought to "cure" that sense of unknowing will undermine the inquiry. A willingness to remain in unguarded curiosity is the lamp that lights the way forward.

Empirical: One definition of empirical is, "verifiable by observation or experience rather than theory or logic." When conducting self-inquiry, it's best to forego comparing your experience to any idealized experience or expectation. We're here to discover. So any description we've read or heard about what is supposed to happen when we self-inquire is useless. We're only interested in what we directly discover. If you're willing to take a strictly empirical approach, then only immediate, obvious, and self-explanatory experience matters. When you really get the spirit of this, it is quite a relief. How nice it is to not to have to stress over whether your experience is the "right" one. In a sense, you're putting realization in the hot seat. You're saying, "Okay, I trust that you really can show me something that is beyond my own capacity to construct it as a mental image. I will keep my slate clean and not compare my experience to any ideal, regardless of where I acquired that ideal."

Fresh: When you begin this inquiry, just let go of everything you know. Let go of past inquiries and results. Let go of any insights you might have had, even the last time you meditated or engaged in inquiry. In fact, let go of what happened five minutes ago. Just this one question. Just this one experiential observation. Do this every time you return to inquiry. Then do this as you go about inquiry. It's like writing on a chalkboard and there is an eraser immediately following the chalk. In this way every moment is fresh. Every time a question is asked, it's asked from complete innocence and unknowing. We carry no baggage in this way. When we free ourselves from the bondage of the past, we are free to synchronize with the moment-to-moment flow of reality.

Consistent: Initially, you might approach this inquiry during seated meditation, or when you feel inclined to introspect. Over time, as the curiosity and desire to wake up build, you will find that you can carry this inquiry with you for longer periods of time. You might be surprised as it becomes quite enjoyable to carry this throughout daily activities such as cooking, working, exercising, and even talking with others. With consistency, a certain momentum builds. When I was close to awakening (though I didn't know it at the time), I would even carry inquiry off into sleep. I would try to stay with the query even as my consciousness seemed to disappear into nothingness. I would then pick it up just as soon as I remembered to do so upon waking. There's no need to judge yourself if you can't stay with it constantly, but as your passion to penetrate the barrier of illusion grows, you will find that it can be carried with you a lot of the time. After all, if you've come this far you've realized there is nothing more important than this, right?

Here is the basic Process:

1. Become receptive to thought:

    It's so common for us to attempt suppress or avoid thoughts when we want to relax and rest. We often conclude that if all those

434

thoughts weren't there, we'd be at peace. Well, when it comes to self-inquiry, we actually want the thoughts to come. We orient toward thoughts as if we can't wait for the next thought to arrive. This might sound counterintuitive, but when you truly embrace the arrival of thoughts (regardless of their content), it can relax you in a different way than you might be used to. It's not a checked-out sort of relaxation; it's a checked-in relaxation. To put it simply, a lot of strain is involved in resisting thoughts, and we resist thoughts to various degrees all day long. So the first step is to simply become thought-receptive. Turn your attention to that inner movie screen. You can even affirm inwardly, I choose to be completely receptive to thoughts. They have all of my attention right now. I welcome them. You make the awareness of thoughts as thoughts, the most interesting thing to you in this moment. Also, this is not about daydreaming. When we daydream, we are not aware of thoughts as such. Instead, we are taking them to be reality. To clarify, let's suppose that thoughts about the Bahamas appear. The goal is not to daydream endlessly about a beach trip to the Bahamas. Rather, we should become fascinated as the thought of the Bahamas forms on that inner screen. Oh, so this is a thought! It's showing a sort of inner movie of the Bahamas, and yet I can see it's made out of some sort of nebulous thought-stuff. That's what it means to become fascinated with thought as thought.

2. Take a neutral stance:

As a thought arrives, don't evaluate its content. There's no need to assign a value to it, such as, "This is a good thought or a bad thought." For example, if a thought arrives that says, I'm confused, we needn't assign a negative connotation to it. Just take it as a neutral experience. You can consider the thought to be like a pad of paper with the message "I'm confused" written on it. We could say that the pad of paper is primary to the message, meaning the pad of paper could be there with any message on it or no

435

message at all. In that sense it's neutral. When we see a thought as a thought, we have this opportunity to perceive its neutrality. It's when we believe a thought points to some reality "out there" that we begin to struggle with polarity. As you practice with one thought at a time, you will get better at perceiving this neutrality.

3.   Clarify the thought:

This step can take a bit of practice because we usually have a dynamic relationship with thought inside consciousness. We tend to move past certain thoughts that are uncomfortable or partially unconscious. This is even more marked when we are feeling restless and our monkey-mind is swinging from branch to branch so quickly that we're not fully aware of what thought branches it's swinging from. So slow down. Take one thought at a time as it arrives. Once you recognize a thought (whether conceptual, auditory, or visual image), try to clarify it a bit. If it's conceptual you can speak it in your mind. If you think of this like watching a slide show of thoughts on a movie screen, you want to slow down the slides. Then you want to move closer to the screen and clarify exactly what that thought/image/slide is. As you get better at holding a single thought in your mind, you might be surprised how simple and even relaxing it becomes. You might also be surprised that the closer you look at a thought, the less substance it seems to have. This is analogous to walking so close to the screen that all you see are soft forms, shapes, and light.

4.   Notice how the thought feels like it's about "me."

The previous steps can become somewhat passive once you get the hang of them. This step requires active engagement with each thought, if only for a moment. This is because this step addresses the precise moment when we become unconscious meaning the moment we become identified with thought. It's a subtle transition, so we must train ourselves to recognize it if we want to finally be free of it. Here you may feel like you are doing a bit of detective work, but it's essential to do it every time. Initially it can feel somewhat awkward, like you're going against the habit force of the thought stream. What you're really doing here is undermining a false perspective. The key is to observe the thought and identify the sense that this thought is about "me." Let's look at an example. Let's say we've become receptive to thought (step one). We turn our attention inward, and within a short time we are starting to form a visual memory of eating a sandwich ten minutes ago. We remember thinking about what a good sandwich it was at the time we were eating it. As we become aware of this thought, we recognize, "Okay, in this thought/memory there is a visual replaying of eating a sandwich. There is also self-dialogue saying it is a good sandwich-eating experience. It is clear that this self-talk occurred ten minutes ago. At this moment it is simply one thought in my mind, neither good nor bad." This last part is step two. Now we clarify the visual experience of that thought, somewhat like we are squaring ourselves up to the internal movie screen and stepping closer (step three). We notice the colors and textures of the room, the sandwich, and our hand holding it. We see the movement and recall the chewing as well as the internal dialogue: What a delicious sandwich this is. We see how peculiar it is that this is all made out of thought-stuff and yet it is quite vivid.

Now for step four. In this step we recognize that this thought, this internal movie, appears to be about me. It seems that I was the one eating the sandwich, doesn't it? Of course, in the past I did eat a sandwich, but in this thought it seems that it is referring to "me." It's not Joe or Jessica eating that sandwich. I understand this may seem so obvious as to be absurd, but it's key to recognize that this thought clearly appears to refer to someone called "me." In addition, it seems and feels like this thought is occurring to "me." This means that the sense of me is not only implied in the thought (the one eating the sandwich), but also it is implied by

437

there being a thought at all. Let me explain. Not only does the thought appear to suggest it is about "me" as the star of the internal movie eating a sandwich, but it also suggests that there is a "me" that is interested in the thought at all. Can you see that distinction? More importantly, can you find that sense with your own thought, whatever that happens to be? It appears as if the thought is happening to a "me," the thinker. It suggests a "me" right here and now that is aware of and viewing the thought. You could say it suggests a "me" in two different respects. One is a remembered me (as a thought subject). The other is an immediate me that is aware of that thought right in this moment. Can you feel into both of those? Is your internal experience starting to feel a bit different? Do you feel the edges of identity starting to soften or distort? If you do, that's totally normal. If you don't yet, that's okay too. Give this some practice, and sooner or later those perceptual frameworks will start to loosen and fragment. If you've gone through this step along with me (using your own immediate thought experience), and you understand and can experience directly that a thought implies both a subject "me," which is the main character in the thought, as well as the immediate "me," which is the viewer/thinker of the thought, then you've completed step four. I know this can be confusing or disorienting at first, but it's imperative to go through this process for this type of self-inquiry to really do its magic. It will get much simpler with a bit of practice.

5. Now, look for the "me:"

All of the steps up until this one were preparatory steps. They are all necessary, and you shouldn't skip over them using this approach. However, they are merely a means to orient you properly for this final step. This step is quite simple. Now that you have a sense that the thought you have become aware of is about "me," look for that me. That's it. The thought says there's a me there that it's about, right? Now look for it in your immediate experience. By that I mean don't think about who/where/what that sense of me is. You have to look for evidence of it right in your experience. It helps to start by looking in the place where it feels like you are right now. Look right in the center of the one that feels like the "me" that thought was about. Do you find something there? Is there something definite you can identify and say, "There's the 'me.' There's exactly what I am?" If you can, then what is it that you found there? If you don't find anything specific, then just keep looking.

Here are some common immediate results and how to navigate them:

1. You immediately start thinking again.

   "Well, I know who I am. This practice is silly. It doesn't work for me." When this happens, great! That is your next thought. Start from step two with that thought and proceed through the inquiry. It doesn't matter what the next thought is. If it is a thought, it is obviously not you, right? It can't be you because you were there before that thought and you will be there after that thought, correct? Also, that thought says it's about you, so clearly it isn't actually you. Lastly, you are aware of the thought so it can't be equivalent to what you are, right? Keep looking, and if a thought sucks you in, then just start at step two with the new thought.

2. You totally forget what you're doing.

   This is fine. It can be confusing to put your mind on the rack in this way. It's not used to it. If at any point you've totally lost track of what you're doing or you find yourself daydreaming, just start again at number one.

3. You go to look for the "me" that the thought says it's about, and you can't find it.

It's important to make a distinction here between the thought, I can't find it / I can't find myself, and a looking that just keeps on going with no landing on anything solid or specific. In the first case, just start with that thought at step two again. If it's the second case, and looking goes on and there is genuine curiosity even though nothing is found, then great! Just keeping doing that. You've figured out the point of self-inquiry. If you find yourself in that pure looking-seeing-being but landing nowhere specific and there are no thoughts, you are doing pure self-inquiry. Just keep at it. Stay in the gap. It might happen only for a few seconds at first. Then a thought will come. At that point, start at step two again. Over time you might go from several seconds to a few minutes or longer. The key is thoughtless looking-seeing-being. Neither rejecting thoughts nor getting entangled in their content. A pure movement of innocent curiosity. It might feel dynamic or it might feel quite still. Either is fine. Just keep that looking going.

Fine-Tuning

Once you get the hang of these steps and can move through them in a short time, you will notice it's not hard to get that thoughtless gap, even if it is for a short time. The following suggestions can help you to fine-tune to that frequency of pure self-inquiry. It's something like tuning a radio between stations. You neither land at this thought nor at that thought, yet you aren't rejecting any thought. Perhaps it could be said that attention moves toward a thought so quickly that it has no time to fully form. Attention becomes the thought. Over time it will become far more spontaneous and relaxing to remain in this thoughtless gap of pure looking, pure knowing without thought, and pure being. Here are a few pointers:

➢ Recognize when another thought has emerged and has bound your attention. Often the thought will be about the immediate inquiry practice. This is often the moment we become reidentified with thought and don't realize it simply because the content of the thought is about the practice itself.

➢ Review the chapters on attention, thoughts, and inquiry. They contain many nuances and pointers that can be helpful to this process.

➢ Recognize that anything you can put into words is a thought. Also, any image, even vaguely defined images, are thoughts.

➢ Reinvigorate your curiosity periodically. You don't want to practice this mechanically.

➢ Use the body as a gauge to assure you are doing this in a nonstraining (relaxed) manner. You can periodically put attention into various parts of the body to see if you're holding tension anywhere or straining. This is especially useful if the inquiry feels strained, frustrating, or tense. Once you get the hang of doing self-inquiry without straining, it may not be necessary to check in with the body in this way.

➢ Don't make distance. Keep in mind that the pure looking in a thoughtless gap doesn't mean that you are out of contact with the stuff thoughts are made of (consciousness). It's quite the opposite. It's more like all of experience gets replaced by thought-stuff, which is also you-stuff. It's all one endless continuum of pure conscious experience. The looking/ questioning, the sense of you, the gap, and the thought-stuff, are all the same flowing substance.

➢ Don't try to arrive. Even though we're using a question as a launch vehicle, we're not looking for a specific arrival place, a conceptual understanding, or a certain predefined experience. We're more interested in "settling in" to pure experience itself, which is not apart from the experiencer. The pure experience is infused with curiosity and fascination. However, it's a satisfied curiosity, so it doesn't require resolution like a typical question would.

Potential Pitfalls

➤ Asking, "Who am I?" or "Where am I?" and then looking around for a conceptual answer. This simply leads to more inner dialogue, thinking, and frustration.

➤ Concluding, "Oh there is no I/me/self." This will lead to a dull inquiry with little interest in actually looking for the sense of "me." The reason this happens is because we've become identified with the thought, There is no I/me/self. When we are identified with that thought, we don't recognize it as just another thought. Another way of saying this is that when we adopt the belief, "There is no I/me/self," the view from which that belief is held remains completely intact. The unseen (and assumed) sense of subjective self holds the view that there is no self. The self we are investigating is not a mere thought or belief. It's a sense, a frame of reference, and a feeling-assumption. It's also a complex web of impressions and beliefs. It's also an ongoing perceptual distortion that is extremely easy to overlook. You can't just make it disappear by adopting a belief that it doesn't exist. If you find yourself concluding this, you can recognize that conclusion as a mere thought. Then you can start at step two again using that thought.

➤ Getting frustrated. It doesn't feel like anything is happening, so we feel frustration, impatience, or even anger. If this occurs, it doesn't mean you're doing anything wrong. In fact, when we start digging into our identity structures, it's common for emotions to come to the surface. Just take a breath and relax for a minute. Then acknowledge the emotion. Feel it in your body. See if you can relax any tension in the body associated with the emotion. Then look for the thought or belief associated with the experience. It might be something like, "I'm feeling frustration." Then proceed with the inquiry starting with step two. If the emotion is constantly distracting and demanding of your attention, you may want to reference the chapter on emotions and do some work with that particular emotion before returning to self-inquiry

➤ Staring at the thought/question, "Who am I?" endlessly without realizing that the one who feels like you doing this practice, and having a history and a spiritual path, is what you are supposed to try to investigate. Whenever that dawns on you, look there!

➤ Concluding that because you haven't found a "me," an I, or a self, there is no value in continuing to look. This is not true. The nonconceptual looking is the point. You could say that in this instance the hidden thought is, This is useless. When you recognize that, or a similar thought, then you can begin the inquiry again.

➤ Being uncomfortable with the thoughtless state, then reengaging thoughts. This happens very frequently. When it occurs, we rarely realize that the mind re-engaged thought to avoid the fear response that can arise with thoughtless gaps. If we keep at self-inquiry, returning to the thoughtless gap again and again, we will often realize there is a certain fear associated with letting go of the addiction to thoughts. We are so used to clinging to the next thought, and then the next, that we often don't recognize an underlying uneasiness that we are habitually using thoughts to avoid. If we persist in spite of any uneasiness or fear, then these emotions will settle with time and experience. If we just keep returning to this gap and remain there beyond the fear and physical responses, then things will start to change experientially. This is where magic can happen, but you have to keep at it.

"The cave you fear to enter holds the treasure you seek."

—Joseph Campbell

A Practice Example

Above we looked at the example of a thought about eating a sandwich. I started with a visual thought because they are the simplest to describe. Let's look at another example with a thought that is a bit more obscure. Let's assume we start the self-inquiry process. We begin by becoming receptive to thought. We become aware of our inner thought-space and wait. After a short time, we think, Inquiry never works for me. This is where the rubber meets the road. Many people will get exactly this far and give up. They give up by not recognizing that the thought, Inquiry never works for me was their entry point. If you don't catch it, and you believe that you were the thinker of that thought, you will give in to the stream of thoughts that follow. How do I know this happens so frequently? Well, because people tell me. It's common for someone to attempt self-inquiry and then report, "Every time I do inquiry it starts out well, but then I can't get past _____." Then they proceed to tell me the rest of the thought that bound them. I don't blame them; the hypnotic pull of thought i far more powerful than most of us realize. When this happens, I try as nicely as possible to point out that the thought that came up during self-inquiry, saying, Every time I do inquiry it starts out well, but then I can't get past _____ was just a thought like any other. However, at the moment they failed to recognize it as a thought; they hypnotized themself back into the thought stream and abandoned the inquiry process.

So with that background information, let's look at the thought, Inquiry never works for me. Step two is to take a neutral stance. If we believe this thought is a statement of truth, we might feel frustrated and might judge it as undesirable. However, now that we're out of the business of judging thoughts, we can regard it as neutral, because it is. It's a thought like any other in that it's made of the same thought-stuff that every thought is made of. That thought-stuff is neutral in quality. The next step is to clarify it. Just repeat it once in your mind and annunciate the inner dialogue. "Self-inquiry never works for me." Can you see how it's just like some mysterious substance of mind that can seemingly form internal sounds (dialogue) where there are none? That internal dialogue is clear somehow, but also not there at all. It's also the same stuff that made up the sandwich thought isn't it?

Proceeding to step four, we notice this thought appears to be about "me." In this case it becomes more clear why this is important. It has to do with the story I told about how people commonly get this far and then end up getting dragged down the thought-stream. If you don't slow down enough and go through these steps, then when a thought like this comes, it can really hook you and take you for a ride. There is a certain momentum to our relationship with thoughts. The stepwise approach slows this momentum down enough to truly disentangle ourselves from thoughts. When a thought like this catches us and drags us into the thought-stream, such that we abandon the entire process of self-inquiry, it is because that momentum has caused us to take that thought as a statement of fact. We experience that thought as if it's defining reality. Moreover, we take it as if it's defining reality for "me." The "me" becomes assumed and solidified when this momentum is ongoing. This is the step where we have an opportunity to truth-test the "me" that this thought claims to be about.

Now let's perform step four. The thought was, Self-inquiry never works for me. We can easily recognize that the thought seems to be referring to "me." In fact, it states that assertion explicitly, doesn't it? That's the assumed me that is the subject of the thought. More importantly, there is an assumed, a felt "me," that seems to be aware of that thought the moment it arises. This is the sense of the one that feels disappointed or frustrated if that thought is believed.

Now we proceed to step five: Look for that "me." You'll notice that the "me" we are looking for isn't in the thought. How do we know this? We know because clearly you don't disappear when that thought subsides. Furthermore, you were clearly here before that thought arose. So where else can you look? You can look where it feels like you are. What's there? Well, you might notice a sensation, such as a pressure in the head or a subtle feeling in some other part of the body. Is that you? Well, the sense of you can be here when you aren't noticing that specific sensation, right? So just keep looking. Stay in that curiosity. Stay in the feeling of that place that seems to be aware of thoughts, seems to form thoughts, and yet is still there even when there are no thoughts for a moment.

"I'm trying to free your mind, Neo. But I can only show you the door. You're the one that has to walk through it."

—*Morpheus, The Matrix*

Stay here and you'll be physically experiencing where the sense of you the thinker, the sense of the thoughts on the inner movie screen, and the gap between thoughts are all seamlessly one. Just stay there. It might feel dynamic, and it might feel very still. It might feel both simultaneously. Once you get the feel of this, you need do nothing more than stay right here. Stay here during meditation. Stay here as you get up from meditation. Stay with this through various activities to whatever degree is possible. See if you can carry this off into sleep, then pick it up right as you awaken.

One-Pointed

In its essence, the one-pointed approach isn't that different from self-inquiry. More importantly, it leads to exactly the same place. Once you come to that place, all other approaches will vanish. There will be effortless, brilliant clarity. The manner and degree to which we exert ourselves to come upon this placeless place can vary considerably. It's something like a mountain with multiple paths beginning at the base. Some paths may start in the plains, others in the forest. Some are steep, and others are flat. Some are meandering, and others seem to head straight up the mountainside. As the various paths make their way farther up the terrain, they begin to converge. Many paths turn into few paths. At some point, when you are near the top, the remaining two or three paths are quite close to one another and thus begin to resemble one another. Nearing awakening is much like this. As you approach the threshold, things start to converge. Whether you climbed the mountain through effort and determination or through curiosity and questioning becomes irrelevant. At the very top of that mountain, all of those paths that began in diverse terrains at the base, have fully converged, and simultaneously ceased. From this vantage point, you won't care which path you took up the mountain. You'll know the universal view, and you will be able to appreciate each of the paths in their own right. Further, there will no longer be a mountain. Where a mountain once stood, now only peace remains.

As I begin to describe the one-pointed approach, it might sound quite distinct from self-inquiry. Once you give yourself fully to it, however, it will converge with the path of self-inquiry. Whereas the self-inquiry approach has more of an inquisitive, curious, and discerning tone, the one-pointed approach is based more on determination, focus, and sheer will. I might call it the warrior's way.

"If you cut up a large diamond into little bits, it will entirely lose the value it had as a whole; and an army divided up into small bodies of soldiers, loses all its strength. So, a great intellect sinks to the level of an ordinary one, as soon as it is interrupted and disturbed, its attention distracted and drawn off from the matter in hand; for its superiority depends upon its power of concentration—of bringing all its strength to bear upon one theme."

—Arthur Schopenhauer

This path is often taken up out of frustration and desperation. We sometimes turn to it instinctually once we have come to the end of what our mind can do. Sometimes we need to engage the emotions to propel us beyond where our mind can take us. Harnessing the physical forces of frustration, desperation, and anger, and bringing them to bear, can sometimes be what's needed to break this open. Here comes another paradox. This works because we fully exhaust all of our resources, mental as well as physical, and when we see that we still can't force reality to do what we want it to, we finally collapse in exhaustion and our awake nature hits us over the head in the most surprising of ways. Hearing this, one might be compelled to think that they can just take a short cut and "give up" without exerting all of this effort in hopes that they would wake up. Unfortunately, there's still too much unconscious control operating for that to happen. So, we need to go through the physical process of emptying ourselves and our will into the practice. This is exactly how it went for me.

I had pushed against life as long as I could remember. Most of the time I hadn't realized I was doing that. Once I realized it, I harnessed all of that struggle into the practice. I figured if I'm going to struggle consciously, I'm going to struggle in a way that is deeply truthful. I knew I couldn't just stop struggling, so I harnessed it and turned it into a burning intention to break through whatever barrier it was that was keeping me looking through a veil all the time. I knew the truth was there somewhere, but I wasn't going to settle for a thought that had always failed me. This had to be the real thing. So I put my frustration, stubbornness, and anger behind this practice.

"Knowing what must be done does away with fear."

—Rosa Parks

I didn't direct this anger at the Universe, I directed it at whatever divisive mechanism was keeping me from coming into communion with the universe! I became one-pointed. Interestingly, just doing that was a sort of relief in and of itself. I was finally putting all of my energy into what really mattered the most to me in life.

There's something very freeing about not giving yourself choices and just pouring your will into one thing. In addition, there was something very mysterious going on because I was pouring all of my will into something that I could not think about or define, and yet I fully trusted it. This is the nice thing about the one-pointed approach; the act itself is trust. You can feel it. Even while there is still doubt, confusion, and discursive thoughts, you know you're onto something. For me it was a relief because by this point, I knew it was awakening or death. This means that I was so committed, I knew I would do this the rest of my life if I had to. I wasn't going to live the old way by choice any longer. I was going to wake up or die trying. Can you feel into this? You may not think about it exactly like I did, but if you can relate to this desperation and determination, this may be the way for you. It's sort of an alchemical process of turning doubt into one-pointed determination.

So how do you do it? What is the practice specifically? First of all, the most important part of this approach is the emotional charge and the resolve. I didn't tell that story merely to share my path with you. I also wanted to use a personal approach to explaining what the fuel behind the one-pointed approach consists of. Once you feel that kind of resolve, that deep sense that this priority is what matters above all else, then the rest is simple. Here it is: You distill all of that resolve, intention, frustration, and desperation down into a single point. It can be like a point of light where multiple lasers converge. It can be the tip of an exceptionally powerful drill. It can be the exact point that is the center of gravity for your body. Can you feel into this? Don't worry that this one-pointed image may be imaginary. What's behind it is not imaginary. What's driving this is powerful beyond your imagination. Once you've distilled that drive down into a one-pointed singularity, just stay right there. Don't deviate. Don't daydream. Don't mind-wander. Let that singularity burn through all layers of your mind. Let it dissolve layer after layer of memory and identity. Don't contemplate its action. Don't think about it. Just absorb yourself fully into it. Carry it with you day and night. Wake up to it. Carry it off into sleep and even into dreams if you can. Don't worry about progress. Progress is thought. Don't even worry about awakening. Awakening is thought. Just that one point. Hold onto it as if letting it go for even a moment would be the end of your life. Don't separate yourself in the least. Let that focal point absorb all of your life energy. That one point is the beginning and the end of your life. It is the beginning and the end of the Universe. Don't deviate!

Anything can be your focus of practice if it feels right to you. If you usually use a mantra to meditate, then let that be your focal point. If you use an inquiry question, then let that be the focal point. Instead of asking, "Who am I?" Just ask, "Who?" Then just listen to the sound "who" with no question and without trying to go anywhere beyond it. Then feel the impulse. Take this all the way down to one point and don't ever separate yourself. No matter what thoughts, emotions, or sensations come, don't be distracted; stay with that singularity.

You have to take this all the way until there's nothing left. Until you don't exist outside that singularity. Until the Universe doesn't exist outside that singularity. Even if you notice all of that has happened, you can still recognize that even that noticing is a thought. Just pour yourself even more fully into the singularity.

The Final Technique

The mind is hungry; it wants something to chew on. It might have devoured all the techniques, pointers, and inquiries that you've read in this book, and yet it's telling you, "Yeah but where's the big one? The one that's going to finally do it for me?" If this line of thinking is familiar to you, then pay close attention to what I'm about to say: You don't need any more techniques or knowledge to wake up. You have plenty.

"It's too late to be ready."

—Dogen

What you really need to do is to see that if you're waiting until "later, when," then you are still under the spell of some very sneaky thoughts and beliefs. The hungry mind is somewhat two-faced. One face tells you, "Well, for whatever reason I haven't found the proper inquiry, technique, or turning word yet, but let's keep looking. It's all so interesting!" The other face that we usually don't see is saying, "I want to know exactly what it's going to be like to go through this. I want to know what it's going to take, and I want to know what it's going to look like on the other side. I want to decide when and how I wake up." Buying into this narrative won't get you there. That narrative describes the curiosity of safety and predictability. It's the illusion of control co-opting your authentic aspiration to awaken. When you see that the mind is hopelessly incapable of bringing about awakening, or even perceiving what it truly is, and yet proclaims to know a whole lot about it as if it is in control, then you have an opportunity to do something revolutionary: stop listening to it!

A Personal Message

We've come a long way since we set out on this journey. Maybe you've already made this transition we're calling awakening. If you haven't, I want to offer a few words of acknowledgment and encouragement. I know this process can be confusing. I know there's a lot of doubt. I know that it's scary at times. I know how many dead ends you've come to inside your mind. I know the frustration and disappointment. This work is not for the faint of heart, so I want to acknowledge that you've sacrificed a lot of time, comfort, and certainty. Indeed, there may be more disappointments to come. Yet I want to remind you not to lose sight of the fact that awakening doesn't take time. It happens now or not at all. I know, it's a paradox, but it's a divine paradox.

I also know you've doubted whether this can actually happen for you. You've entertained the possibility that it's something that only happens to special "spiritual" people, lucky people, or people with more will than you have. We've all had these thoughts. They come with the territory. The thing is, this is such a personal journey that referencing anyone else's experience is unnecessary and unhelpful. Awakening for you won't play out in the ways that it did for others. It's an instinctual and intimate process. It can only look like what it looks like for you. Awake nature naturally comes forth when you trust your deepest instinct and then follow it beyond everything you know about yourself and beyond all memories and identities you've acquired. You can and will cross this threshold as long as you keep at it and give priority to this part of your life.

"No matter how difficult and painful it may be,
nothing sounds as good to the soul as the truth."

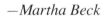
—*Martha Beck*

What you've taken yourself to be for so long is but a shadow of the infinitude of your undivided nature. The feeling of isolation is not intrinsic to what you truly are. The experience of life being divided up into parts and being hindered by struggle at every turn is not the only way to experience reality. You have the capacity to dissolve the constraints of the images you've carried around about who you are, who you're supposed to be, how you're supposed to act, and how you're supposed to experience life. These weigh you down far more than you realize.

Even though it feels like you're back at the beginning sometimes, your efforts and your commitment to truth have not been in vain. Salvation is closer than you can imagine. Don't abandon the path. Keep working at it, keep inquiring, keep questioning until you get your answer. Don't settle for a new view or a new way of thinking about yourself and life. The answer must be living truth. Don't settle for anything less.

There's no cheating this system. You can't just learn about presence, clarity, and flow and expect to cross over. The transformation has to be experientially clear and beyond any doubt. Many people try to negotiate with reality, which just keeps them asleep. Reality is nonnegotiable. You can't negotiate with reality and expect to get your way, but you can wake up to reality. Once you've breeched this veil, it will be undeniable and self-evident that there is nowhere to go from here. It will be obvious that there never was a path nor was there anything to struggle against. There is only uninhibited flow, presence, and clarity. This clarity excludes nothing, effortlessly accommodating all the textures of life, including thoughts, emotions, and sense phenomena.

Let's walk right to the edge together. Let's stare into the abyss together. What's in there? In fact, where is there? Is it in front, behind, above, or below? Or . . . is it what is looking through your eyes right now? Maybe the abyss is what has been looking, thinking, searching all along. Maybe the abyss itself is what steps off into the abyss.

I won't be stepping off with you. I've already crossed, as have many others. You have to leave me behind, just like you have to leave all other images behind to cross over. I can't tell you what happens

454

when you step in. You can't know. You have to step to find out. You can never be prepared for this, but you can be willing. This is the end of self-imposed struggle. This is where you let go of the old ways of knowing yourself. Let the Universe show you what you can never construct in your own mind. Let the universal will take over where your will has come to the end of what it can do. Trust . . . and step . . .

Meet me on the other side. Where there no sides. Where you and I are not two. Where the shackles of time cannot be found. Where closeness loses all meaning. Where contact is infinite within and without.

Love of two is one,
Here but now they're gone.
Came the last night of sadness,
And it was clear she couldn't go on.

Then the door was opened and the wind appeared,
The candles blew then disappeared.
The curtains flew then he appeared, saying don't be
afraid,
Come on baby, and she had no fear.

And she ran to him, then they started to fly.
They looked backward and said goodbye, she had
become like they are.
She had taken his hand, she had become like they
are.
Come on baby, don't fear the reaper.

— "Don't Fear the Reaper" by Blue Oyster Cult

Chapter 17:

Post-Awakening Guidance

As I mentioned in chapter three, I will leave detailed discussions about the refinements that occur after initial awakening for the next volume. Most of the inquiries and investigations that are useful after awakening can be found in this book, specifically in the chapters on attention, inquiry, thoughts, and emotions. The next book will include when and how to apply them as pertains the natural progression that occurs once one has had an awakening. Furthermore, it will address the common pitfalls that occur after awakening when one traverses the spiritual "no-person's land" that tends to follow the awakening honeymoon period.

With that said, I don't want to leave anyone who has already had an awakening hanging. I will divide this chapter into two short sections to address, in general terms, approaches that are helpful both immediately after awakening, and then when that honeymoon period has passed. I'll begin with wonderful piece of writing a friend sent me the morning of her first awakening:

The body is tired, but it doesn't sleep much.
It shakes.

I wake up in the middle of the night to cry. The
tears keep coming.

It actually isn't me crying, it's the Universe crying.

It's shedding all the tears that my family had to
hold back,
all the tears that my friends innocently swallowed.

What grace to be broken open like this
Nobody is doing anything.

This has nothing to do with me.
What is me? Is it still here? Was it ever here?
I don't know. I can't tell. 'Me' sounds like a pet
dog.

Something is dying. But I am here. Alive. There is
nothing more obvious.

At times thought is quiet. At times thought is loud.
Thoughts come.

The mind is active. The mind is adorable.
All I see are dreams. Mere whispers on the stage.

Desire and aversion come and go, but they belong
to no one.

There are hopes and wishes, fears and concerns.
And here they all converge,
they meet and kiss and dissolve into each other.

Ava is changing and not changing. It's a beautiful
show.

She's still here, apparently.

She still loves to work her ass off,
and eat chocolate and exercise and laugh and fall
apart.
She loves to fall apart. So what?

There is nothing to overcome. Suffering is
perfection.
The most mundane is the most sacred.
Imagination is sacred. Delusion is sacred. Pretense
is sacred.

In this play I meet myself again and again and
again. Hi there, you.

I'm on my death bed and outside the sun is rising.
This is where the end meets the beginning.

I've never heard the birds sing so clearly. So
effortlessly.

I'm exhausted and heavy and I'm vital and light.
How can this be?
There's a coexistence. Sameness. I'm moving so
rapidly and yet unwaveringly still.

I'm naked and absolutely held. Held by the
unknown.
Kidnapped. Conquered by the unknown.
Home.

———————

Thank YOU for lighting the way.
Thank you for your willingness to take everything
away so gently and so radically.

Thank you for feeling when I couldn't feel.

Thank you for getting out of the way, for showing up relentlessly,

for the lack of filters, for everything you didn't do. I don't know what the fuck you did, but I suspect you didn't do anything.

Thank you for a selfless, agenda-less offering from no one to no one.

Words are cheap here.

Immediately Post-Awakening

This guidance refers specifically to that period immediately following awakening. It's sometimes called the honeymoon period, but when you're there it won't feel like anything specific. The advice here is very simple:

❖ A window is open. You are in a good place. This is a place where nothing needs doing. You recognize fluidity and peace as natural expression. It isn't earned or caused; it simply is. This is the great relief. While this window is open, I usually recommend just steeping yourself in this clarity. Make room for it. You have the opportunity to drive this insight far deeper in a short time. How do you do that? By not doing a damn thing. Orient your attention to this marvelous display of brilliant, fluid presence. A sound is a sound; a sensation is a sensation; and a thought is a thought. If you notice this, then the penetration is effortless, a movement of pure fascination, pure love. Give yourself the gift of not "doing anything" with this. Let it overtake you again and again. Keep a bit of alertness to your immediate experience, but don't add, subtract, or conclude.

❖ Whereas before there may have been an inquiry or a technique or a meditative practice, now practice proceeds from no-practice, from no-effort, from no-orientation. Orient to no-orientation, then let the realization itself carry you forward, inward, outward.

❖ Don't concern yourself with what happened, what's happening, or what will happen. That's all a waste of time. You see now awaking is not an event. It's not even a thing. There is only life, and life knows no boundary, no separation, no time.

❖ Avoid philosophical or spiritual conversations with people. Even though there is uncaused peace, natural flow, and pristine presence, it's still not too hard to get twisted up in the mind. The quickest way to do this is conceptualize and discuss philosophy, spirituality, awakening, reality, etc.

❖ If your situation allows, avoid unnecessary activities for a time; instead, sit in presence and/or natural mediation. It's easy in this state to get overly involved in intense and dramatic situations without realizing what you are doing. The spontaneity and fluidity you are enjoying can be a bit of a double-edged sword until you get good at navigating emotional or heady situations. While you can never "lose" this presence you've realized, you can definitely get yourself into situations where you rev up the machinery of the mind and the ego, which can be particularly disorienting in this state.

❖ If you begin to experience fixation, intense emotions, or sticky mental constructs, you can use the techniques in the corresponding chapters to work with them. Even then, try to approach these practices from this instinctual knowing of ease, spontaneity, and fluid contact. It is also helpful in these situations to talk with a good teacher who knows this territory well. If you do engage a teacher and they don't feel as clear as you, then they may not be helpful. There are enough good teachers around that if you do a bit of looking, you can find one who can help you navigate these waters.

❖ Here is a simple and effective approach if something feels heavy or contracted, and it doesn't naturally dissolve through sitting in presence or through natural meditation. Come into contact with each component of the experience. Start with the body sensations. Scan the body and find any sensations arising in the momentary experience. Then just saturate your attention with those sensations for a few moments. Now move your attention to the sound field. Similarly, let the sound field saturate your experience without adding, subtracting, or analysis. Next, investigate the visual field. Just take in all of those colors, shapes, and textures. Don't judge or comment internally. Just allow yourself to see. Now move your attention to consciousness and/or thought. Notice that the fluidity, immediacy, and vividness of that immediate experience of thought/consciousness is of a similar quality to the other sense fields. Let the flow of consciousness wash over and through all of experience. That's it. You can move through those sense fields as many times as you want to. If you do this gently, with curiosity and love for mere experience, you might start to notice that this becomes more instinctual than intentional.

Spiritual No-Person's Land

This is my tongue-in-cheek term for that bizarre and often confusing period that comes after the awakening honeymoon, but before liberation. This phase can last months to years. Clarifying what was glimpsed during the initial awakening is far more a matter of what you don't do than it is a matter of what you do. Even so, there are practices and contemplations that can be quite helpful during this period, but they tend to be deceptively simple.

❖ For most of us, this period requires a lot of emotion work. I would venture to say that this area is the biggest barrier to the natural clarification that occurs after awakening. The avoidance patterns and mistrust of emotion is pervasive and deeply rooted among humans. To not recognize this is to continue to put energy into identities and resistance patterns that are in place specifically to assure we never delve deeply into this territory. Worse, we can convince ourselves that realization is about not feeling or transcending emotions, and now we've spiritualized these identities and resistance patterns. The acknowledgement and acceptance that this phase is not about chasing mystical states or trying to cultivate enjoyable experiences will serve you well. Be prepared to feel rather unenlightened for some time. This is shadow work; it cannot be avoided. The emotions chapter contains many good approaches.

❖ Don't try to recreate your awakening. It will never happen. The past is gone. All you have left of that experience and event is a memory. The truth you realized has never gone anywhere, and it is with you right now. Don't judge the form that truth arises in. It knows exactly what to show you moment by moment.

❖ A daily practice of natural meditation, simple meditation with or without a technique, or similar, is quite valuable.

❖ Spending time in unbound consciousness (sometimes experienced as the pure sense of I or I AM, on a daily basis is also quite helpful. This will help to relax and ultimately dissolve fixations and resistance patterns. Be selfish and give yourself this space. Enjoy it.

❖ As things clarify, consider taking up a direct investigation of the senses. This is exquisitely simple and can be done any time. It can be done during meditation, and it can be done while performing daily activities. Similar to what was described in the previous section, we simply cycle through the sense fields. The key is that when our attention is in a specific sense field, we make a point to clarify that sense experience as a solitary experience. This means we aren't thinking about or contemplating anything, there is just that sense. For instance, when we move attention to the body sensations, we notice that the sense field begins to clarify. We can inwardly affirm "feeling," but it's not necessary to do so. We notice those sensations aren't in a certain place, and they don't require any effort to be as they are. You could say that they are self-obvious or self-propagating. Just feel into that field for a few moments. Then cycle attention into the sound field. Take in all the sounds. Let there be just sound, without mental comment or labeling. You can affirm "hearing" if that helps. Similarly, you cycle through the visual field and then the field of consciousness/thought. As you repeat this process, you will likely notice the senses begin to clarify. You might also notice there is less attention or concern for the inner world of contemplation, monitoring, self-reflection, and the chatter of the mind. Keep at this, and eventually the gap between the sense fields will close. This will naturally lead to further insights. The descriptions of the insights beyond stage three in the stages of awakening chapter can give you a sense of how this plays out.

❖ Have fun, and don't take any of this too seriously.

"God is a comedian playing to an audience that is too afraid to laugh."

—Voltaire

About the Author

Angelo DiLullo works full time as a physician, and in his spare time works with people who are undergoing the processes of awakening and deepening realization. These interactions began to occur organically about 15 years after his own awakening. In casual conversations with friends and acquaintances, the subject of the possibility of living one's life without the burden of perceptual filters would arise on occasion. Over time, this led to writing this book to facilitate the process of awakening in people who are inclined in that way. Development of the website SimpyAlwaysAwake.com as well as a YouTube channel by the same name soon followed.

Made in the USA
Coppell, TX
05 June 2021

56923023R00262